Study and Solutions Guide for

TRIGONOMETRY
THIRD EDITION

Larson/Hostetler

Dianna L. Zook

Indiana University
Purdue University at Fort Wayne, Indiana

D. C. Heath and Company

Lexington, Massachusetts   Toronto

TO THE STUDENT

The *Study and Solutions Guide for Trigonometry* is a supplement to the text by Roland E. Larson and Robert P. Hostetler.

As a mathematics instructor, I often have students come to me with questions about the assigned homework. When I ask to see their work, the reply often is "I didn't know where to start." The purpose of the *Study Guide* is to provide brief summaries of the topics covered in the textbook and enough detailed solutions to problems so that you will be able to work the remaining exercises.

This *Study Guide* is the result of the efforts of Richard Bambauer, Lisa Bickel, Linda Bollinger, Laurie Brooks, Patti Jo Campbell, Darin Johnson, Linda Kifer, Deanna Larson, Timothy Larson, Amy Marshall, John Musser, Scott O'Neil, Louis Rieger, Paula Sibeto Steinhart, and Evelyn Wedzikowski. I would like to thank my husband Edward L. Schlindwein for his support during the several months I worked on this project.

If you have any corrections or suggestions for improving this *Study Guide*, I would appreciate hearing from you.

Good luck with your study of trigonometry.

Dianna L. Zook
Indiana University,
Purdue University
at Fort Wayne, Indiana 46805

STUDY STRATEGIES

- Attend all classes and come prepared. Have your homework completed. Bring the text, paper, pen or pencil, and a calculator (scientific or graphing) to each class.

- Read the section in the text that is to be covered before class. Make notes about any questions that you have and, if they are not answered during the lecture, ask them at the appropriate time.

- Participate in class. As mentioned above, ask questions. Also, do not be afraid to answer questions.

- Take notes on all definitions, concepts, rules, formulas and examples. After class, read your notes and fill in any gaps, or make notations of any questions that you have.

- DO THE HOMEWORK!!! You learn mathematics by doing it yourself. Allow **at least** two hours outside of each class for homework. Do not fall behind.

- Seek help when needed. Visit your instructor during office hours and come prepared with specific questions; check with your school's tutoring service; find a study partner in class; check additional books in the library for more examples—just do something before the problem becomes insurmountable.

- Do not cram for exams. Each chapter in the text contains a chapter review and this study guide contains a practice test at the end of each chapter. (The answers are at the back of the study guide.) Work these problems a few days before the exam and review any areas of weakness.

CONTENTS

CHAPTER 1

Prerequisites for Trigonometry

SECTION 1.1

The Real Number System

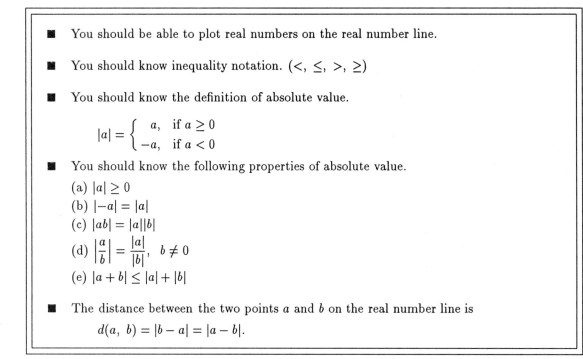

■ You should be able to plot real numbers on the real number line.

■ You should know inequality notation. ($<$, $\leq$, $>$, $\geq$)

■ You should know the definition of absolute value.

$$|a| = \begin{cases} a, & \text{if } a \geq 0 \\ -a, & \text{if } a < 0 \end{cases}$$

■ You should know the following properties of absolute value.

(a) $|a| \geq 0$

(b) $|-a| = |a|$

(c) $|ab| = |a||b|$

(d) $\left|\dfrac{a}{b}\right| = \dfrac{|a|}{|b|}$, $b \neq 0$

(e) $|a + b| \leq |a| + |b|$

■ The distance between the two points a and b on the real number line is

$$d(a, b) = |b - a| = |a - b|.$$

Solutions to Selected Exercises

5. Given $\{-\pi, , -\frac{1}{3}, \frac{6}{3}, \frac{1}{2}\sqrt{2}, -7.5\}$, determine which numbers are (a) natural numbers, (b) integers, (c) rational numbers, and (d) irrational numbers.

Solution:

(a) Natural numbers: $\frac{6}{3} = 2$

(b) Integers: $\frac{6}{3} = 2$

(c) Rational numbers: $-\frac{1}{3}$, $\frac{6}{3}$, -7.5

(d) Irrational numbers: $-\pi$, $\frac{1}{2}\sqrt{2}$

11. Plot the two real numbers $\frac{5}{6}$ and $\frac{2}{3}$ on the real number line and place the appropriate inequality sign between them.

Solution:

$$\frac{5}{6} > \frac{2}{3}$$

15. Verbally describe the subset of real numbers represented by the inequality $x < 0$. Then sketch the subset on the real number line.

Solution:

$x < 0$: Read "x is less than zero" or "the set of all negative real numbers."

21. Verbally describe the subset of real numbers represented by the inequality $-1 \le x < 0$. Then sketch the subset on the real number line.

Solution:

$-1 \le x < 0$: Read "x is greater than or equal to -1 AND x is less than zero."

25. Write $|3 - \pi|$ without absolute value signs.

Solution:

Since $3 < \pi$, $3 - \pi$ is negative. Therefore, $|3 - \pi| = -(3 - \pi) = \pi - 3 \approx 0.1416$.

29. Write $-3|-3|$ without absolute value signs.

Solution:

$$-3|-3| = -3(3) = -9$$

33. Place the correct symbol ($<$, $>$, or $=$) between $|-3|$ and $-|-3|$.

Solution:

$$|-3| > -|-3| \text{ since } 3 > -3.$$

37. Place the correct symbol ($<$, $>$, or $=$) between $-|-2|$ and $-|2|$.

Solution:

$$-|-2| = -|2| \text{ since } -2 = -2.$$

41. Find the distance between the points $-\frac{5}{2}$ and 0 on the real number line.

Solution:

$$d\left(-\tfrac{5}{2},\ 0\right) = \left|0 - \left(-\tfrac{5}{2}\right)\right| = \left|\tfrac{5}{2}\right| = \tfrac{5}{2}$$

45. Find the distance between the points 9.34 and −5.65 on the real number line.

Solution:

$$d(9.34,\ -5.65) = |9.34 - (-5.65)|$$

$$= |9.34 + 5.65|$$

$$= |14.99|$$

$$= 14.99$$

49. Match $x < 4$ with its graph.

Solution:

$x < 4$ matches graph (a).

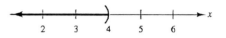

55. The accounting department of a company is checking to see whether the actual expenses of a department differ from the budgeted expenses by more than $500 or 5%. Complete the missing parts of the table and determine whether the actual expense passes the "budget variance test."

	Budgeted expense, b	Actual expense, a	$\|a - b\|$	$0.05b$
Taxes	$37,640.00	$37,335.80		

Solution:

$$|a - b| = |37,335.80 - 37,640.00| = \$304.20$$

$$0.05b = 0.05(37,640) = \$1882.00$$

The actual expense for taxes passes the "budget variance test."

61. Use a calculator to order the following real numbers, from smallest to largest.

$$\frac{7071}{5000},\ \frac{584}{413},\ \sqrt{2},\ \frac{47}{33},\ \frac{127}{90}$$

Solution:

$$\frac{7071}{5000} = 1.4142$$

$$\frac{584}{413} \approx 1.414043584$$

$$\sqrt{2} \approx 1.414213562$$

$$\frac{47}{33} = 1.42\overline{42}$$

$$\frac{127}{90} = 1.41\overline{1}$$

$$\frac{127}{90} < \frac{584}{413} < \frac{7071}{5000} < \sqrt{2} < \frac{47}{33}$$

65. Use a calculator to find the decimal form of $\frac{41}{333}$. If it is a nonterminating decimal, write the repeating pattern.

Solution:

$$\frac{41}{333} = 0.\overline{123}$$

67. Determine whether the statement "the reciprocal of a nonzero integer is an integer" is true or false.

Solution:

The statement is false. The reciprocal of every nonzero integer, except 1 and −1, is **not** an integer.

SECTION 1.2

Solving Equations

- To solve an equation you may:
  - (a) Remove symbols of grouping, combine like terms, or reduce fractions on both sides of the equation.
  - (b) Add or subtract the same quantity to both sides of the equation.
  - (c) Multiply or divide both sides of the equation by the same nonzero quantity.
  - (d) Interchange the two sides of the equation.

- Be sure to check your answers for extraneous solutions.

- You should be able to factor special polynomial forms.
  - (a) $u^2 - v^2 = (u + v)(u - v)$
  - (b) $u^2 + 2uv + v^2 = (u + v)^2$
  - (c) $u^2 - 2uv + v^2 = (u - v)^2$
  - (d) $u^3 + v^3 = (u + v)(u^2 - uv + v^2)$
  - (e) $u^3 - v^3 = (u - v)(u^2 + uv + v^2)$

- You should know the Quadratic Formula. For $ax^2 + bx + c = 0, \ a \neq 0$, the solutions are

$$x = \frac{-b \pm \sqrt{b^2 - 4ac}}{2a}.$$

- Use the discriminant to determine the type of solutions of a quadratic equation.
  - (a) If $b^2 - 4ac > 0$, there are two distinct real solutions.
  - (b) If $b^2 - 4ac = 0$, there is one repeated real solution.
  - (c) If $b^2 - 4ac < 0$, there are no real solutions.

- Be able to solve polynomial equations of higher degree.
  - (a) Factor into linear and quadratic factors.
  - (b) Use the Quadratic Formula on polynomials that are similar to quadratics.
  - (c) Factor by grouping.

Solutions to Selected Exercises

5. Determine whether the equation $3x^2 - 8x + 5 = (x - 4)^2 - 11$ is an identity or a conditional equation.

Solution:

$$3x^2 - 8x + 5 = (x - 4)^2 - 11$$

$$3x^2 - 8x + 5 = x^2 - 8x + 16 - 11$$

$$3x^2 - 8x + 5 = x^2 - 8x + 5$$

$$2x^2 = 0$$

$$x = 0$$

The equation is conditional since zero is the only solution.

9. Determine whether the given value of x is a solution of the equation $3x^2 + 2x - 5 = 2x^2 - 2$.

    (a) $x = -3$ (b) $x = 1$ (c) $x = 4$ (d) $x = -5$

Solution:

    (a) $3(-3)^2 + 2(-3) - 5 \stackrel{?}{=} 2(-3)^2 - 2$ (b) $3(1)^2 + 2(1) - 5 \stackrel{?}{=} 2(1)^2 - 2$

                         $16 = 16$ $0 = 0$

       $x = -3$ *is* a solution. $x = 1$ *is* a solution.

    (c) $3(4)^2 + 2(4) - 5 \stackrel{?}{=} 2(4)^2 - 2$ (d) $3(-5)^2 + 2(-5) - 5 \stackrel{?}{=} 2(-5)^2 - 2$

                      $51 \neq 30$ $60 \neq 48$

       $x = 4$ *is not* a solution. $x = -5$ *is not* a solution.

13. Solve the equation $2(x + 5) - 7 = 3(x - 2)$ and check your answer.

Solution:

$$2(x + 5) - 7 = 3(x - 2)$$

$$2x + 10 - 7 = 3x - 6$$

$$2x + 3 = 3x - 6$$

$$-x + 3 = -6$$

$$-x = -9$$

$$x = 9$$

Check: $2(9 + 5) - 7 \stackrel{?}{=} 3(9 - 2)$

$$2(14) - 7 \stackrel{?}{=} 3(7)$$

$$28 - 7 \stackrel{?}{=} 21$$

$$21 = 21$$

15. Solve the following equation and check your answer.

$$\frac{5x}{4} + \frac{1}{2} = x - \frac{1}{2}$$

Solution:

$$\frac{5x}{4} + \frac{1}{2} = x - \frac{1}{2}$$

$$4\left(\frac{5x}{4} + \frac{1}{2}\right) = 4\left(x - \frac{1}{2}\right)$$

$$5x + 2 = 4x - 2$$

$$x + 2 = -2$$

$$x = -4$$

Check: $\dfrac{5(-4)}{4} + \dfrac{1}{2} \overset{?}{=} -4 - \dfrac{1}{2}$

$$-\frac{20}{4} + \frac{1}{2} \overset{?}{=} -\frac{8}{2} - \frac{1}{2}$$

$$-\frac{10}{2} + \frac{1}{2} \overset{?}{=} -\frac{9}{2}$$

$$-\frac{9}{2} = -\frac{9}{2}$$

17. Solve the equation $x + 8 = 2(x - 2) - x$, if possible.

Solution:

$$x + 8 = 2(x - 2) - x$$

$$x + 8 = 2x - 4 - x$$

$$x + 8 = x - 4$$

$$8 = -4 \qquad \text{Not possible}$$

Thus, the equation has no solution.

21. Solve the following equation and check your answer.

$$\frac{5x - 4}{5x + 4} = \frac{2}{3}$$

Solution:

$$\frac{5x - 4}{5x + 4} = \frac{2}{3}$$

$$3(5x - 4) = 2(5x + 4) \qquad \text{Cross multiply}$$

$$15x - 12 = 10x + 8$$

$$5x = 20$$

$$x = 4$$

Check: $\dfrac{5(4) - 4}{5(4) + 4} \overset{?}{=} \dfrac{2}{3}$

$$\frac{16}{24} \overset{?}{=} \frac{2}{3}$$

$$\frac{2}{3} = \frac{2}{3}$$

23. Solve the following equation and check your answer.

$$\frac{1}{x-3} + \frac{1}{x+3} = \frac{10}{x^2-9}$$

Solution:

$$\frac{1}{x-3} + \frac{1}{x+3} = \frac{10}{x^2-9}$$

$$\frac{(x+3)+(x-3)}{(x-3)(x+3)} = \frac{10}{x^2-9}$$

$$(x^2-9)\left(\frac{2x}{x^2-9}\right) = \left(\frac{10}{x^2-9}\right)(x^2-9)$$

$$2x = 10$$

$$x = 5$$

Check:

$$\frac{1}{5-3} + \frac{1}{5+3} \overset{?}{=} \frac{10}{5^2-9}$$

$$\frac{1}{2} + \frac{1}{8} \overset{?}{=} \frac{10}{16}$$

$$\frac{10}{16} = \frac{10}{16}$$

$$\frac{5}{8} = \frac{5}{8}$$

25. Solve the following equation and check your answer.

$$\frac{7}{2x+1} - \frac{8x}{2x-1} = -4$$

Solution:

$$\frac{7}{2x+1} - \frac{8x}{2x-1} = -4$$

$$(2x+1)(2x-1)\left[\frac{7}{2x+1} - \frac{8x}{2x-1}\right] = -4(2x+1)(2x-1)$$

$$7(2x-1) - 8x(2x+1) = -4(4x^2-1)$$

$$14x - 7 - 16x^2 - 8x = -16x^2 + 4$$

$$-16x^2 + 6x - 7 = -16x^2 + 4$$

$$6x - 7 = 4$$

$$6x = 11$$

$$x = \frac{11}{6}$$

Check:

$$\frac{7}{2\left(\frac{11}{6}\right)+1} - \frac{8\left(\frac{11}{6}\right)}{2\left(\frac{11}{6}\right)-1} \overset{?}{=} -4$$

$$\frac{7}{\frac{11}{3}+\frac{3}{3}} - \frac{\frac{44}{3}}{\frac{11}{3}-\frac{3}{3}} \overset{?}{=} -4$$

$$\frac{21}{14} - \frac{44}{8} \overset{?}{=} -4$$

$$\frac{3}{2} - \frac{11}{2} \overset{?}{=} -4$$

$$-\frac{8}{2} \overset{?}{=} -4$$

$$-4 = -4$$

27. Solve the equation $(x+2)^2 + 5 = (x+3)^2$ and check your answer.

Solution:

$$(x+2)^2 + 5 = (x+3)^2$$

$$x^2 + 4x + 4 + 5 = x^2 + 6x + 9$$

$$4x + 9 = 6x + 9$$

$$4x = 6x$$

$$-2x = 0$$

$$x = 0$$

Check: $(0+2)^2 + 5 \overset{?}{=} (0+3)^2$

$$4 + 5 \overset{?}{=} 9$$

$$9 = 9$$

33. Solve $x^2 - 2x - 8 = 0$ by factoring.

Solution:

$$x^2 - 2x - 8 = 0$$

$$(x+2)(x-4) = 0$$

$$x = -2 \quad \text{or} \quad x = 4$$

37. Solve $2x^2 = 19x + 33$ by factoring.

Solution:

$$2x^2 = 19x + 33$$

$$2x^2 - 19x - 33 = 0$$

$$(2x+3)(x-11) = 0$$

$$2x + 3 = 0 \quad \text{or} \quad x - 11 = 0$$

$$2x = -3 \qquad\qquad x = 11$$

$$x = -\tfrac{3}{2}$$

41. Use the Quadratic Formula to solve $16x^2 + 8x - 3 = 0$.

Solution:

$$16x^2 + 8x - 3 = 0$$

$$a = 16, \ b = 8, \ c = -3$$

$$x = \frac{-8 \pm \sqrt{8^2 - 4(16)(-3)}}{2(16)}$$

$$= \frac{-8 \pm \sqrt{256}}{32} = \frac{-8 \pm 16}{32}$$

$$x = \frac{-8 + 16}{32} = \frac{1}{4}$$

$$x = \frac{-8 - 16}{32} = -\frac{3}{4}$$

47. Use the Quadratic Formula to solve $4x^2 + 4x = 7$.

Solution:

$$4x^2 + 4x = 7$$

$$4x^2 + 4x - 7 = 0$$

$$a = 4, \ b = 4, \ c = -7$$

$$x = \frac{-4 \pm \sqrt{(4)^2 - 4(4)(-7)}}{2(4)}$$

$$= \frac{-4 \pm \sqrt{16 + 112}}{8} = \frac{-4 \pm \sqrt{128}}{8}$$

$$= \frac{-4 \pm 8\sqrt{2}}{8} = \frac{4(-1 \pm 2\sqrt{2})}{8}$$

$$= \frac{-1 \pm 2\sqrt{2}}{2} = -\frac{1}{2} \pm \sqrt{2}$$

51. Use the Quadratic Formula to solve

$$\frac{1}{x} - \frac{1}{x+1} = 3.$$

Solution:

$$\frac{1}{x} - \frac{1}{x+1} = 3$$

$$\frac{(x+1) - x}{x(x+1)} = 3$$

$$\frac{1}{x^2 + x} = 3$$

$$1 = 3(x^2 + x)$$

$$0 = 3x^2 + 3x - 1; \ a = 3, \ b = 3, \ c = -1$$

$$x = \frac{-3 \pm \sqrt{(3)^2 - 4(3)(-1)}}{2(3)} = \frac{-3 \pm \sqrt{21}}{6} = -\frac{1}{2} \pm \frac{\sqrt{21}}{6}$$

53. Use a calculator to solve $5.1x^2 - 1.7x - 3.2 = 0$. Round your answer to three decimal places.

Solution:

$$5.1x^2 - 1.7x - 3.2 = 0; \ a = 5.1, \ b = -1.7, \ c = -3.2$$

$$x = \frac{-(-1.7) \pm \sqrt{(-1.7)^2 - 4(5.1)(-3.2)}}{2(5.1)}$$

$$x = \frac{1.7 \pm \sqrt{68.17}}{10.2} \approx \frac{1.7 \pm 8.2565}{10.2}$$

$$x \approx 0.976 \quad \text{or} \quad x \approx -0.643$$

57. Find all solutions of $4x^4 - 9x^2 = 0$.

Solution:

$$4x^4 - 9x^2 = 0$$

$$x^2(4x^2 - 9) = 0$$

$$x^2(2x + 3)(2x - 3) = 0$$

$$x = 0, \ x = -\frac{3}{2}, \ \text{or } x = \frac{3}{2}$$

61. Find all solutions of $x^4 - 81 = 0$.

Solution:

$$x^4 - 81 = 0$$

$$(x^2 + 9)(x^2 - 9) = 0$$

$$(x^2 + 9)(x + 3)(x - 3) = 0$$

$$x = \pm 3$$

65. Find all solutions of $x^6 + 7x^3 - 8 = 0$.

Solution:

$$x^6 + 7x^3 - 8 = 0$$

$$(x^3 + 8)(x^3 - 1) = 0$$

$$(x + 2)(x^2 - 2x + 4)(x - 1)(x^2 + x + 1) = 0$$

$$x = -2, \qquad x = \frac{2 \pm \sqrt{4 - 16}}{2}, \qquad x = 1, \quad \text{or} \quad x = \frac{-1 \pm \sqrt{1 - 4}}{2}$$

$$x = -2, \qquad \text{No real solution}, \qquad x = 1, \qquad \text{No real solution}$$

69. A rancher has 200 feet of fencing to enclose two adjacent rectangular corrals (see figure). Find the dimensions that would create an enclosed area of 1400 square feet.

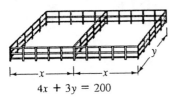

$$4x + 3y = 200$$

Solution:

$$4x + 3y = 200 \Rightarrow y = \frac{200 - 4x}{3}$$

$$A = l \cdot w = (2x)y = 2xy$$

$$1400 = 2x \left(\frac{200 - 4x}{3} \right)$$

$$4200 = 400x - 8x^2$$

$$8x^2 - 400x + 4200 = 0$$

$$8(x^2 - 50x + 525) = 0$$

$$8(x - 15)(x - 35) = 0$$

$$x = 15 \qquad \text{or} \qquad x = 35$$

$$y = \frac{140}{3} \qquad\qquad y = 20$$

Two solutions: 30 feet by $46\frac{2}{3}$ feet or 70 feet by 20 feet

SECTION 1.3

The Cartesian Plane and Graphs of Equations

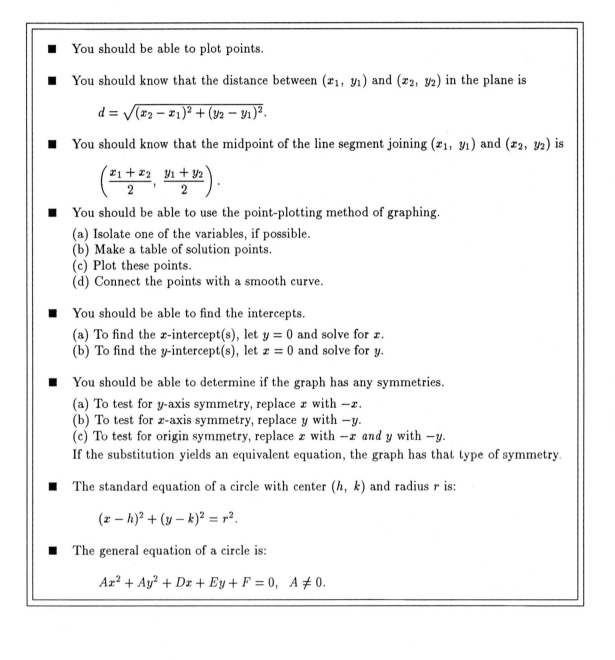

■ You should be able to plot points.

■ You should know that the distance between $(x_1,\ y_1)$ and $(x_2,\ y_2)$ in the plane is

$$d = \sqrt{(x_2 - x_1)^2 + (y_2 - y_1)^2}.$$

■ You should know that the midpoint of the line segment joining $(x_1,\ y_1)$ and $(x_2,\ y_2)$ is

$$\left(\frac{x_1 + x_2}{2},\ \frac{y_1 + y_2}{2}\right).$$

■ You should be able to use the point-plotting method of graphing.

(a) Isolate one of the variables, if possible.
(b) Make a table of solution points.
(c) Plot these points.
(d) Connect the points with a smooth curve.

■ You should be able to find the intercepts.

(a) To find the x-intercept(s), let $y = 0$ and solve for x.
(b) To find the y-intercept(s), let $x = 0$ and solve for y.

■ You should be able to determine if the graph has any symmetries.

(a) To test for y-axis symmetry, replace x with $-x$.
(b) To test for x-axis symmetry, replace y with $-y$.
(c) To test for origin symmetry, replace x with $-x$ *and* y with $-y$.
If the substitution yields an equivalent equation, the graph has that type of symmetry.

■ The standard equation of a circle with center $(h,\ k)$ and radius r is:

$$(x - h)^2 + (y - k)^2 = r^2.$$

■ The general equation of a circle is:

$$Ax^2 + Ay^2 + Dx + Ey + F = 0,\quad A \neq 0.$$

Solutions to Selected Exercises

3. Sketch the square with vertices
(2, 4), (5, 1), (2, −2), and (−1, 1).

Solution:

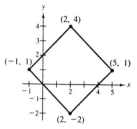

9. Find the distance between the points (−3, −1) and (2, −1).

Solution:

Since the points (−3, −1) and (2, −1) lie on the same vertical line, the distance between the points is given by the absolute value of the difference of their x-coordinates.

$$d = |-3 - 2| = 5$$

13. For the indicated triangle (a) find the length of the two sides of the right triangle and use the Pythagorean Theorem to find the length of the hypotenuse, and (b) use the Distance Formula to find the length of the hypotenuse of the triangle.

Solution:

(a) $a = |-3 - 7| = 10$

$\quad b = |4 - 1| = 3$

$\quad c = \sqrt{10^2 + 3^2} = \sqrt{109}$

(b) $c = \sqrt{(7 - (-3))^2 + (4 - 1)^2}$

$\quad = \sqrt{10^2 + 3^2}$

$\quad = \sqrt{109}$

15. (a) Plot the points $(-4, 10)$ and $(4, -5)$, (b) find the distance between the points, and (c) find the midpoint of the line segment joining the points.

Solution:

(a)

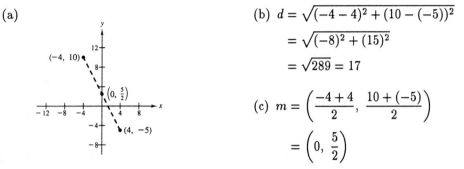

(b) $d = \sqrt{(-4 - 4)^2 + (10 - (-5))^2}$

$= \sqrt{(-8)^2 + (15)^2}$

$= \sqrt{289} = 17$

(c) $m = \left(\dfrac{-4 + 4}{2}, \dfrac{10 + (-5)}{2}\right)$

$= \left(0, \dfrac{5}{2}\right)$

19. (a) Plot the points $(6.2, 5.4)$, and $(-3.7, 1.8)$, (b) find the distance between the points, and (c) find the midpoint of the line segment joining the points.

Solution:

(a)

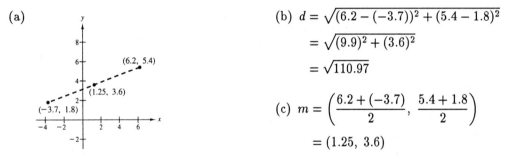

(b) $d = \sqrt{(6.2 - (-3.7))^2 + (5.4 - 1.8)^2}$

$= \sqrt{(9.9)^2 + (3.6)^2}$

$= \sqrt{110.97}$

(c) $m = \left(\dfrac{6.2 + (-3.7)}{2}, \dfrac{5.4 + 1.8}{2}\right)$

$= (1.25, 3.6)$

23. Show that the points $(4, 0)$, $(2, 1)$, and $(-1, -5)$ form the vertices of a right triangle.

Solution:

$d_1 = \sqrt{(-1 - 2)^2 + (-5 - 1)^2} = \sqrt{45}$

$d_2 = \sqrt{(2 - 4)^2 + (1 - 0)^2} = \sqrt{5}$

$d_3 = \sqrt{(4 - (-1))^2 + (0 - (-5))^2} = \sqrt{50}$

Since $d_1{}^2 + d_2{}^2 = d_3{}^2$, we can conclude by the Pythagorean Theorem that the triangle is a right triangle.

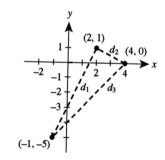

25. Find x so that the distance between $(1, 2)$ and $(x, -10)$ is 13.

Solution:

$$\sqrt{(x-1)^2 + (-10-2)^2} = 13$$
$$\sqrt{x^2 - 2x + 1 + 144} = 13$$
$$x^2 - 2x + 145 = 169$$
$$x^2 - 2x - 24 = 0$$
$$(x+4)(x-6) = 0$$
$$x = -4 \quad \text{or} \quad x = 6$$

27. Find a relationship between x and y so that (x, y) is equidistant from the points $(4, -1)$ and $(-2, 3)$.

Solution:

The distance between $(4, -1)$ and (x, y) is equal to the distance between $(-2, 3)$ and (x, y).

$$\sqrt{(x-4)^2 + (y+1)^2} = \sqrt{(x+2)^2 + (y-3)^2}$$
$$(x-4)^2 + (y+1)^2 = (x+2)^2 + (y-3)^2$$
$$x^2 - 8x + 16 + y^2 + 2y + 1 = x^2 + 4x + 4 + y^2 - 6y + 9$$
$$4 = 12x - 8y$$
$$1 = 3x - 2y$$
$$0 = 3x - 2y - 1$$

31. Determine the quadrant(s) in which (x, y) is located so that the conditions $x = -4$ and $y > 0$ are satisfied.

Solution:

$x = -4 \Rightarrow x$ lies in Quadrant II or Quadrant III.

$y > 0 \Rightarrow y$ lies in Quadrant I or Quadrant II.

$x = -4$ AND $y > 0 \Rightarrow (x, y)$ lies in Quadrant II.

35. A line segment has (x_1, y_1) as one endpoint and (x_m, y_m) as its midpoint. Find the other endpoint (x_2, y_2) of the line segment in terms of x_1, x_m, y_1, and y_m.

Solution:

Since $(x_m, y_m) = \left(\dfrac{x_1 + x_2}{2}, \dfrac{y_1 + y_2}{2} \right)$, we have:

$$x_m = \frac{x_1 + x_2}{2} \quad \text{and} \quad y_m = \frac{y_1 + y_2}{2}$$

$$2x_m = x_1 + x_2 \qquad\qquad 2y_m = y_1 + y_2$$

$$2x_m - x_1 = x_2 \qquad\qquad 2y_m - y_1 = y_2$$

Thus, $(x_2, y_2) = (2x_m - x_1, 2y_m - y_1)$.

41. Plot the points $(2, 1)$, $(-3, 5)$, and $(7, -3)$ on the rectangular coordinate system. Now plot the corresponding points when the sign of the x-coordinate is reversed. What can you infer about the result of the location of a point when the sign of the x-coordinate is changed?

Solution:

The points (x, y) and $(-x, y)$ are symmetric with respect to the y-axis.

45. Determine whether the indicated points lie on the graph of $2x - y - 3 = 0$.

(a) $(1, 2)$ (b) $(1, -1)$

Solution:

$$2x - y - 3 = 0$$

(a) $2(1) - (2) - 3 \overset{?}{=} 0$ (b) $2(1) - (-1) - 3 \overset{?}{=} 0$

$-3 \neq 0$ $0 = 0$

The point $(1, 2)$ is **not** on the graph.   The point $(1, -1)$ **is** on the graph.

49. Find the x- and y-intercepts of the graph of the equation $y = x^2 + x - 2$.

Solution:

Let $y = 0$. Then $0 = x^2 + x - 2 = (x + 2)(x - 1)$ and $x = -2$ or $x = 1$.
x-intercepts: $(-2, \ 0)$ and $(1, \ 0)$

Let $x = 0$. Then $y = -2$.
y-intercept: $(0, \ -2)$

53. Find the x- and y-intercepts of the graph of the equation $xy - 2y - x + 1 = 0$.

Solution:

Let $y = 0$. Then $-x + 1 = 0$ and $x = 1$.
x-intercept: $(1, \ 0)$

Let $x = 0$. Then $-2y + 1 = 0$ and $y = \frac{1}{2}$.
y-intercept: $\left(0, \ \frac{1}{2}\right)$

57. Check for symmetry with respect to both axes and the origin for $x - y^2 = 0$.

Solution:

By replacing y with $-y$, we have

$$x - (-y)^2 = 0$$
$$x - y^2 = 0$$

which is the original equation. Replacing x with $-x$ or replacing both x and y with $-x$ and $-y$ does not yield equivalent equations. Thus, $x - y^2 = 0$ is symmetric with respect to the x-axis.

65. Match $y = x^3 - x$ with its graph.

Solution:

$y = x^3 - x$
x-intercepts: $(-1, \ 0)$, $(0, \ 0)$, $(1, \ 0)$
y-intercept: $(0, \ 0)$
Symmetry: Origin
Matches graph (e)

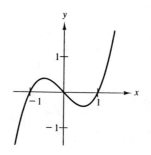

67. Sketch the graph of $y = -3x + 2$. Identify any intercepts and test for symmetry.

Solution:

$$y = -3x + 2$$

x-intercept: $\left(\frac{2}{3},\ 0\right)$

y-intercept: $(0,\ 2)$

No symmetry

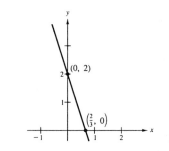

73. Sketch the graph of $y = \sqrt{x - 3}$. Identify any intercepts and test for symmetry.

Solution:

$$y = \sqrt{x - 3}$$

x-intercept: $(3,\ 0)$

No y-intercept

No symmetry

x	3	4	7	12
y	0	1	2	3

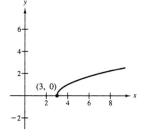

Note: The domain is $[3,\ \infty)$ and the range is $[0,\ \infty)$.

77. Sketch the graph of $x = y^2 - 1$. Identify any intercepts and test for symmetry.

Solution:

$$x = y^2 - 1$$

x-intercept: $(-1,\ 0)$

y-intercepts: $(0,\ -1),\ (0,\ 1)$

x-axis symmetry

x	-1	0	3
y	0	± 1	± 2

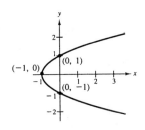

81. Find the standard form of the equation of the circle with center $(-1, 2)$ passing through the point $(0, 0)$.

Solution:

$$(x + 1)^2 + (y - 2)^2 = r^2$$
$$(0 + 1)^2 + (0 - 2)^2 = r^2 \Rightarrow r^2 = 5$$
$$(x + 1)^2 + (y - 2)^2 = 5$$

83. Find the center and radius, and sketch the graph of the equation $x^2 + y^2 - 2x + 6y + 6 = 0$.

Solution:

$$x^2 + y^2 - 2x + 6y + 6 = 0$$
$$(x^2 - 2x + 1^2) + (y^2 + 6y + 3^2) = -6 + 1 + 9$$
$$(x - 1)^2 + (y + 3)^2 = 4$$

Center: $(1, -3)$

Radius: 2

85. Find the center and radius, and sketch the graph of the equation $16x^2 + 16y^2 + 16x + 40y - 7 = 0$.

Solution:

$$16x^2 + 16y^2 + 16x + 40y - 7 = 0$$
$$x^2 + y^2 + x + \frac{5}{2}y - \frac{7}{16} = 0$$
$$\left(x^2 + x + \left(\frac{1}{2}\right)^2\right) + \left(y^2 + \frac{5}{2}y + \left(\frac{5}{4}\right)^2\right) = \frac{7}{16} + \frac{1}{4} + \frac{25}{16}$$
$$\left(x + \frac{1}{2}\right)^2 + \left(y + \frac{5}{4}\right)^2 = \frac{36}{16}$$
$$\left(x + \frac{1}{2}\right)^2 + \left(y + \frac{5}{4}\right)^2 = \frac{9}{4}$$

Center: $\left(-\frac{1}{2}, -\frac{5}{4}\right)$

Radius: $\frac{3}{2}$

SECTION 1.4
Lines in the Plane: Slope

- The slope, m, of a nonvertical line passing through the points (x_1, y_1) and (x_2, y_2) is

$$m = \frac{y_2 - y_1}{x_2 - x_1}.$$

  Any two points on a line can be used to calculate its slope.

- Types of slope:
  (a) If $m > 0$, the line rises (from left to right).
  (b) If $m < 0$, the line falls (from left to right).
  (c) If $m = 0$, the line is horizontal.
  (d) A vertical line has undefined slope.

- Equations of lines:
  (a) Point-slope form   (b) Two-point form   (c) Slope-intercept form
  $$y - y_1 = m(x - x_1)$$ $$y - y_1 = \frac{y_2 - y_1}{x_2 - x_1}(x - x_1)$$ $$y = mx + b$$

  (d) Vertical line   (e) Horizontal line   (f) General form
  $$x = a$$ $$y = b$$ $$Ax + By + C = 0$$

Solutions to Selected Exercises

7. Sketch the graph of the lines through the point $(2, 3)$ with the indicated slope. Make the sketches on the same set of coordinate axes.

   (a) 0   (b) 1   (c) 2   (d) −3

   Solution:

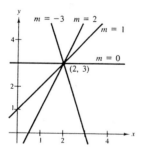

11. Plot the points $(-6, -1)$ and $(-6, 4)$ and find the slope of the line passing through the points.

Solution:

$$m = \frac{4 - (-1)}{-6 - (-6)} = \frac{5}{0}$$

The slope is undefined.

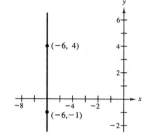

17. Use the point $(5, -6)$ on the line and the slope $m = 1$ of the line to find three additional points that the line passes through. (The solution is not unique.)

Solution:

Since $m = 1 = \frac{1}{1}$, each unit of horizontal change results in one unit of vertical change. Three additional points are:

$$(5 + 1, \ -6 + 1) = (6, \ -5)$$
$$(5 + 2, \ -6 + 2) = (7, \ -4)$$
$$(5 + 3, \ -6 + 3) = (8, \ -3)$$

23. Find the slope and y-intercept, if possible, of the line specified by $5x - y + 3 = 0$. Sketch a graph of the line.

Solution:

$$5x - y + 3 = 0$$
$$-y = -5x - 3$$
$$y = 5x + 3$$

Slope: $m = 5$

y-intercept: $(0, 3)$

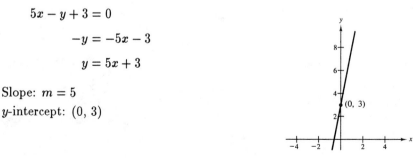

27. Find the slope and y-intercept, if possible, of the line specified by the equation $7x + 6y - 30 = 0$. Sketch a graph of the line.

Solution:

$$7x + 6y - 30 = 0$$

$$6y = -7x + 30$$

$$y = -\frac{7}{6}x + 5$$

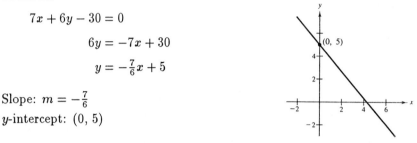

Slope: $m = -\frac{7}{6}$

y-intercept: $(0, 5)$

31. Find an equation for the line passing through the points $(2, \frac{1}{2})$, and $(\frac{1}{2}, \frac{5}{4})$.

Solution:

$$m = \frac{(5/4) - (1/2)}{(1/2) - 2} = \frac{3/4}{-3/2} = -\frac{1}{2}$$

$$y - \frac{1}{2} = -\frac{1}{2}(x - 2)$$

$$2y - 1 = -(x - 2)$$

$$2y - 1 = -x + 2$$

$$x + 2y - 3 = 0$$

33. Find an equation for the line passing through the points $(-8, 1)$ and $(-8, 7)$.

Solution:

$$m = \frac{7 - 1}{-8 - (-8)} = \frac{6}{0} \text{ which is undefined.}$$

The line is vertical since it has no slope. Therefore, we have $x = -8$ or $x + 8 = 0$ since the line passes through $(-8, 1)$ and $(-8, 7)$.

39. Find an equation of the line that passes through the point $(-3, 6)$ and has a slope of $m = -2$. Sketch a graph of the line.

Solution:

$$y - 6 = -2\left[x - (-3)\right]$$

$$y - 6 = -2x - 6$$

$$y = -2x$$

$$2x + y = 0$$

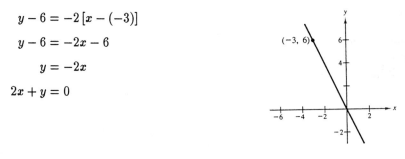

43. Find an equation of the line that passes through the point $(6, -1)$ and has an undefined slope. Sketch a graph of the line.

Solution:

Since the slope is undefined, the line is vertical and since the line passes through $(6, -1)$, its equation is $x = 6$ or $x - 6 = 0$.

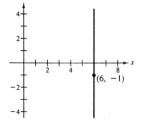

47. Use the intercept form, $(x/a) + (y/b) = 1$, $a \neq 0$, $b \neq 0$, to find an equation of the line with x-intercept $(2, 0)$ and y-intercept $(0, 3)$.

Solution:

$$\frac{x}{2} + \frac{y}{3} = 1$$

$$3x + 2y = 6$$

$$3x + 2y - 6 = 0$$

51. Use the intercept form, $(x/a) + (y/b) = 1$, $a \neq 0$, $b \neq 0$, to find an equation of the line through $(1, 2)$ with x-intercept $(a, 0)$ and y-intercept $(0, a)$.

Solution:

$$\frac{x}{a} + \frac{y}{a} = 1$$

$$x + y = a$$

Since the line passes through $(1, 2)$ we have $1 + 2 = a \Rightarrow a = 3$. The equation of the line is

$$x + y = 3$$

$$x + y - 3 = 0.$$

57. Match the description "A person is paying \$10 per week to a friend to repay a \$100 loan" with a graph. Determine the slope and how it is interpreted in the situation.

Solution:

$$y = 100 - 10x$$

The description matches graph (b). The slope of -10 represents the weekly decrease in the amount of the loan.

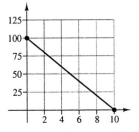

61. Find the equation of the line giving the relationship between the temperature in degrees Celsius, C, and degrees Fahrenheit, F. Use the fact that water freezes at 0° Celsius (32° Fahrenheit) and boils at 100° Celsius (212° Fahrenheit).

Solution:

Using the points (0, 32) and (100, 212), we have

$$m = \frac{212 - 32}{100 - 0} = \frac{180}{100} = \frac{9}{5}$$

$$F - 32 = \frac{9}{5}(C - 0)$$

$$F = \frac{9}{5}C + 32.$$

65. A salesperson receives a monthly salary of \$2500 plus a commission of 7% of his sales. Write a linear equation for the salesperson's monthly wage, W, in terms of his monthly sales, S.

Solution:

$$W = 2500 + 7\% \text{ of } S$$

$$= 2500 + 0.07S$$

SECTION 1.5
Functions

- ■ Given an equation, you should be able to determine if it represents a function.

- ■ Given a function, you should be able to do the following.
  - (a) Find the domain.
  - (b) Find the range.
  - (c) Evaluate it at specific values.

Solutions to Selected Exercises

5. Evaluate the function $f(x) = 2x - 3$ at the specified value of the independent variable and simplify.

   (a) $f(1)$ (b) $f(-3)$ (c) $f(x - 1)$

   Solution:

   (a) $f(1) = 2(1) - 3$
   $$= -1$$

   (b) $f(-3) = 2(-3) - 3$
   $$= -9$$

   (c) $f(x - 1) = 2(x - 1) - 3$
   $$= 2x - 5$$

9. Evaluate the function $f(y) = 3 - \sqrt{y}$ at the specified value of the independent variable and simplify.

   (a) $f(4)$ (b) $f(0.25)$ (c) $f(4x^2)$

   Solution:

   (a) $f(4) = 3 - \sqrt{4}$
   $$= 1$$

   (b) $f(0.25) = 3 - \sqrt{0.25}$
   $$= 2.5$$

   (c) $f(4x^2) = 3 - \sqrt{4x^2}$
   $$= 3 - 2|x|$$

11. For $f(x) = x^2 - x + 1$, find $\dfrac{f(2 + h) - f(2)}{h}$ and simplify your answer.

    Solution:

    $$f(x) = x^2 - x + 1$$
    $$f(2 + h) = (2 + h)^2 - (2 + h) + 1 = 4 + 4h + h^2 - 2 - h + 1 = h^2 + 3h + 3$$
    $$f(2) = (2)^2 - 2 + 1 = 3$$
    $$f(2 + h) - f(2) = h^2 + 3h$$
    $$\frac{f(2 + h) - f(2)}{h} = h + 3$$

15. For $g(x) = 3x - 1$, find $\dfrac{g(x) - g(3)}{x - 3}$ and simplify your answer.

Solution:

$$g(x) = 3x - 1$$

$$g(3) = 3(3) - 1 = 8$$

$$\frac{g(x) - g(3)}{x - 3} = \frac{(3x - 1) - 8}{x - 3} = \frac{3x - 9}{x - 3} = \frac{3(x - 3)}{x - 3} = 3$$

19. Find all real values x such that $f(x) = 0$ for $f(x) = x^2 - 9$.

Solution:

$$x^2 - 9 = 0$$

$$x^2 = 9$$

$$x = \pm 3$$

21. Find all real values x such that $f(x) = 0$ for $f(x) = \dfrac{3}{x - 1} + \dfrac{4}{x - 2}$.

Solution:

$$\frac{3}{x - 1} + \frac{4}{x - 2} = 0$$

$$3(x - 2) + 4(x - 1) = 0$$

$$7x - 10 = 0$$

$$x = \frac{10}{7}$$

25. Find the domain of $h(t) = 4/t$.

Solution:

The domain includes all real numbers except 0, i.e. $t \neq 0$.

31. Assume that the domain of $f(x) = x^2$ is the set $A = \{-2, -1, 0, 1, 2\}$. Determine the set of ordered pairs representing the function f.

Solution:

$$\{(-2,\ f(-2)),\ (-1,\ f(-1)),\ (0,\ f(0)),\ (1,\ f(1)),\ (2,\ f(2))\}$$

$$\{(-2,\ 4),\ (-1,\ 1),\ (0,\ 0),\ (1,\ 1),\ (2,\ 4)\}$$

35. Express the area, A, of a circle as a function of its circumference, C.

Solution:

$$A = \pi r^2, \quad C = 2\pi r$$

$$r = \frac{C}{2\pi}$$

$$A = \pi \left(\frac{C}{2\pi}\right)^2 = \frac{C^2}{4\pi}$$

37. A right triangle is formed in the first quadrant by the x- and y-axes and a line through the point $(1, 2)$, as shown in the figure. Write the area of the triangle as a function of x, and determine the domain of the function.

Solution:

$$A = \frac{1}{2}bh = \frac{1}{2}xy$$

Since $(0, y)$, $(1, 2)$ and $(x, 0)$ all lie on the same line, the slopes between any pair are equal.

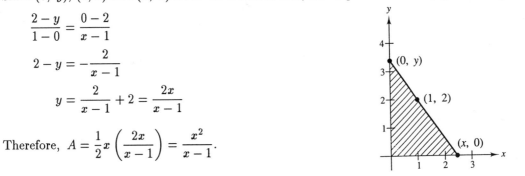

$$\frac{2 - y}{1 - 0} = \frac{0 - 2}{x - 1}$$

$$2 - y = -\frac{2}{x - 1}$$

$$y = \frac{2}{x - 1} + 2 = \frac{2x}{x - 1}$$

Therefore, $A = \frac{1}{2}x\left(\frac{2x}{x - 1}\right) = \frac{x^2}{x - 1}$.

The domain of A includes x-values such that $x^2/(x - 1) > 0$. This results in a domain of $x > 1$.

41. A balloon carrying a transmitter ascends vertically from a point 2000 feet from the receiving station (see figure). Let d be the distance between the balloon and the receiving station. Express the height of the balloon as a function of d. What is the domain of the function?

Solution:

By the Pythagorean Theorem, we have:

$$h^2 + 2000^2 = d^2$$

$$h^2 = d^2 - 2000^2$$

$$h = \sqrt{d^2 - 2000^2}$$

For the domain we have $d^2 - 2000^2 \geq 0$ and $d \geq 0$. Thus, $d \geq 2000$.

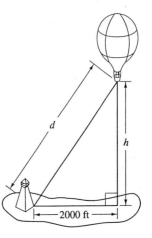

SECTION 1.6

Graphs of Functions

- You should be able to determine the domain and range of a function from its graph.

- You should be able to use the vertical line test for functions.

- You should know that the graph of $f(x) = c$ is a horizontal line through $(0, c)$.

- You should be able to determine when a function is constant, increasing, or decreasing.

- You should know that f is
  (a) Odd if $f(-x) = -f(x)$.
  (b) Even if $f(-x) = f(x)$.

- You should know the basic types of transformations.

- You should be able to graph rational functions using vertical and horizontal asymptotes as sketching aids.

Solutions to Selected Exercises

3. Determine the domain and range of the function $f(x) = \sqrt{25 - x^2}$.

   Solution:

   From the graph we see that the x-values do not extend beyond $x = -5$ (on the left) and $x = 5$ (on the right). The domain is $[-5, 5]$. Similarly, the y-values do not extend beyond $y = 0$ and $y = 5$. The range is $[0, 5]$.

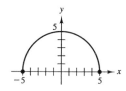

5. Use the vertical line test to determine if y is a function of x where $y = x^2$.

Solution:

Since no vertical line would ever cross the graph more than one time, y **is** a function of x.

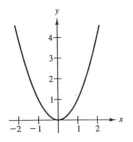

7. Use the vertical line test to determine if y is a function of x where $x = |y|$.

Solution:

Since some vertical lines cross the graph twice, y is **not** a function of x.

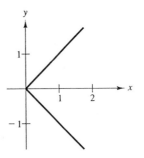

13. (a) Determine the intervals over which the function is increasing, decreasing, or constant, and (b) determine if the function is even, odd, or neither for $f(x) = x\sqrt{x+3}$.

Solution:

(a) By its graph we see that f is increasing on $(-2, \infty)$ and decreasing on $(-3, -2)$.

(b) $f(-x) = -x\sqrt{-x+3}$
$f(-x) \neq f(x)$ and $f(-x) \neq -f(x)$, so the function is neither even nor odd.

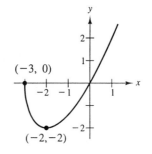

17. Determine whether $g(x) = x^3 - 5x$ is even, odd, or neither.

Solution:

$$g(x) = x^3 - 5x$$
$$g(-x) = (-x)^3 - 5(-x) = -x^3 + 5x = -(x^3 - 5x) = -g(x)$$

Therefore, g is odd.

21. Sketch the graph of $f(x) = 3$ and determine whether the function is even, odd, or neither.

Solution:

$f(x) = 3$

Domain: $(-\infty, \infty)$
Range: $\{3\}$
y-intercept: $(0, 3)$
y-axis symmetry
$\qquad f(-x) = 3 = f(x)$
Therefore, f is even.

25. Sketch the graph of $g(s) = s^3/4$ and determine whether the function is even, odd, or neither.

Solution:

$g(s) = \dfrac{s^3}{4}$

Intercept: $(0, 0)$
Origin symmetry
Domain: $(-\infty, \infty)$
Range: $(-\infty, \infty)$

$\qquad g(-s) = -g(s) = -\dfrac{s^3}{4}$

Therefore, g is odd.

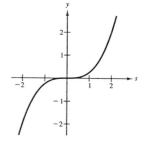

31. Sketch the graph of $h(x) = x\sqrt{4 - x^2}$ and determine whether the function is even, odd, or neither.

Solution:

$h(x) = x\sqrt{4 - x^2}$
Domain: $[-2, 2]$
Intercepts: $(-2, 0)$, $(0, 0)$, $(2, 0)$
Origin symmetry
$\qquad h(-x) = -x\sqrt{4 - x^2} = -h(x)$
Therefore, h is odd.

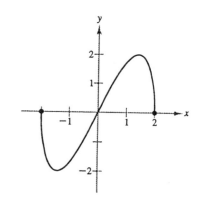

x	-2	-1	0	1	2
$h(x)$	0	$-\sqrt{3}$	0	$\sqrt{3}$	0

33. Sketch the graph of the following function and determine whether it is even, odd, or neither.

$$f(x) = \begin{cases} x+3, & \text{if } x \leq 0 \\ 3, & \text{if } 0 < x \leq 2 \\ 2x-1, & \text{if } x > 2 \end{cases}$$

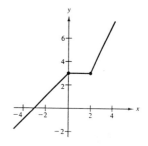

Solution:

For $x \leq 0$, $f(x) = x + 3$. For $0 < x \leq 2$, $f(x) = 3$.
For $x > 2$, $f(x) = 2x - 1$.
Thus, the graph of f is as shown.

$$f(-x) = \begin{cases} -x+3, & \text{if } x \leq 0 \\ 3, & \text{if } 0 < x \leq 2 \\ -2x-1, & \text{if } x > 2 \end{cases}$$

So, f is neither even nor odd.

37. Sketch the graph of $f(x) = x^2 - 9$ and determine the interval(s), if any, on the real axis for which $f(x) \geq 0$.

Solution:

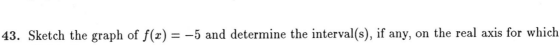

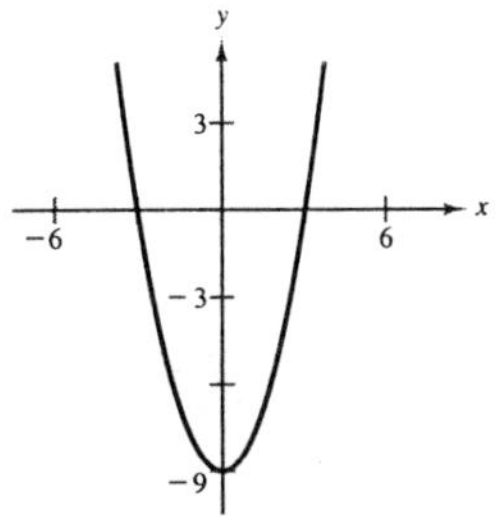

$$f(x) = x^2 - 9$$
x-intercepts: $(-3, 0)$, $(0, 3)$
y-intercept: $(0, -9)$
y-axis symmetry
Domain: $(-\infty, \infty)$
Range: $[-9, \infty)$
$f(x) \geq 0$ on the intervals $(-\infty, -3]$ and $[3, \infty)$ since the
graph is on or above the x-axis on these intervals.

43. Sketch the graph of $f(x) = -5$ and determine the interval(s), if any, on the real axis for which $f(x) \geq 0$.

Solution:

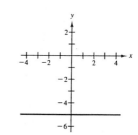

$$f(x) = -5$$
Intercept: $(0, -5)$
y-axis symmetry
Domain: $(-\infty, \infty)$
Range: $\{-5\}$
$f(x) < 0$ for any real value of x.

47. Use the graph of f (see figure) to sketch the graph of each of the following.

(a) $f(x) + 2$
(b) $-f(x)$
(c) $f(x - 2)$
(d) $f(-x)$

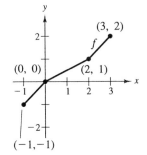

Solution:

(a) $f(x) + 2$
    Vertical shift two units upward

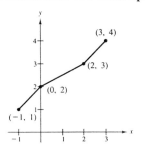

(b) $-f(x)$
    Reflection in the x-axis

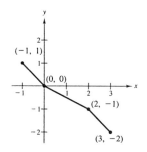

(c) $f(x - 2)$
    Horizontal shift two units to the right

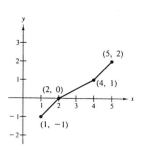

(d) $f(-x)$
    Reflection in the y-axis

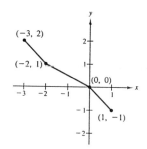

53. Use the graph of $g(x) = 8/x^3$ to sketch the graph of $y = -g(x) = -8/x^3$.

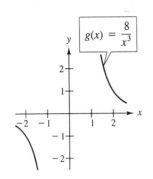

Solution:

Reflection in the x-axis

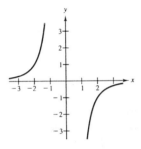

57. Sketch the graph of the following rational function. As sketching aids, check for intercepts, symmetry, vertical asymptotes, and horizontal asymptotes.

$$f(x) = \frac{2 + x}{1 - x}$$

Solution:

$$f(x) = \frac{2 + x}{1 - x}$$

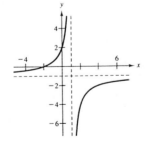

x-intercept: $(-2,\ 0)$
y-intercept: $(0,\ 2)$
No symmetry
Vertical asymptote: $x = 1$
    since $f(x) \Rightarrow \infty$ as $x \Rightarrow 1$ from the left
    and $f(x) \Rightarrow -\infty$ as $x \Rightarrow 1$ from the right.
Horizontal asymptote: $y = -1$
    since $f(x) \Rightarrow -1$ as $x \Rightarrow \pm\infty$.

x	-3	-2	-1	0	2	3	4
$f(x)$	$-\frac{1}{4}$	0	$\frac{1}{2}$	2	-4	$-\frac{5}{2}$	-2

63. Sketch the graph of the following rational function. As sketching aids, check for intercepts, symmetry, vertical asymptotes, and horizontal asymptotes.

$$f(x) = \frac{x^2}{x^2 + 9}$$

Solution:

$$f(x) = \frac{x^2}{x^2 + 9}$$

Intercept: $(0, 0)$

y-axis symmetry

No vertical asymptotes

Horizontal asymptote: $y = 1$
 since $f(x) \Rightarrow 1$ as $x \Rightarrow \pm\infty$.

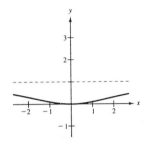

x	± 3	± 2	± 1	0
$f(x)$	$\frac{1}{2}$	$\frac{4}{13}$	$\frac{1}{10}$	0

67. The marketing department for a company estimates that the demand for a product is given by $p = 100 - 0.0001x$ where p is the price per unit and x is the number of units. The cost of producing x units is given by $C = 350{,}000 + 30x$, and the profit for producing and selling x units is given by $P = R - C = xp - C$. Sketch the graph of the profit function and estimate the number of units that would produce a maximum profit.

Solution:

$$P = R - C$$

$$= xp - C$$

$$= x(100 - 0.0001x) - (350{,}000 + 30x)$$

$$= -0.0001x^2 + 70x - 350{,}000$$

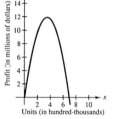

x-intercepts:
$$-0.0001x^2 + 70x - 350{,}000 = 0$$

$$x = \frac{-70 \pm \sqrt{70^2 - 4(-0.0001)(-350{,}000)}}{2(-0.0001)}$$

$$= \frac{-70 \pm \sqrt{4760}}{-0.0002}$$

$$x \approx 5036 \text{ or } x \approx 694{,}964$$

The profit is maximum when $x = 350{,}000$ units.

71. Write the height, h, of the given rectangle as a function of x.

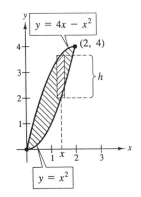

Solution:

$$h = \text{top} - \text{bottom}$$
$$= (4x - x^2) - x^2$$
$$= 4x - 2x^2$$

75. Explain why $f(x) = x^5 - x^3 + x$ is odd and $g(x) = x^5 - x^3 + x + 1$ is not odd.

Solution:

$$f(-x) = (-x)^5 - (-x)^3 + (-x)$$
$$= -x^5 + x^3 - x$$
$$= -(x^5 - x^3 + x)$$
$$= -f(x)$$

Thus, f is odd.

$$g(-x) = (-x)^5 - (-x)^3 + (-x) + 1$$
$$= -x^5 + x^3 - x + 1$$
$$= -(x^5 - x^3 + x - 1)$$
$$\neq -g(x)$$

Thus, g is not odd. The constant term does not change in sign when x is replaced with $-x$.

SECTION 1.7

Combinations of Functions and Inverse Functions

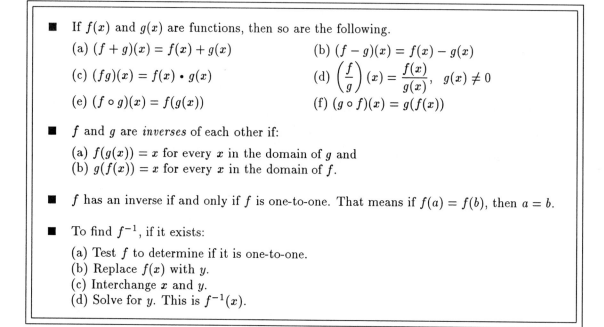

- If $f(x)$ and $g(x)$ are functions, then so are the following.
  - (a) $(f + g)(x) = f(x) + g(x)$
  - (b) $(f - g)(x) = f(x) - g(x)$
  - (c) $(fg)(x) = f(x) \cdot g(x)$
  - (d) $\left(\dfrac{f}{g}\right)(x) = \dfrac{f(x)}{g(x)}, \quad g(x) \neq 0$
  - (e) $(f \circ g)(x) = f(g(x))$
  - (f) $(g \circ f)(x) = g(f(x))$

- f and g are *inverses* of each other if:
  - (a) $f(g(x)) = x$ for every x in the domain of g and
  - (b) $g(f(x)) = x$ for every x in the domain of f.

- f has an inverse if and only if f is one-to-one. That means if $f(a) = f(b)$, then $a = b$.

- To find f^{-1}, if it exists:
  - (a) Test f to determine if it is one-to-one.
  - (b) Replace $f(x)$ with y.
  - (c) Interchange x and y.
  - (d) Solve for y. This is $f^{-1}(x)$.

Solutions to Selected Exercises

1. Given $f(x) = x^2$, $g(x) = 1 - x$, find (a) $(f + g)(x)$, (b) $(f - g)(x)$, (c) $(fg)(x)$, and (d) $(f/g)(x)$. What is the domain of f/g?

   Solution:

   (a) $(f + g)(x) = f(x) + g(x) = x^2 + (1 - x) = x^2 - x + 1$

   (b) $(f - g)(x) = f(x) - g(x) = x^2 - (1 - x) = x^2 + x - 1$

   (c) $(fg)(x) = f(x) \cdot g(x) = x^2(1 - x) = x^2 - x^3$

   (d) $\left(\dfrac{f}{g}\right)(x) = \dfrac{f(x)}{g(x)} = \dfrac{x^2}{1 - x}$

   The domain of f/g is the set of all real numbers except 1, (i.e. $x \neq 1$).

7. Evaluate $(f - g)(2t)$ for $f(x) = x^2 + 1$ and $g(x) = x - 4$.

Solution:

$$(f - g)(2t) = f(2t) - g(2t)$$
$$= [(2t)^2 + 1] - [(2t) - 4]$$
$$= 4t^2 + 1 - 2t + 4$$
$$= 4t^2 - 2t + 5$$

11. Evaluate $(f/g)(-1) - g(3)$ for $f(x) = x^2 + 1$ and $g(x) = x - 4$.

Solution:

$$\left(\frac{f}{g}\right)(-1) - g(3) = \frac{f(-1)}{g(-1)} - g(3)$$
$$= \frac{(-1)^2 + 1}{(-1) - 4} - [3 - 4]$$
$$= -\frac{2}{5} + 1$$
$$= \frac{3}{5}$$

15. Given $f(x) = 3x + 5$ and $g(x) = 5 - x$, find (a) $f \circ g$, (b) $g \circ f$, and (c) $f \circ f$.

Solution:

(a) $f \circ g = f(g(x))$

$\qquad = f(5 - x)$

$\qquad = 3(5 - x) + 5$

$\qquad = 20 - 3x$

(b) $g \circ f = g(f(x))$

$\qquad = g(3x + 5)$

$\qquad = 5 - (3x + 5)$

$\qquad = -3x$

(c) $f \circ f = f(f(x))$

$\qquad = f(3x + 5)$

$\qquad = 3(3x + 5) + 5$

$\qquad = 9x + 20$

19. Use the graphs of f and g to evaluate (a) $(f \circ g)(2)$ and (b) $(g \circ f)(2)$.

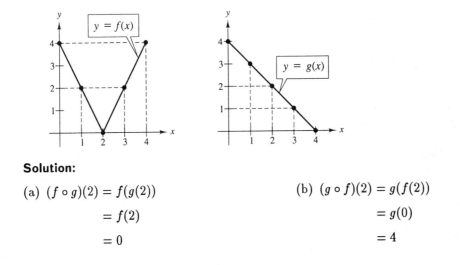

Solution:

(a) $(f \circ g)(2) = f(g(2))$

$\qquad = f(2)$

$\qquad = 0$

(b) $(g \circ f)(2) = g(f(2))$

$\qquad = g(0)$

$\qquad = 4$

23. (a) Show that $f(x) = 2x$ and $g(x) = x/2$ are inverse functions by showing that $f(g(x)) = x$ and $g(f(x)) = x$, and (b) graph f and g on the same set of coordinate axes.

Solution:

$$f(x) = 2x, \quad g(x) = \frac{x}{2}$$

(a) $f(g(x)) = f\left(\frac{x}{2}\right) = 2\left(\frac{x}{2}\right) = x$

$$g(f(x)) = g(2x) = \frac{2x}{2} = x$$

(b)

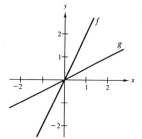

27. (a) Show that $f(x) = x^3$ and $g(x) = \sqrt[3]{x}$ are inverse functions by showing that $f(g(x)) = x$ and $g(f(x)) = x$, and (b) graph f and g on the same set of coordinate axes.

Solution:

$$f(x) = x^3, \quad g(x) = \sqrt[3]{x}$$

(a) $f(g(x)) = f(\sqrt[3]{x}) = (\sqrt[3]{x})^3 = x$

$$g(f(x)) = g(x^3) = \sqrt[3]{x^3} = x$$

(b)

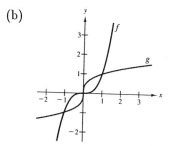

29. (a) Show that $f(x) = \sqrt{x - 4}$ and $g(x) = x^2 + 4, \ x \geq 0$ are inverse functions by showing that $f(g(x)) = x$ and $g(f(x)) = x$, and (b) graph f and g on the same set of coordinate axes.

Solution:

$$f(x) = \sqrt{x - 4}, \quad g(x) = x^2 + 4, \quad x \geq 0$$

(a) $f(g(x)) = f(x^2 + 4)$

$$= \sqrt{(x^2 + 4) - 4}$$

$$= \sqrt{x^2}$$

$$= |x|$$

$$= x, \quad x \geq 0$$

$$g(f(x)) = g(\sqrt{x - 4})$$

$$= (\sqrt{x - 4})^2 + 4$$

$$= (x - 4) + 4$$

$$= x$$

(b)

![graph for problem 29]

33. Determine whether the function shown is one-to-one.

Solution:

Since the function is decreasing on its entire domain, it is one-to-one.

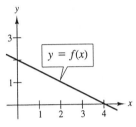

37. Determine whether the function $g(x) = (4 - x)/6$ is one-to-one.

Solution:

Let a and b be real numbers with $g(a) = g(b)$. Then we have

$$\frac{4-a}{6} = \frac{4-b}{6}$$

$$4 - a = 4 - b$$

$$-a = -b$$

$$a = b.$$

Therefore, $g(x)$ is one-to-one.

41. Determine whether the function $f(x) = -\sqrt{16 - x^2}$ is one-to-one.

Solution:

Since $f(4) = 0$ and $f(-4) = 0$, the function is not one-to-one.

45. Find the inverse of the one-to-one function $f(x) = x^5$. Then graph both f and f^{-1} on the same coordinate plane.

Solution:

$$f(x) = x^5$$

$$y = x^5$$

$$x = y^5$$

$$\sqrt[5]{x} = y$$

$$f^{-1}(x) = \sqrt[5]{x}$$

51. Find the inverse of the one-to-one function $f(x) = \sqrt[3]{x} - 1$. Then graph both f and f^{-1} on the same coordinate plane.

Solution:

$$f(x) = \sqrt[3]{x} - 1$$

$$y = \sqrt[3]{x} - 1$$

$$x = \sqrt[3]{y} - 1$$

$$x^3 = y - 1$$

$$x^3 + 1 = y$$

$$f^{-1}(x) = x^3 + 1$$

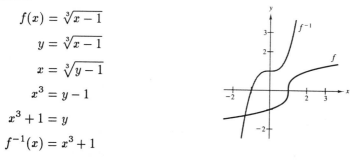

55. Determine whether the function $g(x) = x/8$ is one-to-one. If it is, find its inverse.

Solution:

$$g(a) = g(b)$$

$$\frac{a}{8} = \frac{b}{8}$$

$$a = b \quad \text{Thus, } g \text{ is one-to-one.}$$

$$g(x) = \frac{x}{8}$$

$$y = \frac{x}{8}$$

$$x = \frac{y}{8}$$

$$8x = y$$

$$g^{-1}(x) = 8x$$

59. Determine whether the function $h(x) = 1/x$ is one-to-one. If it is, find its inverse.

Solution:

$$h(a) = h(b)$$

$$\frac{1}{a} = \frac{1}{b}$$

$$a = b \quad \text{Thus, } h \text{ is one-to-one.}$$

$$h(x) = \frac{1}{x}$$

$$y = \frac{1}{x}$$

$$x = \frac{1}{y}$$

$$xy = 1$$

$$y = \frac{1}{x}$$

$$h^{-1}(x) = \frac{1}{x}$$

63. Determine whether the function $f(x) = 25 - x^2$, $x \leq 0$ is one-to-one. If it is, find its inverse.

Solution:

$$f(a) = f(b)$$
$$25 - a^2 = 25 - b^2$$
$$a^2 = b^2 \qquad \text{since } a, \ b \leq 0, \text{ we have } a = b \text{ and } f \text{ is one-to-one.}$$
$$f(x) = 25 - x^2, \quad x \leq 0$$
$$y = 25 - x^2$$
$$x = 25 - y^2$$
$$y^2 = 25 - x$$
$$y = -\sqrt{25 - x} \quad \text{since } x \leq 0 \text{ for } f.$$
$$f^{-1}(x) = -\sqrt{25 - x}$$

69. Use the functions $f(x) = x + 4$ and $g(x) = 2x - 5$ to find $g^{-1} \circ f^{-1}$.

Solution:

$$f(x) = x + 4 \Rightarrow f^{-1}(x) = x - 4$$
$$g(x) = 2x - 5 \Rightarrow g^{-1}(x) = \frac{x + 5}{2}$$

$$(g^{-1} \circ f^{-1})(x) = g^{-1}(f^{-1}(x)) = g^{-1}(x - 4) = \frac{(x - 4) + 5}{2} = \frac{x + 1}{2}$$

73. While traveling in a car at x miles per hour, you are required to stop quickly to avoid an accident. The distance the car travels during your reaction time is given by $R(x) = \frac{3}{4}x$. The distance traveled while braking is given by $B(x) = \frac{1}{15}x^2$. Find the function giving the total stopping distance T. Graph the functions R, B, and T on the same set of coordinate axes for $0 \leq x \leq 60$.

Solution:

$$R(x) = \frac{3}{4}x, \ B(x) = \frac{1}{15}x^2, \ T(x) = R(x) + B(x) = \frac{3}{4}x + \frac{1}{15}x^2$$

x	0	10	20	30	40	50	60
R	0	7.5	15	22.5	30	37.5	45
B	0	6.67	26.67	60	106.67	166.67	240
T	0	14.17	41.67	82.5	136.67	204.17	285

77. Prove that the product of two even functions is an even function.

Solution:

Let $h(x) = f(x) \cdot g(x)$ where f and g are even functions.
Then $h(-x) = f(-x)g(-x)$

$$= f(x)g(x) \quad \text{since } f \text{ and } g \text{ are even.}$$

$$= h(x).$$

Thus, $h(x)$ is even.

REVIEW EXERCISES FOR CHAPTER 1

Solutions to Selected Exercises

5. Give a verbal description of the subset of real numbers that is represented by the inequality $x \leq 7$, and sketch the subset on the real number line.

Solution:

The inequality $x \leq 7$ represents all real numbers less than or equal to seven.

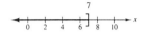

9. Determine whether the value of x is a solution of $3x^2 + 7x + 5 = x^2 + 9$.

   (a) $x = 0$ (b) $x = -4$ (c) $x = \frac{1}{2}$ (d) $x = -1$

Solution:

(a) $3(0)^2 + 7(0) + 5 \overset{?}{=} (0)^2 + 9$

$$5 \neq 9$$

$x = 0$ is **not** a solution.

(c) $3\left(\frac{1}{2}\right)^2 + 7\left(\frac{1}{2}\right) + 5 = \left(\frac{1}{2}\right)^2 + 9$

$$\frac{37}{4} = \frac{37}{4}$$

$x = \frac{1}{2}$ **is** a solution.

(b) $3(-4)^2 + 7(-4) + 5 \overset{?}{=} (-4)^2 + 9$

$$25 = 25$$

$x = -4$ **is** a solution.

(d) $3(-1)^2 + 7(-1) + 5 \overset{?}{=} (-1)^2 + 9$

$$1 \neq 10$$

$x = -1$ is **not** a solution.

13. Solve the equation

$$3\left(1 - \frac{1}{5t}\right) = 0.$$

Solution:

$$3\left(1 - \frac{1}{5t}\right) = 0$$

$$1 - \frac{1}{5t} = 0$$

$$1 = \frac{1}{5t}$$

$$5t = 1$$

$$t = \frac{1}{5}$$

19. Solve the equation $5x^4 - 12x^3 = 0$.

Solution:

$$5x^4 - 12x^3 = 0$$

$$x^3(5x - 12) = 0$$

$$x^3 = 0 \quad \text{or} \quad 5x - 12 = 0$$

$$x = 0 \quad \text{or} \quad x = \frac{12}{5}$$

21. Solve the equation $4t^3 - 12t^2 + 8t = 0$.

   Solution:

$$4t^3 - 12t^2 + 8t = 0$$
$$4t(t^2 - 3t + 2) = 0$$
$$4t(t - 1)(t - 2) = 0$$
$$t = 0, \ t = 1, \ t = 2$$

25. For the points $(2, 1)$ and $(14, 6)$, find (a) the distance between the two points, (b) the coordinates of the midpoint of the line segment between the two points, (c) an equation of the line through the points, and (d) an equation of the circle whose diameter is the line segment between the two points.

   Solution:

(a) $d = \sqrt{(14 - 2)^2 + (6 - 1)^2}$ (b) $m = \left(\dfrac{2 + 14}{2}, \dfrac{1 + 6}{2}\right)$ (c)

$\qquad = \sqrt{144 + 25}$ $= \left(8, \dfrac{7}{2}\right)$

$\qquad = \sqrt{169}$

$\qquad = 13$

$$m = \frac{6 - 1}{14 - 2} = \frac{5}{12}$$
$$y - 1 = \frac{5}{12}(x - 2)$$
$$12y - 12 = 5x - 10$$
$$5x - 12y + 2 = 0$$

(d) The length of the diameter is 13, so the length of the radius is $\frac{13}{2}$. The midpoint of the line segment is the center of the circle. The center is $(8, \frac{7}{2})$ and the radius is $\frac{13}{2}$.

$$(x - 8)^2 + \left(y - \frac{7}{2}\right)^2 = \frac{169}{4}$$

31. Find the intercepts of the graph of $2y^2 = x^3$ and check for symmetry with respect to each of the coordinate axes and the origin.

   Solution:

The only intercept is the origin, $(0, 0)$. The graph is symmetric with respect to the x-axis since $2(-y)^2 = x^3$ results in the original equation. Replacing x with $-x$ or replacing both x and y with $-x$ and $-y$ does not yield equivalent equations. Thus, the graph is not symmetric with respect to either the y-axis or the origin.

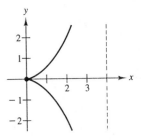

35. Find the intercepts of the graph of $y = x\sqrt{4 - x^2}$ and check for symmetry with respect to each of the coordinate axes and the origin.

Solution:

Let $y = 0$, then $0 = x\sqrt{4 - x^2}$ and $x = 0, \pm 2$.
  x-intercepts: $(0, 0)$, $(2, 0)$, $(-2, 0)$

Let $x = 0$, then $y = 0\sqrt{4 - 0^2}$ and $y = 0$.
  y-intercept: $(0, 0)$

The graph is symmetric with respect to the origin since

$$-y = -x\sqrt{4 - (-x)^2}$$

$$-y = -x\sqrt{4 - x^2}$$

$$y = x\sqrt{4 - x^2}.$$

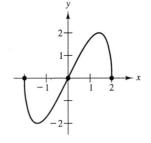

The graph is not symmetric with respect to either axis.
Domain: $[-2, 2]$

39. Determine the center and radius of the circle. Then, sketch the graph of
$4x^2 + 4y^2 - 4x - 40y + 92 = 0$.

Solution:

$$4x^2 + 4y^2 - 4x - 40y + 92 = 0$$

$$x^2 + y^2 - x - 10y + 23 = 0$$

$$\left(x^2 - x + \tfrac{1}{4}\right) + \left(y^2 - 10y + 25\right) = -23 + \tfrac{1}{4} + 25$$

$$\left(x - \tfrac{1}{2}\right)^2 + (y - 5)^2 = \tfrac{9}{4}$$

Center: $\left(\tfrac{1}{2}, 5\right)$
Radius: $\tfrac{3}{2}$

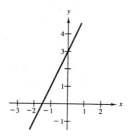

41. Sketch a graph of the equation
$y - 2x - 3 = 0$.

Solution:

$$y - 2x - 3 = 0$$

$$y = 2x + 3$$

x-intercept: $\left(-\tfrac{3}{2}, 0\right)$
y-intercept: $(0, 3)$

49. Sketch a graph of the equation $y = \sqrt{25 - x^2}$.

Solution:

$y = \sqrt{25 - x^2}$

x-intercepts: $(5, 0)$, $(-5, 0)$

y-intercept: $(0, 5)$

y-axis symmetry

Domain: $[-5, 5]$

Range: $[0, 5]$

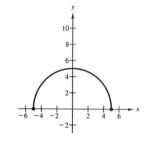

x	0	± 3	± 4	± 5
y	5	4	3	0

51. Sketch a graph of the equation $y = \frac{1}{4}(x + 1)^3$.

Solution:

$y = \frac{1}{4}(x + 1)^3$

x-intercept: $(-1, 0)$

y-intercept: $\left(0, \frac{1}{4}\right)$

Domain: $(-\infty, \infty)$

Range: $(-\infty, \infty)$

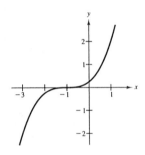

x	-3	-2	-1	0	1
y	-2	$-\frac{1}{4}$	0	$\frac{1}{4}$	2

55. Sketch a graph of the equation $y = x/(x^2 - 1)$.

Solution:

$$y = \frac{x}{x^2 - 1}$$

Intercept: $(0, 0)$

Origin symmetry

Domain: $(-\infty, -1) \cup (-1, 1) \cup (1, \infty)$

Vertical asymptotes: $x = 1$, $x = -1$

Horizontal asymptote: $y = 0$

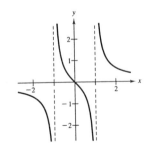

x	-3	-2	$-\frac{1}{2}$	0	$\frac{1}{2}$	2	3
y	$-\frac{3}{8}$	$-\frac{2}{3}$	$\frac{2}{3}$	0	$-\frac{2}{3}$	$\frac{2}{3}$	$\frac{3}{8}$

61. Determine the domain of the function

$$g(s) = \frac{5}{3s - 9}.$$

Solution:

The domain of $g(s) = 5/(3s - 9)$ includes all real numbers except $s = 3$ since this value would yield a zero in the denominator.

65. For $f(x) = \sqrt{x+1}$ (a) find f^{-1}, (b) sketch the graphs of f and f^{-1} on the same coordinate plane, and (c) verify that $f^{-1}(f(x)) = x = f(f^{-1}(x))$.

Solution:

(a) $\qquad y = \sqrt{x+1}, \ x \geq -1, \ y \geq 0$ $\qquad\qquad$ (b)

$\qquad\qquad x = \sqrt{y+1}$

$\qquad\qquad x^2 = y + 1$

$\qquad\qquad x^2 - 1 = y$

$\qquad\qquad f^{-1}(x) = x^2 - 1, \ x \geq 0$

(c) $f^{-1}[f(x)] = f^{-1}(\sqrt{x+1})$

$\qquad\qquad = (\sqrt{x+1})^2 - 1 = (x+1) - 1 = x$

$\qquad f[f^{-1}(x)] = f(x^2 - 1)$

$\qquad\qquad = \sqrt{(x^2 - 1) + 1} = \sqrt{x^2} = x, \ x \geq 0$

69. Restrict the domain of the function $f(x) = 2(x - 4)^2$ to an interval where the function is increasing and determine f^{-1} over that interval.

Solution:

$f(x) = 2(x - 4)^2$ is increasing on the interval $(4, \infty)$. It is decreasing on the interval $(-\infty, 4)$.

$\qquad\qquad f(x) = 2(x - 4)^2, \ x \geq 4$

$\qquad\qquad y = 2(x - 4)^2, \ x \geq 4, \ y \geq 0$

$\qquad\qquad x = 2(y - 4)^2$

$\qquad\qquad \sqrt{x} = \sqrt{2}(y - 4)$

$\qquad\qquad \sqrt{\frac{x}{2}} + 4 = y$

$\qquad\qquad f^{-1}(x) = \sqrt{\frac{x}{2}} + 4, \ x \geq 0$

73. Let $f(x) = 3 - 2x$, $g(x) = \sqrt{x}$, and $h(x) = 3x^2 + 2$. Find $(f - g)(4)$.

Solution:

$$(f - g)(4) = f(4) - g(4) = [3 - 2(4)] - \sqrt{4} = -7$$

77. Let $f(x) = 3 - 2x$, $g(x) = \sqrt{x}$, and $h(x) = 3x^2 + 2$. Find $(h \circ g)(7)$.

Solution:

$$(h \circ g)(7) = h(g(7)) = h(\sqrt{7}) = 3(\sqrt{7})^2 + 2 = 23$$

81. The total profit for a company in October was 12% more than it was in September. The total profit for the two months was $689,000. Find the profit for each month.

Solution:

Let $x =$ the profit for September. Then,

$$x + 12\% \text{ of } x = 1.12x = \text{the profit for October.}$$

$$x + 1.12x = 689,000$$

$$2.12x = 689,000$$

$$x = 325,000$$

$$1.12x = 364,000$$

The profit for September was $325,000 and for October was $364,000.

87. A wire 24 inches long is to be cut into four pieces to form a rectangle whose shortest side has a length of x. Express the area A of the rectangle as a function of x. Determine the domain of the function and sketch its graph over that domain.

Solution:

Let y be the longer side of the rectangle. Then we have $A = xy$. Since the perimeter is 24 inches, we have $2x + 2y = 24$ or $y = (24 - 2x)/2 = 12 - x$. The area equation now becomes: $A = xy = x(12 - x)$. To find the domain of A, we realize that area is a nonnegative quantity. Thus, $x(12 - x) > 0$. This gives us the interval $(0, 12)$. We also have the further restriction that x is the shortest side. This occurs on the interval $(0, 6]$.

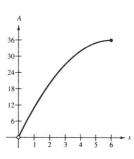

Practice Test for Chapter 1

1. Evaluate $-|-17|-17$.

2. Find the distance between a and b;
   $a = \frac{12}{5}$, $b = -\frac{7}{15}$.

3. Use absolute value notation to describe the expression "The distance between z and -5 is no more than 12."

4. Use absolute value notation to define the given interval on the real line.

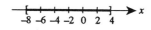

5. Solve the following equation.
   $$\frac{6x+5}{2x-9} = \frac{3}{5}.$$

6. Use the Quadratic Formula to solve the equation $4x^2 + 3x - 5 = 0$.

7. Use a calculator to solve the equation $21.4x^2 + 6.9x - 1.4 = 0$. Round your answers to three decimal places.

8. Find all real solutions to the equation $x^6 - 7x^3 - 8 = 0$.

9. Find the distance between the points $(4, 7)$ and $(-2, 5)$.

10. Find the midpoint of the line segment joining $(-1, 16)$ and $(3, -5)$.

11. Find x so that the distance between the points $(2, 0)$ and $(-6, x)$ is 9.

12. Find the x- and y-intercepts of the graph of the equation $y = x\sqrt{3-x}$.

13. Check for symmetry with respect to both axes and the origin:
    $$y = \frac{x^2}{x^3 - 1}.$$

14. Graph $y = \sqrt{x+2}$.

15. Graph $y = |x - 3|$.

16. Write the equation of the circle in standard form:
    $$x^2 + y^2 - 14x + 6y + 42 = 0.$$

17. Given $f(x) = 5x + 11$, find $\dfrac{f(x) - f(2)}{x - 2}$.

18. Find the domain of $f(x) = \sqrt{\dfrac{x-1}{x+3}}$.

19. An open box is to be made from a rectangular piece of cardboard, 16 inches by 11 inches, by cutting equal squares from each corner and turning up the sides. Write an equation for the volume V of the box as a function of its height x.

In Exercises 20–22, sketch the graph of the given function.

20. $f(x) = x^2 - 9$

21. $f(x) = -1 + |x|$

22. $f(x) = \dfrac{3x^2}{x^2 - 4}$

23. Given $f(x) = x^2 + 2$ and $g(x) = 3x - 8$, find $(f \circ g)(x)$.

24. Find the inverse of $f(x) = \dfrac{x + 3}{x}$.

25. Given $f(x) = \dfrac{x^3}{4}$ and $g(x) = 3x$, find $g^{-1} \circ f^{-1}$.

CHAPTER 2

Trigonometry

SECTION 2.1

Radian and Degree Measure

- If two angles have the same initial and terminal sides, they are coterminal angles.

- The radian measure of a central angle θ is found by taking the arc length s and dividing it by the radius r.

$$\theta = \frac{s}{r}$$

- You should know the following about angles:

  (a) θ is acute if $0 < \theta < \pi/2$.
  (b) θ is a right angle if $\theta = \pi/2$.
  (c) θ is obtuse if $\pi/2 < \theta < \pi$.
  (d) α and β are complementary if $\alpha + \beta = \pi/2$.
  (e) α and β are supplementary if $\alpha + \beta = \pi$.

- To convert degrees to radians, multiply by $\pi/180$.

- To convert radians to degrees, multiply by $180/\pi$.

- You should be able to convert angles to degrees, minutes, and seconds.

  (a) One minute: $1' = \dfrac{1}{60}(1°)$

  (b) One second: $1'' = \dfrac{1}{60}(1') = \dfrac{1}{3600}(1°)$

- Speed $= \dfrac{\text{distance}}{\text{time}} = \dfrac{s}{t}$

- Angular speed $= \dfrac{\theta}{t}$

Solutions to Selected Exercises

3. Determine the quadrant in which the terminal side of the angle lies. The angle is given in radians.

(a) -1 (b) -2

Solution:

(a) Since $-\pi/2 \approx -1.57$ and $-\pi/2 < -1 < 0$, the terminal side of $\theta = -1$ lies in Quadrant IV.

(b) Since $-\pi/2 \approx -1.57$, $-\pi \approx -3.14$ and $-\pi < -2 < -\pi/2$, the terminal side of $\theta = -2$ lies in Quadrant III.

7. Sketch the angle in standard position.

(a) $\dfrac{5\pi}{4}$ (b) $\dfrac{2\pi}{3}$

Solution:

(a) $\dfrac{5\pi}{4} = \pi + \dfrac{\pi}{4}$

The terminal side lies in Quadrant III.

(b) $\dfrac{2\pi}{3} = \pi - \dfrac{\pi}{3}$

The terminal side lies in Quadrant II.

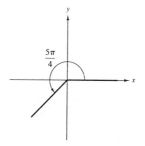 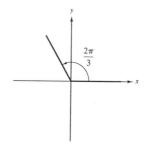

11. Determine two coterminal angles (one positive and one negative) for (a) $\theta = \pi/9$ and (b) $\theta = 4\pi/3$. Give the answers in radians.

Solution:

(a) Coterminal angles for $\dfrac{\pi}{9}$:

$$\dfrac{\pi}{9} + 2\pi = \dfrac{19\pi}{9}$$

$$\dfrac{\pi}{9} - 2\pi = -\dfrac{17\pi}{9}$$

(b) Coterminal angles for $\dfrac{4\pi}{3}$:

$$\dfrac{4\pi}{3} + 2\pi = \dfrac{10\pi}{3}$$

$$\dfrac{4\pi}{3} - 2\pi = -\dfrac{2\pi}{3}$$

13. Determine two coterminal angles (one positive and one negative) for (a) $\theta = 36°$ and (b) $\theta = -45°$. Give the answers in degrees.

Solution:

a) Coterminal angles for $36°$:

$$36° + 360° = 396°$$
$$36° - 360° = -324°$$

(b) Coterminal angles for $-45°$:

$$-45° + 360° = 315°$$
$$-45° - 360° = -405°$$

17. Find (if possible) the positive angle complement and the positive angle supplement of the angles (a) $\pi/3$ and (b) $3\pi/4$.

Solution:

(a) Complement: $\dfrac{\pi}{2} - \dfrac{\pi}{3} = \dfrac{\pi}{6}$

Supplement: $\pi - \dfrac{\pi}{3} = \dfrac{2\pi}{3}$

(b) Complement: Not possible since

$$\frac{3\pi}{4} > \frac{\pi}{2}.$$

Supplement: $\pi - \dfrac{3\pi}{4} = \dfrac{\pi}{4}$

23. Express (a) $7\pi/3$ and (b) $-11\pi/30$ in degree measure. (Do not use a calculator.)

Solution:

(a) $\dfrac{7\pi}{3} = \dfrac{7\pi}{3}\left(\dfrac{180}{\pi}\right) = 420°$

(b) $-\dfrac{11\pi}{30} = -\dfrac{11\pi}{30}\left(\dfrac{180}{\pi}\right) = -66°$

27. Express (a) $-20°$ and (b) $-240°$ in radian measure as a multiple of π. (Do not use a calculator.)

Solution:

(a) $-20° = -20\left(\dfrac{\pi}{180}\right) = -\dfrac{\pi}{9}$

(b) $-240° = -240\left(\dfrac{\pi}{180}\right) = -\dfrac{4\pi}{3}$

31. Convert (a) $532°$ and (b) $0.54°$ to radian measure. List your answer to three decimal places.

Solution:

(a) $532° = 532\left(\dfrac{\pi}{180}\right) \approx 9.285$ radians

(b) $0.54° = 0.54\left(\dfrac{\pi}{180}\right) \approx 0.009$ radian

33. Convert (a) $\pi/7$ and (b) $5\pi/11$ from radian to degree measure. List your answer to three decimal places.

Solution:

(a) $\dfrac{\pi}{7} = \dfrac{\pi}{7}\left(\dfrac{180}{\pi}\right) \approx 25.714°$

(b) $\dfrac{5\pi}{11} = \dfrac{5\pi}{11}\left(\dfrac{180}{\pi}\right) \approx 81.818°$

35. Convert (a) -4.2π and (b) 4.8 from radian to degree measure. List your answer to three decimal places.

Solution:

(a) $-4.2\pi = -4.2\pi\left(\dfrac{180}{\pi}\right) = -756°$

(b) $4.8 = 4.8\left(\dfrac{180}{\pi}\right) \approx 275.020°$

39. Convert (a) $240.6°$ and (b) $-145.8°$ to $D° M' S''$ form.

Solution:

(a) $240.6° = 240 + 0.6(60) = 240° 36'$

(b) $-145.8° = -[145 + 0.8(60)] = -145° 48'$

43. Find the radian measure of the central angle of a circle with radius $r = 15$ inches which intercepts an arc of length $s = 4$ inches.

Solution:

$$\theta = \frac{s}{r} = \frac{4 \text{ inches}}{15 \text{ inches}} = \frac{4}{15} \text{ radian}$$

49. Find the length of the arc intercepted by the central angle $\theta = 2$ radians on the circle of radius $r = 6$ meters.

Solution:

$$s = r\theta$$

$$s = (6)(2) = 12 \text{ m}$$

53. Find the distance between the two cities. Assume that earth is a sphere of radius 4000 miles and that the cities are on the same meridian (one city is due north of the other).

City	Latitude
Miami	25°46'37" N
Erie	42°7'15" N

Solution:

The central angle is the difference in latitudes.

$$\theta = 42°7'15" - 25°46'37"$$

$$= \left(42 + \tfrac{7}{60} + \tfrac{15}{3600}\right) - \left(25 + \tfrac{46}{60} + \tfrac{37}{3600}\right)$$

$$= 16.343\overline{8}° \approx 0.28525 \text{ radian}$$

The distance between the cities is found by calculating the arc length.

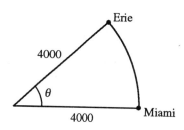

$$s = r\theta = 4000(0.28525) = 1141 \text{ miles}$$

The cities are approximately 1141 miles apart.

55. Assuming that the earth is a sphere of radius 4000 miles, what is the difference in latitude of two cities, one of which is 325 miles due north of the other?

Solution:

Use the formula $\theta = s/r$.

$$\theta = \frac{325}{4000} \cdot \frac{180}{\pi} \approx 4.655°$$

The difference in latitude is approximately 4.655°.

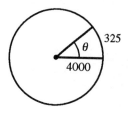

59. A car is moving at the rate of 50 miles per hour, and the diameter of each wheel is 2.5 feet.

(a) Find the number of revolutions per minute of the rotating wheels.

(b) Find the *angular speed* of the wheels in radians per minute.

Solution:

(a) 50 miles per hour $= 50(5280)/60 = 4400$ feet per minute
The circumference of the tire is $C = 2.5\pi$ feet.
The number of revolutions per minute is $r = 4400/2.5\pi \approx 560.2$

(b) The angular speed is θ/t.

$$\theta = \frac{4400}{2.5\pi}(2\pi) = 3520 \text{ radians}$$

$$\text{Angular speed} = \frac{3520 \text{ radians}}{1 \text{ minute}} = 3520 \text{ rad/min}$$

SECTION 2.2

The Trigonometric Functions and the Unit Circle

■ You should know the definition of the trigonometric functions. Let t be a real number and (x, y) the point on the unit circle corresponding to t.

(a) $\sin t = y$ (b) $\cos t = x$
(c) $\tan t = y/x, \quad x \neq 0$ (d) $\cot t = x/y, \quad y \neq 0$
(e) $\sec t = 1/x, \quad x \neq 0$ (f) $\csc t = 1/y, \quad y \neq 0$

■ The cosine and secant functions are even.

(a) $\cos(-t) = \cos t$ (b) $\sec(-t) = \sec t$

■ The other four trigonometric functions are odd.

(a) $\sin(-t) = -\sin t$ (b) $\tan(-t) = -\tan t$
(c) $\cot(-t) = -\cot t$ (d) $\csc(-t) = -\csc t$

■ You should be able to evaluate trigonometric functions with a calculator.

Solutions to Selected Exercises

3. Find the point (x, y) on the unit circle that corresponds to $t = 5\pi/6$.

Solution:

Using Figure 5.19 in the text, move counterclockwise to obtain the second quadrant point

$$(x, y) = \left(-\frac{\sqrt{3}}{2}, \frac{1}{2}\right).$$

5. Find the point (x, y) on the unit circle that corresponds to $\theta = 4\pi/3$.

Solution:

Using Figure 5.19 again and the fact that $4\pi/3 = 8\pi/6$, we obtain the point

$$(x, y) = \left(-\frac{1}{2}, -\frac{\sqrt{3}}{2}\right).$$

9. Evaluate the sine, cosine, and tangent of $t = \pi/4$.

Solution:

$t = \dfrac{\pi}{4}$ corresponds to the point

$\left(\dfrac{\sqrt{2}}{2}, \dfrac{\sqrt{2}}{2} \right)$.

$$\sin \frac{\pi}{4} = y = \frac{\sqrt{2}}{2}$$

$$\cos \frac{\pi}{4} = x = \frac{\sqrt{2}}{2}$$

$$\tan \frac{\pi}{4} = \frac{y}{x} = \frac{\sqrt{2}/2}{\sqrt{2}/2} = 1$$

13. Evaluate the sine, cosine, and tangent of $t = 11\pi/6$.

Solution:

$t = \dfrac{11\pi}{6}$ corresponds to the point

$\left(\dfrac{\sqrt{3}}{2}, -\dfrac{1}{2} \right)$.

$$\sin \frac{11\pi}{6} = y = -\frac{1}{2}$$

$$\cos \frac{11\pi}{6} = x = \frac{\sqrt{3}}{2}$$

$$\tan \frac{11\pi}{6} = \frac{y}{x} = \frac{-1/2}{\sqrt{3}/2} = -\frac{1}{\sqrt{3}} = -\frac{\sqrt{3}}{3}$$

17. Evaluate the six trigonometric functions of $t = 3\pi/4$.

Solution:

$t = \dfrac{3\pi}{4}$ corresponds to the point $\left(-\dfrac{\sqrt{2}}{2}, \dfrac{\sqrt{2}}{2} \right)$.

$$\sin \frac{3\pi}{4} = y = \frac{\sqrt{2}}{2}$$

$$\cos \frac{3\pi}{4} = x = -\frac{\sqrt{2}}{2}$$

$$\tan \frac{3\pi}{4} = \frac{y}{x} = \frac{\sqrt{2}/2}{-\sqrt{2}/2} = -1$$

$$\csc \frac{3\pi}{4} = \frac{1}{y} = \frac{1}{\sqrt{2}/2} = \frac{2}{\sqrt{2}} = \sqrt{2}$$

$$\sec \frac{3\pi}{4} = \frac{1}{x} = \frac{1}{-\sqrt{2}/2} = -\frac{2}{\sqrt{2}} = -\sqrt{2}$$

$$\cot \frac{3\pi}{4} = \frac{x}{y} = \frac{-\sqrt{2}/2}{\sqrt{2}/2} = -1$$

23. Evaluate $\sin 3\pi$ using its period as an aid.

Solution:

$$\sin 3\pi = \sin(2\pi + \pi)$$

$$= \sin \pi$$

$$= 0$$

27. Evaluate $\cos(19\pi)/6$ using its period as an aid.

Solution:

$$\cos \frac{19\pi}{6} = \cos\left(2\pi + \frac{7\pi}{6} \right)$$

$$= \cos \frac{7\pi}{6}$$

$$= -\frac{\sqrt{3}}{2}$$

31. Use $\sin t = \frac{1}{3}$ to evaluate the functions (a) $\sin(-t)$ and (b) $\csc(-t)$.

Solution:

(a) $\sin(-t) = -\sin t = -\dfrac{1}{3}$

(b) $\csc(-t) = -\csc t$

$$= -\frac{1}{\sin t} = -\frac{1}{1/3} = -3$$

35. Use $\sin t = \frac{4}{5}$ to evaluate the functions (a) $\sin(\pi - t)$ and (b) $\sin(t + \pi)$.

Solution:

(a) $\sin(\pi - t) = \sin t = \frac{4}{5}$

If t is in Quadrant I, $\pi - t$ is in Quadrant II and they both have the same y-value on the unit circle. If t is in Quadrant II, $\pi - t$ is in Quadrant I and they both have the same y-value on the unit circle. (t cannot be in Quadrant III or Quadrant IV since $\sin t = \frac{4}{5}$ is positive.)

(b) $\sin(t + \pi) = -\sin t = -\frac{4}{5}$

If t is in Quadrant I, $\pi + t$ is in Quadrant III and has a negative y-value on the unit circle. If t is in Quadrant II, $\pi + t$ is in Quadrant IV and has a negative y-value on the unit circle.

39. Use a calculator to evaluate $\cos(-3)$. [Set your calculator in radian mode and round your answer to four decimal places.]

Solution:

$\cos(-3) = \cos 3 \approx -0.9899925 \approx -0.9900$

43. Use a calculator to evaluate $\csc 0.8$. [Set your calculator in radian mode and round your answer to four decimal places.]

Solution:

$\csc 0.8 = \dfrac{1}{\sin 0.8} \approx 1.3940078 \approx 1.3940$

49. The displacement from equilibrium of an oscillating weight suspended by a spring is $y(t) = \frac{1}{4} \cos 6t$ where y is the displacement in feet and t is the time in seconds. Find the displacement when (a) $t = 0$, (b) $t = \frac{1}{4}$, and (c) $t = \frac{1}{2}$.

Solution:

(a) $y(0) = \frac{1}{4} \cos[6(0)] = \frac{1}{4} \cos 0 = \frac{1}{4}(1) = 0.2500$ foot

(b) $y\left(\frac{1}{4}\right) = \frac{1}{4} \cos\left[6\left(\frac{1}{4}\right)\right] = \frac{1}{4} \cos \frac{3}{2} \approx 0.0177$ foot

(c) $y\left(\frac{1}{2}\right) = \frac{1}{4} \cos\left[6\left(\frac{1}{2}\right)\right] = \frac{1}{4} \cos 3 \approx -0.2475$ foot

SECTION 2.3

Trigonometric Functions and Right Triangles

■ You should know the right triangle definition of trigonometric functions.

(a) $\sin\theta = \dfrac{\text{opp}}{\text{hyp}}$ (b) $\cos\theta = \dfrac{\text{adj}}{\text{hyp}}$

(c) $\tan\theta = \dfrac{\text{opp}}{\text{adj}}$ (d) $\cot\theta = \dfrac{\text{adj}}{\text{opp}}$

(e) $\sec\theta = \dfrac{\text{hyp}}{\text{adj}}$ (f) $\csc\theta = \dfrac{\text{hyp}}{\text{opp}}$

■ You should know the sine, cosine, and tangent of the special angles 30°, 45°, and 60°.

(a) For 45°, use the triangle   (b) For 30° and 60°, use the triangle

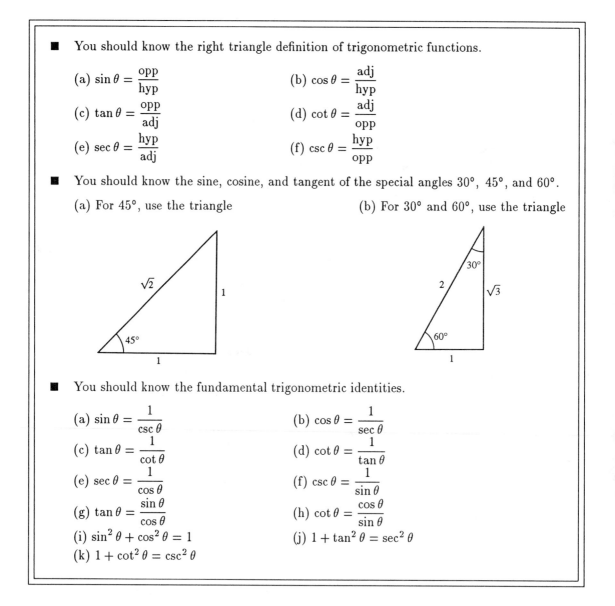

■ You should know the fundamental trigonometric identities.

(a) $\sin\theta = \dfrac{1}{\csc\theta}$ (b) $\cos\theta = \dfrac{1}{\sec\theta}$

(c) $\tan\theta = \dfrac{1}{\cot\theta}$ (d) $\cot\theta = \dfrac{1}{\tan\theta}$

(e) $\sec\theta = \dfrac{1}{\cos\theta}$ (f) $\csc\theta = \dfrac{1}{\sin\theta}$

(g) $\tan\theta = \dfrac{\sin\theta}{\cos\theta}$ (h) $\cot\theta = \dfrac{\cos\theta}{\sin\theta}$

(i) $\sin^2\theta + \cos^2\theta = 1$ (j) $1 + \tan^2\theta = \sec^2\theta$

(k) $1 + \cot^2\theta = \csc^2\theta$

Solutions to Selected Exercises

5. Sketch a right triangle corresponding to $\sin\theta = \frac{2}{3}$. Use the Pythagorean Theorem to determine the third side and then find the other five trigonometric functions of θ.

Solution:

$$\sin\theta = \frac{2}{3}$$

$$2^2 + (\text{adj})^2 = 3^2$$

Adjacent side $= \sqrt{9 - 4} = \sqrt{5}$

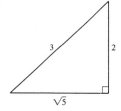

$$\cos\theta = \frac{\sqrt{5}}{3} \qquad\qquad \sec\theta = \frac{3}{\sqrt{5}} = \frac{3\sqrt{5}}{5}$$

$$\tan\theta = \frac{2}{\sqrt{5}} = \frac{2\sqrt{5}}{5} \qquad \csc\theta = \frac{3}{2}$$

$$\cot\theta = \frac{\sqrt{5}}{2}$$

7. Sketch a right triangle corresponding to $\tan\theta = 3$. Use the Pythagorean Theorem to determine the third side and then find the other five trigonometric functions of θ.

Solution:

$$\tan\theta = 3 = \frac{3}{1}$$

$$3^2 + 1^2 = (\text{hyp})^2$$

Hypotenuse $= \sqrt{1 + 9} = \sqrt{10}$

$$\sin\theta = \frac{3}{\sqrt{10}} = \frac{3\sqrt{10}}{10} \qquad \csc\theta = \frac{\sqrt{10}}{3}$$

$$\cos\theta = \frac{1}{\sqrt{10}} = \frac{\sqrt{10}}{10} \qquad \sec\theta = \sqrt{10}$$

$$\cot\theta = \frac{1}{3}$$

11. Use $\csc \theta = 3$ and $\sec \theta = \frac{3\sqrt{2}}{4}$ and trigonometric identities to find the following trigonometric functions.

(a) $\sin \theta$ (b) $\cos \theta$ (c) $\tan \theta$ (d) $\sec(90° - \theta)$

Solution:

(a) $\sin \theta = \dfrac{1}{\csc \theta} = \dfrac{1}{3}$ (b) $\cos \theta = \dfrac{1}{\sec \theta} = \dfrac{4}{3\sqrt{2}} = \dfrac{2\sqrt{2}}{3}$

(c) $\tan \theta = \dfrac{\sin \theta}{\cos \theta}$ (d) $\sec(90° - \theta) = \csc \theta = 3$

$= \dfrac{1/3}{(2\sqrt{2})/3} = \dfrac{1}{2\sqrt{2}} = \dfrac{\sqrt{2}}{4}$

13. Evaluate (a) $\cos 60°$ and (b) $\tan \pi/6$ by memory or by constructing an appropriate triangle.

Solution:

(a) $\cos 60° = \dfrac{1\cdot}{2}$

(b) $\tan \dfrac{\pi}{6} = \dfrac{1}{\sqrt{3}} = \dfrac{\sqrt{3}}{3}$

19. Use a calculator to evaluate (a) $\cot(\pi/16)$ and (b) $\tan(\pi/16)$. Round your answers to four decimal places.

Solution:

Make sure that your calculator is in radian mode.

(a) $\cot \dfrac{\pi}{16} = \dfrac{1}{\tan(\pi/16)} \approx 5.0273$ (b) $\tan \dfrac{\pi}{16} \approx 0.1989$

23. Find the value of θ in degrees ($0° < \theta < 90°$) and radians ($0 < \theta < \pi/2$) for (a) $\sin\theta = 1/2$ and (b) $\csc\theta = 2$ without a calculator.

Solution:

(a) $\sin\theta = \dfrac{1}{2}$

$\theta = 30° = \dfrac{\pi}{6}$

(b) $\csc\theta = 2 \Rightarrow \sin\theta = \dfrac{1}{2}$ Same as (a)

$\theta = 30° = \dfrac{\pi}{6}$

27. Find the value of θ in degrees ($0° < \theta < 90°$) and radians ($0 < \theta < \pi/2$) for (a) $\csc\theta = (2\sqrt{3})/3$ and (b) $\sin\theta = \sqrt{2}/2$ without a calculator.

Solution:

(a) $\csc\theta = \dfrac{2\sqrt{3}}{3} = \dfrac{2}{\sqrt{3}}$

$\theta = 60° = \dfrac{\pi}{3}$

(b) $\sin\theta = \dfrac{\sqrt{2}}{2} = \dfrac{1}{\sqrt{2}}$

$\theta = 45° = \dfrac{\pi}{4}$

31. Find the value of θ in degrees ($0° < \theta < 90°$) and radians ($0 < \theta < \pi/2$) by using the inverse key on a calculator for (a) $\tan\theta = 1.1920$ and (b) $\tan\theta = 0.4663$.

Solution:

(a) $\tan\theta = 1.1920$

$\theta = \tan^{-1} 1.1920$

$\theta \approx 50.01° \approx 0.873$ radian

(b) $\tan\theta = 0.4663$

$\theta = \tan^{-1} 0.4663$

$\theta \approx 25° \approx 0.436$ radian

35. Solve for x.

Solution:

$\tan 60° = \dfrac{25}{x}$

$\sqrt{3} = \dfrac{25}{x}$

$x = \dfrac{25}{\sqrt{3}} = \dfrac{25\sqrt{3}}{3} \approx 14.43$

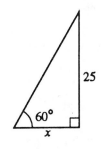

39. Solve for y.

Solution:

$$\sin 50° = \frac{y}{12}$$

$$0.7660 \approx \frac{y}{12}$$

$$y \approx 9.19$$

41. A six-foot person standing 12 feet from a streetlight casts an eight-foot shadow, as shown in the figure. What is the height of the streetlight?

Solution:

$$\frac{h}{6} = \frac{20}{8}$$

$$h = \frac{120}{8} = 15 \text{ ft}$$

The height of the streetlight is 15 feet.

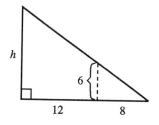

45. From a 150-foot observation tower on the coast, a Coast Guard officer sights a boat in difficulty. The angle of depression of the boat is 4°, as shown in the figure. How far is the boat from the shoreline?

Solution:

Let x = distance from the boat to the shoreline.

$$\tan 4° = \frac{150}{x}$$

$$x = \frac{150}{\tan 4°} \approx 2145 \text{ ft}$$

The boat is approximately 2145 feet from shore.

53. Determine whether the statement is true or false, and give a reason for your answer.

$$\sin 45° + \cos 45° = 1$$

Solution:

False; $\sin 45° + \cos 45° = \dfrac{\sqrt{2}}{2} + \dfrac{\sqrt{2}}{2} = \sqrt{2} \neq 1$

55. Determine whether the statement is true or false, and give a reason for your answer.

$$\dfrac{\sin 60°}{\sin 30°} = \sin 2°$$

Solution:

False; $\dfrac{\sin 60°}{\sin 30°} = \dfrac{\sqrt{3}/2}{1/2} = \sqrt{3} \approx 1.732$ and $\sin 2° \approx 0.035$

Thus, $\dfrac{\sin 60°}{\sin 30°} \neq \sin 2°$.

SECTION 2.4

Trigonometric Functions of Any Angle

- You should know the trigonometric functions of any angle θ in standard position with $(x,\ y)$ on the terminal side of θ and $r = \sqrt{x^2 + y^2}$.

  (a) $\sin \theta = \dfrac{y}{r}$ (b) $\cos \theta = \dfrac{x}{r}$ (c) $\tan \theta = \dfrac{y}{x},\ \ x \neq 0$

  (d) $\cot \theta = \dfrac{x}{y},\ \ y \neq 0$ (e) $\sec \theta = \dfrac{r}{x},\ \ x \neq 0$ (f) $\csc \theta = \dfrac{r}{y},\ \ y \neq 0$

- You should know the signs of the trigonometric functions in the four quadrants.

- You should be able to find the trigonometric functions of the quadrant angles (if they exist).

  (a) For 0, use (1, 0).   (b) For $\dfrac{\pi}{2}$, use (0, 1).

  (c) For π, use $(-1,\ 0)$.   (d) For $\dfrac{3\pi}{2}$, use $(0,\ -1)$.

- You should be able to use reference angles with the special angles to find trigonometric values.

Solutions to Selected Exercises

3. Determine the exact value of the six trigonometric functions of the given angle θ.

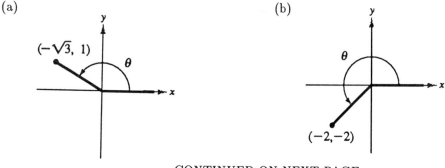

(a) $(-\sqrt{3},\ 1)$ θ

(b) θ $(-2, -2)$

–CONTINUED ON NEXT PAGE–

3. –CONTINUED–

Solution:

(a) $x = -\sqrt{3}, \ y = 1, \ r = \sqrt{3+1} = 2$

$$\sin\theta = \frac{y}{r} = \frac{1}{2} \qquad\qquad \csc\theta = \frac{r}{y} = 2$$

$$\cos\theta = \frac{x}{r} = -\frac{\sqrt{3}}{2} \qquad\qquad \sec\theta = \frac{r}{x} = -\frac{2}{\sqrt{3}} = -\frac{2\sqrt{3}}{3}$$

$$\tan\theta = \frac{y}{x} = -\frac{1}{\sqrt{3}} = -\frac{\sqrt{3}}{3} \qquad \cot\theta = \frac{x}{y} = -\sqrt{3}$$

(b) $x = -2, \ y = -2, \ r = \sqrt{4+4} = 2\sqrt{2}$

$$\sin\theta = \frac{y}{r} = -\frac{2}{2\sqrt{2}} = -\frac{\sqrt{2}}{2} \qquad \csc\theta = \frac{r}{y} = \frac{2\sqrt{2}}{-2} = -\sqrt{2}$$

$$\cos\theta = \frac{x}{r} = -\frac{2}{2\sqrt{2}} = -\frac{\sqrt{2}}{2} \qquad \sec\theta = \frac{r}{x} = \frac{2\sqrt{2}}{-2} = -\sqrt{2}$$

$$\tan\theta = \frac{y}{x} = \frac{-2}{-2} = 1 \qquad\qquad \cot\theta = \frac{x}{y} = \frac{-2}{-2} = 1$$

7. The point is on the terminal side of an angle in standard position. Determine the exact value of the six trigonometric functions of the angle.

(a) $(-4, \ 10)$ \qquad\qquad\qquad\qquad\qquad (b) $(3, \ -5)$

Solution:

(a) $x = -4, \ y = 10, \ r = \sqrt{16 + 100} = 2\sqrt{29}$

$$\sin\theta = \frac{10}{2\sqrt{29}} = \frac{5\sqrt{29}}{29} \qquad \csc\theta = \frac{2\sqrt{29}}{10} = \frac{\sqrt{29}}{5}$$

$$\cos\theta = \frac{-4}{2\sqrt{29}} = -\frac{2\sqrt{29}}{29} \qquad \sec\theta = \frac{2\sqrt{29}}{-4} = -\frac{\sqrt{29}}{2}$$

$$\tan\theta = \frac{10}{-4} = -\frac{5}{2} \qquad\qquad \cot\theta = \frac{-4}{10} = -\frac{2}{5}$$

(b) $x = 3, \ y = -5, \ r = \sqrt{9 + 25} = \sqrt{34}$

$$\sin\theta = \frac{-5}{\sqrt{34}} = -\frac{5\sqrt{34}}{34} \qquad \csc\theta = -\frac{\sqrt{34}}{5}$$

$$\cos\theta = \frac{3}{\sqrt{34}} = \frac{3\sqrt{34}}{34} \qquad \sec\theta = \frac{\sqrt{34}}{3}$$

$$\tan\theta = -\frac{5}{3} \qquad\qquad\qquad \cot\theta = -\frac{3}{5}$$

9. Use the two similar triangles in the figure to find (a) the unknown sides of the triangles and (b) the six trigonometric functions of the angles α_1 and α_2.

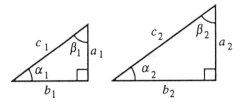

Solution:

Given $a_1 = 3$, $b_1 = 4$, $a_2 = 9$,

(a) $c_1 = \sqrt{a_1{}^2 + b_1{}^2} = \sqrt{9 + 16} = 5$

$$\frac{a_1}{a_2} = \frac{b_1}{b_2}$$

$$\frac{3}{9} = \frac{4}{b_2}$$

$$b_2 = 12$$

$$c_2 = \sqrt{a_2{}^2 + b_2{}^2}$$

$$= \sqrt{81 + 144} = 15$$

(b) $\sin \alpha_1 = \sin \alpha_2 = \frac{3}{5}$ $\csc \alpha_1 = \csc \alpha_2 = \frac{5}{3}$

$\cos \alpha_1 = \cos \alpha_2 = \frac{4}{5}$ $\sec \alpha_1 = \sec \alpha_2 = \frac{5}{4}$

$\tan \alpha_1 = \tan \alpha_2 = \frac{3}{4}$ $\cot \alpha_1 = \cot \alpha_2 = \frac{4}{3}$

13. Determine the quadrant in which θ lies.

(a) $\sin \theta < 0$ and $\cos \theta < 0$ (b) $\sin \theta > 0$ and $\cos \theta < 0$

Solution:

(a) $\sin \theta < 0 \Rightarrow \theta$ lies in Quadrant III or in Quadrant IV.
$\cos \theta < 0 \Rightarrow \theta$ lies in Quadrant II or in Quadrant III.
$\sin \theta < 0$ *and* $\cos \theta < 0 \Rightarrow \theta$ lies in Quadrant III.

(b) $\sin \theta > 0 \Rightarrow \theta$ lies in Quadrant I or in Quadrant II.
$\cos \theta < 0 \Rightarrow \theta$ lies in Quadrant II or in Quadrant III.
$\sin \theta > 0$ *and* $\cos \theta < 0 \Rightarrow \theta$ lies in Quadrant II.

17. Find the values of the six trigonometric functions of θ, given θ lies in Quadrant II and $\sin \theta = \frac{3}{5}$.

Solution:

$y = 3, \ r = 5, \ x = -\sqrt{25 - 9} = -4$

x is negative since θ lies in Quadrant II.

$$\sin \theta = \tfrac{3}{5} \qquad \csc \theta = \tfrac{5}{3}$$

$$\cos \theta = -\tfrac{4}{5} \qquad \sec \theta = -\tfrac{5}{4}$$

$$\tan \theta = -\tfrac{3}{4} \qquad \cot \theta = -\tfrac{4}{3}$$

21. Find the values of the six trigonometric functions of θ, given $\sin \theta > 0$ and $\sec \theta = -2$.

Solution:

θ is in Quadrant II.

$$\sec \theta = \frac{2}{-1}, \ r = 2,$$

$$x = -1, \ y = \sqrt{4 - 1} = \sqrt{3}$$

$$\sin \theta = \frac{\sqrt{3}}{2} \qquad \csc \theta = \frac{2\sqrt{3}}{3}$$

$$\cos \theta = -\frac{1}{2} \qquad \sec \theta = -2$$

$$\tan \theta = -\sqrt{3} \qquad \cot \theta = -\frac{\sqrt{3}}{3}$$

25. Find the values of the six trigonometric functions of θ, given the terminal side of θ is in Quadrant III and lies on the line $y = 2x$.

Solution:

To find a point on the terminal side of θ, use any point on the line $y = 2x$ that lies in Quadrant III. $(-1, -2)$ is one such point.

$$x = -1, \ y = -2, \ r = \sqrt{5}$$

$$\sin \theta = -\frac{2}{\sqrt{5}} = -\frac{2\sqrt{5}}{5} \qquad \csc \theta = \frac{\sqrt{5}}{-2} = -\frac{\sqrt{5}}{2}$$

$$\cos \theta = -\frac{1}{\sqrt{5}} = -\frac{\sqrt{5}}{5} \qquad \sec \theta = \frac{\sqrt{5}}{-1} = -\sqrt{5}$$

$$\tan \theta = \frac{-2}{-1} = 2 \qquad \cot \theta = \frac{-1}{-2} = \frac{1}{2}$$

29. Find the reference angle θ', and draw a sketch for (a) $\theta = -245°$ and (b) $\theta = -72°$.

Solution:

(a) $\theta = -245°$

$\theta' = 245° - 180°$

$\theta' = 65°$

(b) $\theta = -72°$

$\theta' = |-72°| = 72°$

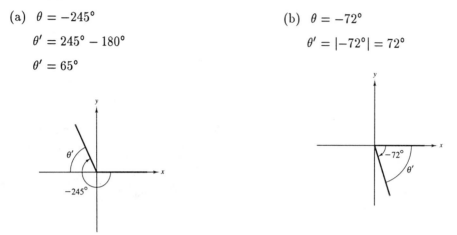

33. Find the reference angle θ' and draw a sketch for (a) $\theta = 3.5$ and (b) $\theta = 5.8$.

Solution:

(a) $\theta = 3.5$

$\theta' = 3.5 - \pi$

$\theta' \approx 0.3584$

(b) $\theta = 5.8$

$\theta' = 2\pi - 5.8$

$\theta' \approx 0.4832$

35. Evaluate the sine, cosine, and tangent of the angles without using a calculator.

(a) 225°   (b) −225°

Solution:

(a) The reference angle of 225° is 45°, and 225° lies in Quadrant III.

$$\sin 225° = -\sin 45° = -\frac{\sqrt{2}}{2}$$

$$\cos 225° = -\cos 45° = -\frac{\sqrt{2}}{2}$$

$$\tan 225° = \tan 45° = 1$$

(b) The reference angle is 45°, and −225° lies in Quadrant II.

$$\sin(-225°) = \sin 45° = \frac{\sqrt{2}}{2}$$

$$\cos(-225°) = -\cos 45° = -\frac{\sqrt{2}}{2}$$

$$\tan(-225°) = -\tan 45° = -1$$

39. Evaluate the sine, cosine, and tangent of the angles without using a calculator.

(a) $\dfrac{4\pi}{3}$ (b) $\dfrac{2\pi}{3}$

Solution:

(a) The reference angle of $4\pi/3$ is $\pi/3$, and $4\pi/3$ lies in Quadrant III.

$$\sin \frac{4\pi}{3} = -\sin \frac{\pi}{3} = -\frac{\sqrt{3}}{2}$$

$$\cos \frac{4\pi}{3} = -\cos \frac{\pi}{3} = -\frac{1}{2}$$

$$\tan \frac{4\pi}{3} = \tan \frac{\pi}{3} = \sqrt{3}$$

(b) The reference angle of $2\pi/3$ is $\pi/3$, and $2\pi/3$ lies in Quadrant II.

$$\sin \frac{2\pi}{3} = \sin \frac{\pi}{3} = \frac{\sqrt{3}}{2}$$

$$\cos \frac{2\pi}{3} = -\cos \frac{\pi}{3} = -\frac{1}{2}$$

$$\tan \frac{2\pi}{3} = -\tan \frac{\pi}{3} = -\sqrt{3}$$

45. Use a calculator to evaluate (a) sin 10° and (b) csc 10° to four decimal places. (Be sure the calculator is set in the correct mode.)

Solution:

(a) $\sin 10° \approx 0.1736$ (b) $\csc 10° = \dfrac{1}{\sin 10°} \approx 5.7588$

47. Use a calculator to evaluate (a) cos(−110°) and (b) cos 250° to four decimal places. (Be sure the calculator is set in the correct mode.)

Solution:

(a) $\cos(-110°) = \cos 110° \approx -0.3420$ (b) $\cos 250° \approx -0.3420$

53. Find two values of θ that satisfy (a) $\sin\theta = \frac{1}{2}$ and (b) $\sin\theta = -\frac{1}{2}$. List your answers in degrees $(0° \le \theta < 360°)$ and radians $(0 \le \theta < 2\pi)$. Do not use a calculator.

Solution:

(a) $\sin\theta = \dfrac{1}{2} > 0$

   θ is in either Quadrant I or Quadrant II.

   $\theta = 30° = \dfrac{\pi}{6}$ or $\theta = 150° = \dfrac{5\pi}{6}$

(b) $\sin\theta = -\dfrac{1}{2} < 0$

   θ is in either Quadrant III or Quadrant IV.

   $\theta = 210° = \dfrac{7\pi}{6}$ or $\theta = 330° = \dfrac{11\pi}{6}$

57. Find two values of θ that satisfy (a) $\tan\theta = 1$ and (b) $\cot\theta = -\sqrt{3}$. List your answers in degrees $(0° \le \theta < 360°)$ and radians $(0 \le \theta < 2\pi)$. Do not use a calculator.

Solution:

(a) $\tan\theta = 1$, θ lies in either Quadrant I or Quadrant III.

   $\theta = 45° = \dfrac{\pi}{4}$ or $\theta = 225° = \dfrac{5\pi}{4}$

(b) $\cot\theta = -\sqrt{3}$, θ lies in either Quadrant II or Quadrant IV.

   $\theta = 150° = \dfrac{5\pi}{6}$ or $\theta = 330° = \dfrac{11\pi}{6}$

61. Use a calculator to approximate two values of θ $(0 \le \theta < 2\pi)$ that satisfy (a) $\cos\theta = 0.9848$ and (b) $\cos\theta = -0.5890$. Round to three decimal places.

Solution:

Make sure the calculator is in radian mode.

(a) $\cos\theta = 0.9848$ θ lies in Quadrant I or Quadrant IV.

   Quadrant I: $\theta = \cos^{-1} 0.9848 \approx 0.175$

   Quadrant IV: $\theta = 2\pi - \cos^{-1} 0.9848 \approx 6.109$

(b) $\cos\theta = -0.5890$ θ lies in Quadrant II or Quadrant III.

   Quadrant II: $\theta = \cos^{-1}(-0.5890) \approx 2.201$

   Quadrant III: $\theta = \pi + \cos^{-1} 0.5890 \approx 4.083$

65. Use $\sin \theta = -\frac{3}{5}$, θ in Quadrant IV, and trigonometric identities to find $\cos \theta$.

Solution:

Since $\sin^2 \theta + \cos^2 \theta = 1$, we have:

$$\cos^2 \theta = 1 - \sin^2 \theta$$

$$\cos \theta = \pm\sqrt{1 - \sin^2 \theta}$$

Also, since θ lies in Quadrant IV, we know that $\cos \theta > 0$. Thus,

$$\cos \theta = +\sqrt{1 - \sin^2 \theta}$$

$$= \sqrt{1 - \left(-\frac{3}{5}\right)^2}$$

$$= \sqrt{1 - \left(\frac{9}{25}\right)}$$

$$= \sqrt{\frac{16}{25}}$$

$$= \frac{4}{5}.$$

71. The average daily temperature (in degrees Fahrenheit) for a city is

$$T = 45 - 23 \cos\left[\frac{2\pi}{365}(t - 32)\right]$$

where t is the time in days with $t = 1$ corresponding to January 1. Find the average temperature on (a) January 1, (b) July 4 ($t = 185$), and (c) October 18 ($t = 291$).

Solution:

(a) $t = 1$

$$T = 45 - 23 \cos\left[\frac{2\pi}{365}(1 - 32)\right] \approx 25.2°\text{F}$$

(b) $t = 185$

$$T = 45 - 23 \cos\left[\frac{2\pi}{365}(185 - 32)\right] \approx 65.1°\text{F}$$

(c) $t = 291$

$$T = 45 - 23 \cos\left[\frac{2\pi}{365}(291 - 32)\right] \approx 50.8°\text{F}$$

SECTION 2.5

Graphs of Sine and Cosine Functions

- You should be able to graph $y = a\sin(bx - c)$ and $y = a\cos(bx - c)$.

- Amplitude: $|a|$

- Period: $\dfrac{2\pi}{|b|}$

- Shift: Solve $bx - c = 0$ and $bx - c = 2\pi$.

- Key Increments: $\dfrac{1}{4}$ (period)

Solutions to Selected Exercises

5. Determine the period and amplitude of $y = \frac{1}{2}\sin \pi x$.

Solution:

$y = \dfrac{1}{2}\sin \pi x; \quad a = \dfrac{1}{2}, \ b = \pi, \ c = 0$

Period: $\dfrac{2\pi}{|b|} = \dfrac{2\pi}{\pi} = 2$

Amplitude: $|a| = \left|\dfrac{1}{2}\right| = \dfrac{1}{2}$

11. Determine the period and amplitude of
$$y = \frac{1}{2}\cos\frac{2x}{3}.$$

Solution:

$y = \dfrac{1}{2}\cos\dfrac{2x}{3}; \quad a = \dfrac{1}{2}, \ b = \dfrac{2}{3}, \ c = 0$

Period: $\dfrac{2\pi}{|b|} = \dfrac{2\pi}{2/3} = 3\pi$

Amplitude: $|a| = \left|\dfrac{1}{2}\right| = \dfrac{1}{2}$

15. Describe the relationship between the graphs of $f(x) = \sin x$ and $g(x) = \sin(x - \pi)$.

Solution:

$f(x) = \sin x$ and $g(x) = \sin(x - \pi)$ both have a period of 2π and an amplitude of 1. However, the graph of $g(x) = \sin(x - \pi)$ is the graph of $f(x) = \sin x$ shifted to the right π units.

19. Describe the relationship between the graphs of $f(x) = \cos x$ and $g(x) = \cos 2x$.

Solution:

$f(x) = \cos x$ and $g(x) = \cos 2x$ both have an amplitude of 1. However, $f(x) = \cos x$ has a period of 2π, whereas $g(x) = \cos 2x$ has a period of π.

23. Sketch the graphs of $f(x) = -2\sin x$ and $g(x) = 4\sin x$ on the same coordinate plane. (Include two full periods.)

Solution:

$f(x) = -2\sin x$

Period: 2π

Amplitude: 2

$g(x) = 4\sin x$

Period: 2π

Amplitude: 4

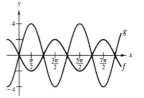

27. Sketch the graphs of the following on the same coordinate plane. (Include two full periods.)

$$f(x) = -\frac{1}{2}\sin\frac{x}{2} \quad \text{and} \quad g(x) = 3 - \frac{1}{2}\sin\frac{x}{2}$$

Solution:

$f(x) = -\dfrac{1}{2}\sin\dfrac{x}{2}$

Period: 4π

Amplitude: $\dfrac{1}{2}$

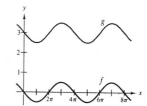

$g(x) = 3 - \dfrac{1}{2}\sin\dfrac{x}{2}$ is the graph of

$f(x)$ shifted vertically three units upward.

31. Sketch f and g on the same coordinate axes and show that $f(x) = g(x)$ for all x. (Include two full periods.)

$$f(x) = \sin x \quad \text{and} \quad g(x) = \cos\left(x - \frac{\pi}{2}\right)$$

Solution:

Since sine and cosine are cofunctions and x and $x - (\pi/2)$ are complementary, we have

$$\sin x = \cos\left(x - \frac{\pi}{2}\right).$$

Period: 2π

Amplitude: 1

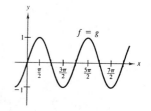

35. Sketch the graph of $y = -2\sin 6x$. (Include two full periods.)

Solution:

$y = -2\sin 6x; \quad a = -2, \ b = 6, \ c = 0$

Period: $\dfrac{2\pi}{6} = \dfrac{\pi}{3}$

Amplitude: $|-2| = 2$

Key points: $(0, \ 0), \ \left(\dfrac{\pi}{12}, \ -2\right), \ \left(\dfrac{\pi}{6}, \ 0\right), \ \left(\dfrac{\pi}{4}, \ 2\right), \ \left(\dfrac{\pi}{3}, \ 0\right)$

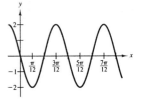

39. Sketch the graph of the following. (Include two full periods.)

$$y = -\sin \dfrac{2\pi x}{3}$$

Solution:

$y = -\sin \dfrac{2\pi x}{3}; \quad a = -1, \ b = \dfrac{2\pi}{3}, \ c = 0$

Period: $\dfrac{2\pi}{2\pi/3} = 3$

Amplitude: 1

Key points: $(0, \ 0), \ \left(\dfrac{3}{4}, \ -1\right), \ \left(\dfrac{3}{2}, \ 0\right), \ \left(\dfrac{9}{4}, \ 1\right), \ (3, \ 0)$

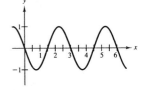

43. Sketch the graph of the following. (Include two full periods.)

$$y = \sin\left(x - \dfrac{\pi}{4}\right)$$

Solution:

$y = \sin\left(x - \dfrac{\pi}{4}\right); \quad a = 1, \ b = 1, \ c = \dfrac{\pi}{4}$

Period: 2π

Amplitude: 1

Shift: Set $x - \dfrac{\pi}{4} = 0 \quad$ and $\quad x - \dfrac{\pi}{4} = 2\pi$

$\qquad\qquad x = \dfrac{\pi}{4} \qquad\qquad\quad x = \dfrac{9\pi}{4}$

Key points: $\left(\dfrac{\pi}{4}, \ 0\right), \ \left(\dfrac{3\pi}{4}, \ 1\right), \ \left(\dfrac{5\pi}{4}, \ 0\right), \ \left(\dfrac{7\pi}{4}, \ -1\right), \ \left(\dfrac{9\pi}{4}, \ 0\right)$

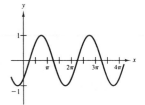

49. Sketch the graph of the following. (Include two full periods.)

$$y = \frac{2}{3}\cos\left(\frac{x}{2} - \frac{\pi}{4}\right)$$

Solution:

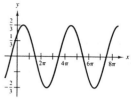

$$y = \frac{2}{3}\cos\left(\frac{x}{2} - \frac{\pi}{4}\right); \quad a = \frac{2}{3}, \; b = \frac{1}{2}, \; c = \frac{\pi}{4}$$

Period: 4π

Amplitude: $\dfrac{2}{3}$

Shift: Set $\dfrac{x}{2} - \dfrac{\pi}{4} = 0$ and $\dfrac{x}{2} - \dfrac{\pi}{4} = 2\pi$

$$x = \frac{\pi}{2} \qquad\qquad x = \frac{9\pi}{2}$$

Key points: $\left(\dfrac{\pi}{2}, \dfrac{2}{3}\right)$, $\left(\dfrac{3\pi}{2}, 0\right)$, $\left(\dfrac{5\pi}{2}, \dfrac{-2}{3}\right)$, $\left(\dfrac{7\pi}{2}, 0\right)$, $\left(\dfrac{9\pi}{2}, \dfrac{2}{3}\right)$

53. Sketch the graph of the following. (Include two full periods.)

$$y = \cos\left(2\pi x - \frac{\pi}{2}\right) + 1$$

Solution:

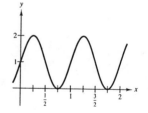

$$y = \cos\left(2\pi x - \frac{\pi}{2}\right) + 1; \quad a = 1, \; b = 2\pi, \; c = \frac{\pi}{2}$$

Period: 1

Amplitude: 1

Shift: Set $2\pi x - \dfrac{\pi}{2} = 0$ and $2\pi x - \dfrac{\pi}{2} = 2\pi$

$$x = \frac{1}{4} \qquad\qquad x = \frac{5}{4}$$

Key points: $\left(\dfrac{1}{4}, 2\right)$, $\left(\dfrac{1}{2}, 1\right)$, $\left(\dfrac{3}{4}, 0\right)$, $(1, 1)$, $\left(\dfrac{5}{4}, 2\right)$

Vertical shift: One unit upward

55. Sketch the graph of the following. (Include two full periods.)

$$y = -0.1 \sin\left(\frac{\pi x}{10} + \pi\right)$$

Solution:

$$y = -0.1 \sin\left(\frac{\pi x}{10} + \pi\right); \quad a = -0.1, \ b = \frac{\pi}{10}, \ c = -\pi$$

Period: $\dfrac{2\pi}{\pi/10} = 20$

Amplitude: $|-0.1| = 0.1$

Shift: Set $\dfrac{\pi x}{10} + \pi = 0 \qquad$ and $\qquad \dfrac{\pi x}{10} + \pi = 2\pi$

$$x = -10 \qquad\qquad\qquad x = 10$$

Key points: $(-10, \ 0), \ (-5, \ -0.1), \ (0, \ 0), \ (5, \ 0.1), \ (10, \ 0)$

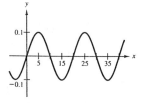

59. Sketch the graph of $y = \frac{1}{10}\cos 60\pi x$. (Include two full periods.)

Solution:

$$y = \frac{1}{10}\cos(60\pi x); \quad a = \frac{1}{10}, \ b = 60\pi, \ c = 0$$

Period: $\dfrac{2\pi}{60\pi} = \dfrac{1}{30}$

Amplitude: $\dfrac{1}{10}$

Key points: $\left(0, \ \dfrac{1}{10}\right), \ \left(\dfrac{1}{120}, \ 0\right), \ \left(\dfrac{1}{60}, \ -\dfrac{1}{10}\right),$

$$\left(\dfrac{1}{40}, \ 0\right), \ \left(\dfrac{1}{30}, \ \dfrac{1}{10}\right)$$

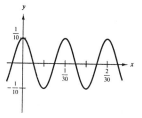

63. Use the graph of $\cos x$ to find all real numbers x in the interval $[-2\pi, \ 2\pi]$ that gives the functional value of $\sqrt{2}/2$.

Solution:

$$\cos x = \frac{\sqrt{2}}{2}$$

$$x = \pm\frac{\pi}{4}, \ \pm\frac{7\pi}{4}$$

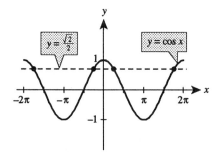

67. Find a, b, and c so that the graph of the function matches the graph in the figure.

Solution:

$y = a\cos(bx - c)$

Amplitude: $1 \Rightarrow a = 1$

Period: $\dfrac{2\pi}{b} = \pi \Rightarrow b = 2$

Shift: The graph begins at $-\dfrac{\pi}{4}$.

$2\left(-\dfrac{\pi}{4}\right) - c = 0 \Rightarrow c = -\dfrac{\pi}{2}$

Thus, $y = \cos\left(2x + \dfrac{\pi}{2}\right)$.

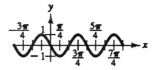

69. For a person at rest, the velocity v (in liters per second) of air flow during a respiratory cycle is

$$v = 0.85\sin\frac{\pi t}{3}$$

where t is the time in seconds. (Inhalation occurs when $v > 0$, and exhalation occurs when $v < 0$.)

(a) Find the time for one full respiratory cycle.

(b) Find the number of cycles per minute.

(c) Sketch the graph of the velocity function.

Solution:

(a) Time for one cycle = one period = $\dfrac{2\pi}{\pi/3} = 6$ sec

(b) Cycles per min = $\dfrac{60}{6} = 10$ cycles per min

(c) Amplitude: 0.85

Period: 6

Key points: $(0,\ 0)$, $\left(\dfrac{3}{2},\ 0.85\right)$, $(3,\ 0)$, $\left(\dfrac{9}{2},\ -0.85\right)$, $(6,\ 0)$

71. When tuning a piano, a technician strikes a tuning fork for the A above middle C and sets up wave motion that can be approximated by

$$y = 0.001 \sin 880\pi t$$

where t is the time in seconds.

(a) What is the period p of this function?
(b) The frequency f is given by $f = 1/p$. What is the frequency of this note?
(c) Sketch the graph of this function.

Solution:

(a) Period: $\dfrac{2\pi}{880\pi} = \dfrac{1}{440}$

(b) $f = \dfrac{1}{p} = 440$

(c) Amplitude: 0.001

Period: $\dfrac{1}{440}$

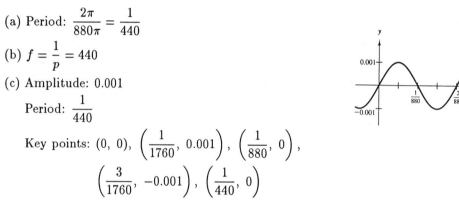

Key points: $(0,\ 0)$, $\left(\dfrac{1}{1760},\ 0.001\right)$, $\left(\dfrac{1}{880},\ 0\right)$,

$\left(\dfrac{3}{1760},\ -0.001\right)$, $\left(\dfrac{1}{440},\ 0\right)$

75. Determine the relationship between the graphs of the functions f and g.

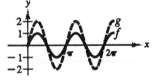

Solution:

The graphs have the same period of π, and the amplitude of g is twice the amplitude of f. Thus, $g = 2f$. On set of possible functions is

$$f(x) = \sin(2x)$$

$$g(x) = 2\sin(2x).$$

SECTION 2.6

Graphs of Other Trigonometric Functions

■ You should be able to graph

$$y = a \tan(bx - c) \quad y = a \cot(bx - c)$$
$$y = a \sec(bx - c) \quad y = a \csc(bx - c)$$

■ When graphing $y = a \sec(bx - c)$ or $y = a \csc(bx - c)$ you should know to first graph $y = a \cos(bx - c)$ or $y = a \sin(bx - c)$ since

(a) The intercepts of sine and cosine are vertical asymptotes of cosecant and secant.

(b) The maximums of sine and cosine are local minimums of cosecant and secant.

(c) The minimums of sine and cosine are local maximums of cosecant and secant.

Solutions to Selected Exercises

5. Match $y = \cot \pi x$ with the correct graph and give the period of the function.

Solution:

Period: $\dfrac{\pi}{\pi} = 1$

Matches graph (d)

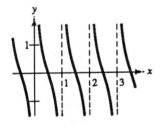

11. Sketch the graph of $y = \tan 2x$ through two periods.

Solution:

Period: $\dfrac{\pi}{2}$

One cycle: $-\dfrac{\pi}{4}$ to $\dfrac{\pi}{4}$

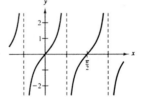

17. Sketch the graph of $y = -2\sec 4x$ through two periods.

Solution:

Graph $y = -2\cos 4x$ first.

Period: $\dfrac{2\pi}{4} = \dfrac{\pi}{2}$

One cycle: 0 to $\dfrac{\pi}{2}$

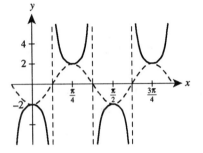

23. Sketch the graph of the following through two periods.

$$y = \csc \dfrac{x}{2}$$

Solution:

Graph $y = \sin \dfrac{x}{2}$ first.

Period: $\dfrac{2\pi}{1/2} = 4\pi$

One cycle: 0 to 4π

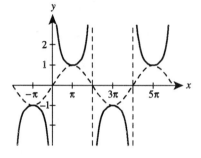

25. Sketch the graph of the following through two periods.

$$y = \cot \dfrac{x}{2}$$

Solution:

Period: $\dfrac{\pi}{1/2} = 2\pi$

One cycle: 0 to 2π

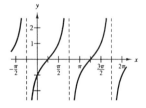

29. Sketch the graph of the following through two periods.

$$y = \tan\left(x - \dfrac{\pi}{4}\right)$$

Solution:

Period: π

Shift: Set $x - \dfrac{\pi}{4} = -\dfrac{\pi}{2}$ and $x - \dfrac{\pi}{4} = \dfrac{\pi}{2}$

$x = -\dfrac{\pi}{4}$ to $x = \dfrac{3\pi}{4}$

33. Sketch the graph of the following through two periods.

$$y = \frac{1}{4}\cot\left(x - \frac{\pi}{2}\right)$$

Solution:

Period: π

Shift: Set $x - \dfrac{\pi}{2} = 0$ and $x - \dfrac{\pi}{2} = \pi$

$\qquad\qquad x = \dfrac{\pi}{2}$ to $\qquad x = \dfrac{3\pi}{2}$

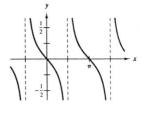

35. Sketch the graph of $y = 2\sec(2x - \pi)$ through two periods.

Solution:

Graph $y = 2\cos(2x - \pi)$ first.

Period: π

Shift: Set $2x - \pi = 0$ and $2x - \pi = 2\pi$

$\qquad\qquad x = \dfrac{\pi}{2}$ to $\qquad x = \dfrac{3\pi}{2}$

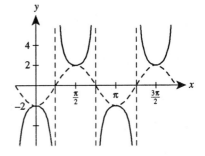

39. Sketch the graph of $y = \csc(\pi - x)$ through two periods.

Solution:

Graph $y = \sin(\pi - x)$ first.

Period: 2π

Shift: Set $\pi - x = 0$ and $\pi - x = 2\pi$

$\qquad\qquad x = \pi$ to $\qquad x = -\pi$

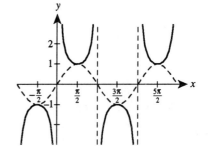

43. Use the graph of $\sec x$ to find all real numbers x in the interval $[-2\pi, \ 2\pi]$ that gives the functional value of -2.

Solution:

$$\sec x = -2$$

$$x = \pm\frac{2\pi}{3}, \ \pm\frac{4\pi}{3}$$

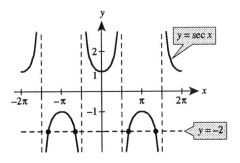

45. A plane flying at an altitude of 6 miles over level ground will pass directly over a radar antenna, as shown in the figure. Let d be the ground distance from the antenna to the point directly under the plane, and let x be the angle of elevation to the plane from the antenna. Write d as a function of x, and sketch the graph of the function over the interval $0 < x < \pi$.

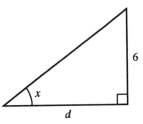

Solution:

$$\tan x = \frac{6}{d}$$

$$d = \frac{6}{\tan x} = 6\cot x$$

SECTION 2.7

Other Graphing Techniques

- ■ You should be able to graph by addition of ordinates.

- ■ You should be able to graph vertical translations.

- ■ You should be able to graph using a damping factor.

Solutions to Selected Exercises

1. Use addition of ordinates to sketch the graph of

$$y = 2 - 2\sin\frac{x}{2}.$$

Solution:

Vertical translation of the graph of $y = -2\sin(x/2)$ by two units

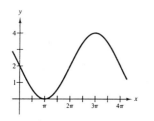

7. Use addition of ordinates to sketch the graph of $y = 1 + \csc x$.

Solution:

Vertical translation of the graph of $y = 1 + \csc x$ by one unit

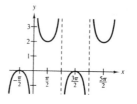

11. Use addition of ordinates to sketch the graph of $y = \frac{1}{2}x - 2\cos x$.

Solution:

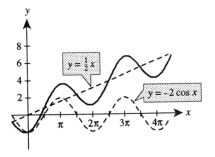

15. Use addition of ordinates to sketch the graph of $y = 2\sin x + \sin 2x$.

Solution:

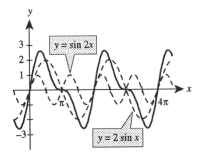

21. Use addition of ordinates to sketch the graph of $y = -3 + \cos x + 2\sin 2x$.

Solution:

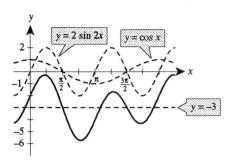

23. Sketch the graph of $y = x\cos x$.

Solution:

$$y = x\cos x$$

$$|x\cos x| = |x||\cos x| \le |x|$$

Thus, the graph lies between the lines $y = -x$ and $y = x$.

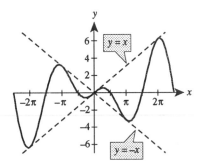

27. Sketch the graph of $y = e^{-x^2/2}\sin x$.

Solution:

$$y = e^{-x^2/2}\sin x$$

$$|e^{-x^2/2}\sin x| = |e^{-x^2/2}||\sin x| \le |e^{-x^2/2}|$$

Thus, $-e^{-x^2/2} \le y \le e^{-x^2/2}$.

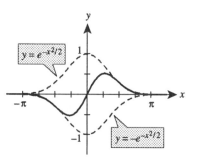

31. The projected monthly sales S (in thousands of units) of a seasonal product is modeled by

$$S = 74 + 3t + 40 \sin \frac{\pi t}{6}$$

where t is the time in months, with $t = 1$ corresponding to January. Sketch the graph of this sales function over one year.

Solution:

t	0	1	2	3	4	5	6
S	74	97	114.64	123	120.64	109	92

t	7	8	9	10	11	12
S	75	63.36	61	69.36	87	110

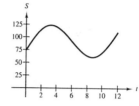

35. An object weighing W pounds is suspended from the ceiling by a steel spring (see figure). The weight is pulled downward (positive direction) from its equilibrium position and released. The resulting motion of the weight is described by the function

$$y = \tfrac{1}{2} e^{-t/4} \cos 4t, \quad t > 0$$

where y is the distance in feet and t is the time in seconds. Sketch the graph of this function.

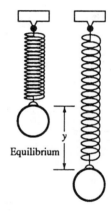

Equilibrium

Solution:

$$y = \tfrac{1}{2} e^{-t/4} \cos 4t, \quad t > 0$$

$$\left| \tfrac{1}{2} e^{-t/4} \cos 4t \right| = \tfrac{1}{2} e^{-t/4} |\cos 4t|$$

$$\leq \tfrac{1}{2} e^{-t/4}$$

Thus, $-\tfrac{1}{2} e^{-t/4} \leq y \leq \tfrac{1}{2} e^{-t/4}$.

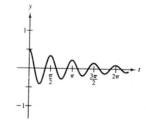

SECTION 2.8

Inverse Trigonometric Functions

- ■ You should know the definitions, domains, and ranges of $y = \arcsin x$, $y = \arccos x$, and $y = \arctan x$.

- ■ You should know the inverse properties of the inverse trigonometric functions.

- ■ You should be able to use the triangle technique to convert trigonometric expressions into algebraic expressions.

Solutions to Selected Exercises

3. Evaluate $\arccos \frac{1}{2}$ without using a calculator.

Solution:

$$\arccos \frac{1}{2} = \theta$$

$$\cos \theta = \frac{1}{2}$$

$$\theta = \frac{\pi}{3}$$

7. Evaluate $\arccos\left(-\frac{\sqrt{3}}{2}\right)$ without using a calculator.

Solution:

$$\arccos\left(-\frac{\sqrt{3}}{2}\right) = \theta$$

$$\cos \theta = -\frac{\sqrt{3}}{2}, \quad \frac{\pi}{2} < \theta < \pi$$

$$\theta = \frac{5\pi}{6}$$

9. Evaluate $\arctan(-\sqrt{3})$ without using a calculator.

Solution:

$$\arctan(-\sqrt{3}) = \theta$$

$$\tan \theta = -\sqrt{3}, \quad -\frac{\pi}{2} < \theta < 0$$

$$\theta = -\frac{\pi}{3}$$

13. Evaluate $\arcsin \frac{\sqrt{3}}{2}$ without using a calculator.

Solution:

$$\arcsin \frac{\sqrt{3}}{2} = \theta$$

$$\sin \theta = \frac{\sqrt{3}}{2}$$

$$\theta = \frac{\pi}{3}$$

17. Use a calculator to approximate $\arccos 0.28$. (Round to two decimal places.)

Solution:

Make sure that your calculator is in radian mode.

$$\arccos 0.28 \approx 1.29$$

21. Use a calculator to approximate arctan(−2). (Round to two decimal places.)

Solution:

$$\arctan(-2) \approx -1.11$$

27. Use a calculator to approximate arctan 0.92. (Round to two decimal places.)

Solution:

$$\arctan 0.92 \approx 0.74$$

31. Use the properties of inverse trigonometric functions to evaluate cos[arccos(−0.1)].

Solution:

$$\cos[\arccos(-0.1)] = -0.1$$

35. Find the exact value of $\sin(\arctan \frac{3}{4})$ without using a calculator. [*Hint:* Make a sketch of a right triangle, as illustrated in Example 6.]

Solution:

Let $y = \arctan \frac{3}{4}$. Then,

$$\tan y = \frac{3}{4}, \quad 0 < y < \frac{\pi}{2}$$

and $\sin y = \frac{3}{5}$.

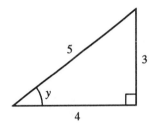

41. Find the exact value of $\sec[\arctan(-\frac{3}{5})]$ without using a calculator. [*Hint:* Make a sketch of a right triangle, as illustrated in Example 6.]

Solution:

Let $y = \arctan\left(-\frac{3}{5}\right)$. Then,

$$\tan y = -\frac{3}{5}, \quad -\frac{\pi}{2} < y < 0$$

and $\sec y = \sqrt{34}/5$.

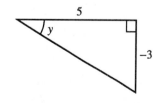

45. Write an algebraic expression that is equivalent to $\cos(\arcsin 2x)$. [*Hint:* Sketch a right triangle, as demonstrated in Example 7.]

Solution:

Let $y = \arcsin(2x)$. Then,

$$\sin y = 2x = \frac{2x}{1}$$

and $\cos y = \sqrt{1 - 4x^2}$.

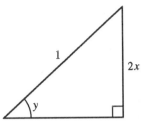

49. Write an algebraic expression that is equivalent to $\tan[\arccos(x/3)]$. [*Hint:* Sketch a right triangle, as demonstrated in Example 7.]

Solution:

Let $y = \arccos(x/3)$. Then,

$$\cos y = \frac{x}{3} \quad \text{and} \quad \tan y = \frac{\sqrt{9 - x^2}}{x}.$$

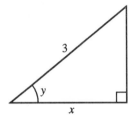

53. Fill in the blank.

$$\arctan \frac{9}{x} = \arcsin (\underline{\quad})$$

Solution:

$$\arctan \frac{9}{x} = \arcsin \frac{9}{\sqrt{x^2 + 81}}$$

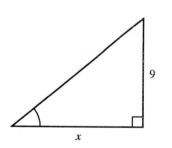

57. Sketch the graph of

$$f(x) = \arcsin(x - 1).$$

Solution:

The graph of $f(x) = \arcsin(x - 1)$ is a horizontal translation of the graph of $y = \arcsin x$ by one unit.

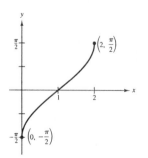

61. A photographer is taking a picture of a four-foot square painting hung in an art gallery. The camera lens is one foot below the lower edge of the painting, as shown in the figure. The angle β subtended by the camera lens x feet from the painting is given by

$$\beta = \arctan \frac{4x}{x^2 + 5}.$$

Find β when (a) $x = 3$ feet and (b) $x = 6$ feet.

Solution:

(a) When $x = 3$, $\beta = \arctan\left(\dfrac{12}{9+5}\right) \approx 0.7086$ radians or $40.6°$.

(b) When $x = 6$, $\beta = \arctan\left(\dfrac{24}{36+5}\right) \approx 0.5296$ radians or $30.3°$.

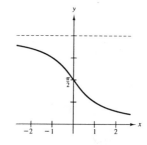

65. Define the inverse cotangent function by restricting the domain of the cotangent to the interval $(0, \pi)$ and sketch its graph.

Solution:

$y = \text{arccot } x$ if and only if $\cot y = x$

Domain: $-\infty < x < \infty$

Range: $0 < y < \pi$

69. Prove the identity of $\arcsin(-x) = -\arcsin x$.

Solution:

Let $y = \arcsin(-x)$. Then,

$$\sin y = -x$$

$$-\sin y = x$$

$$\sin(-y) = x$$

$$-y = \arcsin x$$

$$y = -\arcsin x.$$

Therefore, $\arcsin(-x) = -\arcsin x$.

73. Prove $\arcsin x + \arccos x = \pi/2$.

Solution:

Let $\alpha = \arcsin x$ and $\beta = \arccos x$, then, $\sin \alpha = x$ and $\cos \beta = x$. Thus, $\sin \alpha = \cos \beta$ which implies that α and β are complementary angles and we have

$$\alpha + \beta = \frac{\pi}{2}$$

$$\arcsin x + \arccos x = \frac{\pi}{2}.$$

SECTION 2.9

Applications of Trigonometry

- ■ You should be able to solve right triangles.

- ■ You should be able to solve right triangle applications.

- ■ You should be able to solve applications of simple harmonic motion.

Solutions to Selected Exercises

5. Solve the right triangle, given $A = 12°15'$ and $c = 430.5$. (Round to two decimal places.)

Solution:

$A = 12°15', \quad c = 430.5$

$B = 90° - 12°15' = 77°45'$

$\sin 12°15' = \dfrac{a}{430.5}$

$\qquad a = 430.5 \sin 12°15' \approx 91.34$

$\cos 12°15' = \dfrac{b}{430.5}$

$\qquad b = 430.5 \cos 12°15' \approx 420.70$

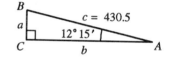

9. Solve the right triangle, given $b = 16$ and $c = 52$. (Round to two decimal places.)

Solution:

$b = 16, \quad c = 52$

$a = \sqrt{52^2 - 16^2}$

$\quad = \sqrt{2448} = 12\sqrt{17} \approx 49.48$

$\cos A = \frac{16}{52}$

$\quad A = \arccos \frac{16}{52} \approx 72.08°$

$\quad B = 90 - 72.08 \approx 17.92°$

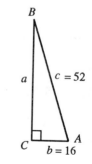

11. An isosceles triangle has two angles of 52°, as shown in the figure. The base of the triangle is 4 inches. Find the altitude of the triangle.

Solution:

Divide the triangle in half. Then

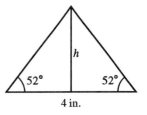

$$\tan 52° = \frac{h}{2}$$

$$h = 2\tan 52°$$

$$\approx 2.56 \text{ inches.}$$

52°   52°

4 in.

15. A ladder of length 16 feet leans against the side of a house (see figure). Find the height h of the top of the ladder if the angle of elevation of the ladder is 74°.

Solution:

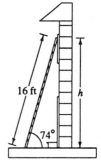

$$\sin 74° = \frac{h}{16}$$

$$16 \sin 74° = h$$

$$h \approx 15.4 \text{ feet}$$

16 ft h

74°

17. An amateur radio operator erects a 75-foot vertical tower for his antenna. Find the angle of elevation to the top of the tower at a point on level ground 50 feet from the base.

Solution:

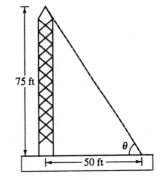

$$\tan \theta = \frac{75}{50}$$

$$\theta = \arctan \frac{3}{2} \approx 56.3°$$

75 ft

θ

50 ft

23. From a point 50 feet in front of a church, the angles of elevation to the base of the steeple and the top of the steeple are $35°$ and $47°40'$, respectively, as shown in the figure. Find the height of the steeple.

Solution:

Let the height of the church $= x$ and the height of the church and steeple $= y$. Then,

$$\tan 35° = \frac{x}{50} \qquad \text{and} \qquad \tan 47°40' = \frac{y}{50}$$

$$x \approx 35.01 \qquad\qquad\qquad y \approx 54.88$$

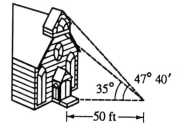

Height of the steeple $= y - x = 19.9$ feet

27. A ship is 45 miles east and 30 miles south of port. If the captain wants to travel directly to port, what bearing should be taken?

Solution:

$$\tan A = \frac{30}{45}$$

$$A = \arctan \frac{2}{3}$$

$$A \approx 33.69°$$

Bearing $= 90 - 33.69 = 56.3° = \text{N } 56.3° \text{ W}$

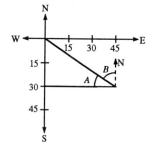

31. An observer in a lighthouse 300 feet above sea level spots two ships directly offshore. The angles of depression to the ships are $4°$ and $6.5°$, as shown in the figure. How far apart are the ships?

Solution:

$$\tan 4° = \frac{300}{y}$$

$$y = \frac{300}{\tan 4°} \approx 4290$$

$$\tan 6.5° = \frac{300}{x}$$

$$x = \frac{300}{\tan 6.5} \approx 2633$$

Distance between ships $= 1657$ feet

37. Use the figure to find the distance y across the flat sides of the hexagonal nut as a function of r.

Solution:

$$\sin 60° = \frac{\text{opp.}}{\text{hyp.}} = \frac{\frac{1}{2}y}{r}$$

$$\frac{\sqrt{3}}{2} = \frac{y}{2r}$$

$$y = \sqrt{3}r$$

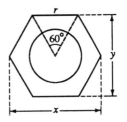

41. For the simple harmonic motion described by $d = 4\cos 8\pi t$, find (a) the maximum displacement, (b) the frequency, and (c) the least positive value of t for which $d = 0$.

Solution:

(a) Maximum displacement = amplitude = 4

(b) Frequency $= \dfrac{\omega}{\text{period}} = \dfrac{8\pi}{2\pi} = 4$ cycles per unit of time

(c) $d = 0$ when $8\pi t = \dfrac{\pi}{2}$ or $t = \dfrac{1}{16}$

45. A point on the end of a tuning fork moves in simple harmonic motion described by $d = a\sin \omega t$. Find ω given that the tuning fork for middle C has a frequency of 264 vibrations per second.

Solution:

$$\text{Frequency} = \frac{\omega}{2\pi} = 264$$

$$\omega = 528\pi$$

REVIEW EXERCISES FOR CHAPTER 2

Solutions to Selected Exercises

3. Sketch the angle $-110°$ in standard position, and list one positive and one negative coterminal angle.

Solution:

$\theta = -110°$

Coterminal angles:

$\theta_1 = 360° + (-110°) = 250°$

$\theta_2 = -360° + (-110°) = -470°$

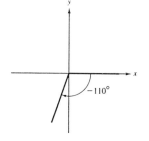

7. Convert $5°22'53''$ to decimal form. Round to two decimal places.

Solution:

$5°22'53'' = \left(5 + \frac{22}{60} + \frac{53}{3600}\right)° \approx 5.38°$

11. Convert $-85.15°$ to $D° \ M' \ S''$ form.

Solution:

$-85.15° = -[85° + .15(60)'] = -85°9'$

15. Convert -3.5 from radians to degrees. Round to two decimal places.

Solution:

$-3.5 = -3.5\left(\frac{180}{\pi}\right)° \approx -200.54°$

19. Convert $-33°45'$ from degrees to radians. Round to four decimal places.

Solution:

$-33°45' = -\left[33 + \frac{45}{60}\right]°$

$= -33.75°$

$= -33.75\left(\frac{\pi}{180}\right)$

$\approx -0.5890 \text{ radians}$

21. Find the reference angle for $252°$.

Solution:

$252°$ is in Quadrant III. The reference angle is $\theta = 252° - 180° = 72°$.

25. Find the six trigonometric functions of the angle θ (in standard position) whose terminal side passes through the point $(12,\ 16)$.

Solution:

$x = 12,\ y = 16,\ r = \sqrt{(12)^2 + (16)^2} = 20$

$$\sin\theta = \frac{y}{r} = \frac{16}{20} = \frac{4}{5} \qquad \csc\theta = \frac{r}{y} = \frac{20}{16} = \frac{5}{4}$$

$$\cos\theta = \frac{x}{r} = \frac{12}{20} = \frac{3}{5} \qquad \sec\theta = \frac{r}{x} = \frac{20}{12} = \frac{5}{3}$$

$$\tan\theta = \frac{y}{x} = \frac{16}{12} = \frac{4}{3} \qquad \cot\theta = \frac{x}{y} = \frac{12}{16} = \frac{3}{4}$$

29. Find the six trigonometric functions of the angle θ (in standard position) whose terminal side passes through the point $(-4,\ -6)$.

Solution:

$x = -4,\ y = -6,\ r = \sqrt{(-4)^2 + (-6)^2} = 2\sqrt{13}$

$$\sin\theta = \frac{y}{r} = \frac{-6}{2\sqrt{13}} = -\frac{3\sqrt{13}}{13} \qquad \csc\theta = \frac{r}{y} = \frac{2\sqrt{13}}{-6} = -\frac{\sqrt{13}}{3}$$

$$\cos\theta = \frac{x}{r} = \frac{-4}{2\sqrt{13}} = -\frac{2\sqrt{13}}{13} \qquad \sec\theta = \frac{r}{x} = \frac{2\sqrt{13}}{-4} = -\frac{\sqrt{13}}{2}$$

$$\tan\theta = \frac{y}{x} = \frac{-6}{-4} = \frac{3}{2} \qquad \cot\theta = \frac{x}{y} = \frac{-4}{-6} = \frac{2}{3}$$

33. Find the remaining five trigonometric functions of θ, given $\sin\theta = \frac{3}{8}$ and $\cos\theta < 0$. [*Hint:* Sketch a right triangle.]

Solution:

$\sin\theta = \frac{3}{8}, \quad \cos\theta < 0, \quad \theta$ is in Quadrant II.

$y = 3,\ r = 8,\ x = -\sqrt{64 - 9} = -\sqrt{55}$

$$\cos\theta = -\frac{\sqrt{55}}{8} \qquad\qquad \sec\theta = \frac{8}{-\sqrt{55}} = -\frac{8\sqrt{55}}{55}$$

$$\tan\theta = \frac{3}{-\sqrt{55}} = -\frac{3\sqrt{55}}{55} \qquad \cot\theta = -\frac{\sqrt{55}}{3}$$

$$\csc\theta = \frac{8}{3}$$

39. Evaluate $\cos 495°$ without the aid of a calculator.

Solution:

The reference angle for $495°$ is $45°$ and $495°$ is in Quadrant II. Therefore,

$$\cos 495° = -\cos 45° = -\frac{\sqrt{2}}{2}.$$

43. Use a calculator to evaluate $\sec(12\pi/5)$. Round your answer to two decimal places.

Solution:

Make sure that your calculator is in radian mode.

$$\sec\left(\frac{12\pi}{5}\right) = \frac{1}{\cos(12\pi/5)} \approx 3.24$$

47. Given $\csc\theta = -2$, find two values of θ in degrees $(0° \leq \theta < 360°)$ and in radians $(0 \leq \theta < 2\pi)$ without using a calculator.

Solution:

Since $\csc\theta < 0$, we know that θ is in either Quadrant III or in Quadrant IV. Also, since $\csc 30° = 2$, we know that $30°$ is the reference angle.

In Quadrant III: $\theta = 180° + 30° = 210° = \dfrac{7\pi}{6}$

In Quadrant IV: $\theta = 360° - 30° = 330° = \dfrac{11\pi}{6}$

51. Given $\sec\theta = -1.0353$, find two values of θ in degrees $(0° \leq \theta < 360°)$ and in radians $(0 \leq \theta < 2\pi)$ by using a calculator.

Solution:

Since $\sec\theta < 0$, we know that θ is in either Quadrant II or in Quadrant III. To find the reference angle θ', use

$$\cos\theta' = \frac{1}{\sec\theta'} = \frac{1}{1.0353}$$

$$\theta' = \cos^{-1}\left(\frac{1}{1.0353}\right).$$

The reference angle θ' is $15°$.

In Quadrant II: $\theta = 180° - 15° = 165° \approx 2.8798$
In Quadrant III: $\theta = 180° + 15° = 195° \approx 3.4034$

55. Write an algebraic expression for

$$\sin\left(\arccos\frac{x^2}{4-x^2}\right).$$

Solution:

Use a right triangle to find $\sin\left(\arccos\dfrac{x^2}{4-x^2}\right)$.

Let $\theta = \arccos\dfrac{x^2}{4-x^2}$, then, $\cos\theta = \dfrac{x^2}{4-x^2}$.

The opposite side is

$$\sqrt{(4-x^2)^2 - (x^2)^2} = \sqrt{16 - 8x^2}$$

$$= 2\sqrt{4 - 2x^2}.$$

Thus, $\sin\theta = \dfrac{2\sqrt{4-2x^2}}{4-x^2}$.

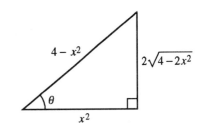

61. Sketch the graph of

$$f(x) = -\frac{1}{4}\cos\frac{\pi x}{4}.$$

Solution:

Amplitude: $\left|-\dfrac{1}{4}\right| = \dfrac{1}{4}$

Period: $\dfrac{2\pi}{\pi/4} = 8$

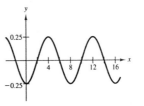

67. Sketch the graph of

$$f(t) = \csc\left(3t - \frac{\pi}{2}\right).$$

Solution:

Period: $\dfrac{2\pi}{3}$

Shift: $3t - \dfrac{\pi}{2} = 0$ and $3t - \dfrac{\pi}{2} = 2\pi$

$\qquad\qquad t = \dfrac{\pi}{6} \qquad\qquad\qquad t = \dfrac{5\pi}{6}$

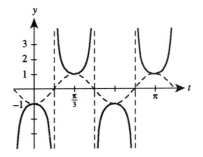

71. Sketch the graph of

$$f(x) = \frac{x}{4} - \sin x.$$

Solution:

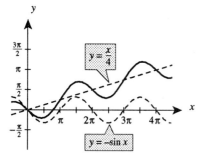

77. Sketch the graph of

$$y = \arcsin \frac{x}{2}.$$

Solution:

Domain: $-2 \le x \le 2$

Range: $-\dfrac{\pi}{2} \le y \le \dfrac{\pi}{2}$

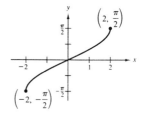

83. An observer 2.5 miles from the launch pad of a space shuttle measures the angle of elevation to the base of the vehicle to be 28° soon after liftoff (see figure). How high is the shuttle at that instant? Assume that the shuttle is still moving vertically.

Solution:

$$\tan 28° = \frac{x}{2.5}$$

$$x = 2.5 \tan 28° \approx 1.33 \text{ miles}$$

The shuttle is approximately 1.33 miles off the ground.

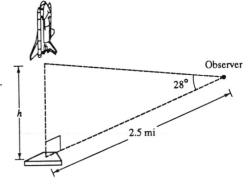

Practice Test for Chapter 2

1. (a) Express $350°$ in radian measure.

   (b) Express $\dfrac{5\pi}{9}$ in degree measure.

2. (a) Convert $135°\,14'12''$ to decimal form.

   (b) Convert $-22.569°$ to $D°\ M'\ S''$ form.

3. Use the unit circle to evaluate the following.

   (a) $\sin\dfrac{5\pi}{6}$

   (b) $\tan\dfrac{5\pi}{4}$

4. Use the unit circle and the periodic nature of sine and cosine to evaluate the following.

   (a) $\sin 7\pi$

   (b) $\cos\left(-\dfrac{13\pi}{3}\right)$

5. If $\cos\theta = \frac{2}{3}$, use the trigonometric identities to find $\tan\theta$ $(0° \le \theta \le 90°)$.

6. Find θ given $\sin\theta = 0.9063$ $(0° \le \theta \le 90°)$.

7. Solve for x.

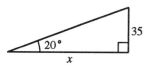

8. Find the magnitude of the reference angle for $\theta = \dfrac{6\pi}{5}$.

9. Evaluate $\csc 3.92$.

10. Find $\sec\theta$ given that θ lies in Quadrant III and $\tan\theta = 6$.

11. Graph $y = 3\sin\dfrac{x}{2}$.

12. Graph $y = -2\cos(x - \pi)$.

13. Graph $y = \tan 2x$.

14. Graph $y = -\csc\left(x + \dfrac{\pi}{4}\right)$.

15. Graph $y = 2x + \sin x$.

16. Graph $y = 3x\cos x$.

17. Evaluate $\arcsin 1$.

18. Evaluate $\arctan(-3)$.

19. Evaluate $\sin\left(\arccos\dfrac{4}{\sqrt{35}}\right)$.

20. Write an algebraic expression for $\cos\left(\arcsin\dfrac{x}{4}\right)$.

For Exercises 21–23, solve the right triangle.

21. $A = 40°$, $c = 12$

22. $B = 6.84°$, $a = 21.3$

23. $a = 5$, $b = 9$

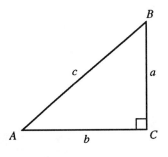

24. A 20-foot ladder leans against the side of a barn. Find the height of the top of the ladder if the angle of elevation of the ladder is 67°.

25. An observer in a lighthouse 250 feet above sea level spots a ship off the shore. If the angle of depression to the ship is 5°, how far out is the ship?

CHAPTER 3

Analytic Trigonometry

SECTION 3.1

Applications of Fundamental Identities

■ You should know the fundamental trigonometric identities.

(a) Reciprocal Identities

$$\sin u = \frac{1}{\csc u} \qquad\qquad \csc u = \frac{1}{\sin u}$$

$$\cos u = \frac{1}{\sec u} \qquad\qquad \sec u = \frac{1}{\cos u}$$

$$\tan u = \frac{1}{\cot u} = \frac{\sin u}{\cos u} \qquad \cot u = \frac{1}{\tan u} = \frac{\cos u}{\sin u}$$

(b) Pythagorean Identities

$$\sin^2 u + \cos^2 u = 1$$

$$1 + \tan^2 u = \sec^2 u$$

$$1 + \cot^2 u = \csc^2 u$$

(c) Cofunction Identities

$$\sin\left(\frac{\pi}{2} - u\right) = \cos u \qquad \cos\left(\frac{\pi}{2} - u\right) = \sin u$$

$$\tan\left(\frac{\pi}{2} - u\right) = \cot u \qquad \cot\left(\frac{\pi}{2} - u\right) = \tan u$$

$$\sec\left(\frac{\pi}{2} - u\right) = \csc u \qquad \csc\left(\frac{\pi}{2} - u\right) = \sec u$$

(d) Negative Angle Identities

$$\sin(-x) = -\sin x \qquad \csc(-x) = -\csc x$$

$$\cos(-x) = \cos x \qquad \sec(-x) = \sec x$$

$$\tan(-x) = -\tan x \qquad \cot(-x) = -\cot x$$

■ You should be able to use these fundamental identities to find function values.

■ You should be able to convert trigonometric expressions to equivalent forms by using the fundamental identities.

Solutions to Selected Exercises

3. Given $\sec\theta = \sqrt{2}$ and $\sin\theta = -\sqrt{2}/2$, use the fundamental identities to find the values of the other trigonometric functions.

Solution:

$$\cos\theta = \frac{1}{\sec\theta} = \frac{1}{\sqrt{2}} = \frac{\sqrt{2}}{2} \qquad \cot\theta = \frac{1}{\tan\theta} = \frac{1}{-1} = -1$$

$$\tan\theta = \frac{\sin\theta}{\cos\theta} = \frac{-\sqrt{2}/2}{\sqrt{2}/2} = -1 \qquad \csc\theta = \frac{1}{\sin\theta} = \frac{1}{-\sqrt{2}/2} = -\sqrt{2}$$

7. Given $\sec\phi = -1$ and $\sin\phi = 0$, use the fundamental identities to find the values of the other trigonometric functions.

Solution:

$$\cos\phi = \frac{1}{\sec\phi} = \frac{1}{-1} = -1 \qquad \cot\phi = \frac{1}{\tan\phi} = \frac{1}{0}, \quad \text{which is undefined}$$

$$\tan\phi = \frac{\sin\phi}{\cos\phi} = \frac{0}{-1} = 0 \qquad \csc\phi = \frac{1}{\sin\phi} = \frac{1}{0}, \quad \text{which is undefined}$$

11. Given $\tan\theta = 2$ and $\sin\theta < 0$, use the fundamental identities to find the values of the other trigonometric functions.

Solution:

θ is in Quadrant III.

$$\sec\theta = -\sqrt{1+\tan^2\theta} = -\sqrt{1+(2)^2} = -\sqrt{5}$$

$$\cot\theta = \frac{1}{\tan\theta} = \frac{1}{2}$$

$$\csc\theta = -\sqrt{1+\cot^2\theta} = -\sqrt{1+(1/2)^2} = -\sqrt{1+(1/4)} = -\frac{\sqrt{5}}{2}$$

$$\sin\theta = \frac{1}{\csc\theta} = -\frac{2}{\sqrt{5}} = -\frac{2\sqrt{5}}{5}$$

$$\cos\theta = \frac{1}{\sec\theta} = -\frac{1}{\sqrt{5}} = -\frac{\sqrt{5}}{5}$$

17. Match $\tan^2 x - \sec^2 x$ with one of the following.

   (a) -1 (b) $\cos x$ (c) $\cot x$

   (d) 1 (e) $-\tan x$ (f) $\sin x$

Solution:

$$\tan^2 x - \sec^2 x = (\sec^2 x - 1) - \sec^2 x = -1$$

Matches (a).

21. Match $\sin x \sec x$ with one of the following.

   (a) $\csc x$ (b) $\tan x$ (c) $\sin^2 x$

   (d) $\sin x \tan x$ (e) $\sec^2 x$ (f) $\sec^2 x + \tan^2 x$

Solution:

$$\sin x \sec x = \sin x \left(\frac{1}{\cos x}\right) = \frac{\sin x}{\cos x} = \tan x$$

Matches (b).

25. Match $\sec^4 x - \tan^4 x$ with one of the following.

   (a) $\csc x$ (b) $\tan x$ (c) $\sin^2 x$

   (d) $\sin x \tan x$ (e) $\sec^2 x$ (f) $\sec^2 x + \tan^2 x$

Solution:

$$\sec^4 x - \tan^4 x = (\sec^2 x + \tan^2 x)(\sec^2 x - \tan^2 x)$$
$$= (\sec^2 x + \tan^2 x)[(1 + \tan^2 x) - \tan^2 x]$$
$$= \sec^2 x + \tan^2 x$$

Matches (f).

29. Use the fundamental identities to simplify $\cos \beta \tan \beta$.

Solution:

$$\cos \beta \tan \beta = \cos \beta \left(\frac{\sin \beta}{\cos \beta}\right) = \sin \beta$$

33. Use the fundamental identities to simplify $\sec^2 x(1 - \sin^2 x)$.

Solution:

$$\sec^2 x(1 - \sin^2 x) = \sec^2 x(\cos^2 x) = \frac{1}{\cos^2 x}(\cos^2 x) = 1$$

39. Use the fundamental identities to simplify

$$\frac{\cos^2 y}{1 - \sin y}.$$

Solution:

$$\frac{\cos^2 y}{1 - \sin y} = \frac{1 - \sin^2 y}{1 - \sin y}$$

$$= \frac{(1 + \sin y)(1 - \sin y)}{1 - \sin y}$$

$$= 1 + \sin y$$

43. Factor $\sin^2 x \sec^2 x - \sin^2 x$ and use the fundamental identities to simplify the result.

Solution:

$$\sin^2 x \sec^2 x - \sin^2 x = \sin^2 x(\sec^2 x - 1)$$

$$= \sin^2 x \tan^2 x$$

47. Factor $\sin^4 x - \cos^4 x$ and use the fundamental identities to simplify the result.

Solution:

$$\sin^4 x - \cos^4 x = (\sin^2 x + \cos^2 x)(\sin^2 x - \cos^2 x)$$

$$= 1(\sin^2 x - \cos^2 x)$$

$$= \sin^2 x - \cos^2 x$$

51. Multiply $(\sec x + 1)(\sec x - 1)$ and use the fundamental identities to simplify the result.

Solution:

$$(\sec x + 1)(\sec x - 1) = \sec^2 x - 1 = \tan^2 x$$

55. Add the following and use the fundamental identities to simplify the result.

$$\frac{\cos x}{1 + \sin x} + \frac{1 + \sin x}{\cos x}$$

Solution:

$$\frac{\cos x}{1 + \sin x} + \frac{1 + \sin x}{\cos x} = \frac{(\cos x)(\cos x) + (1 + \sin x)(1 + \sin x)}{\cos x(1 + \sin x)}$$

$$= \frac{\cos^2 x + 1 + 2\sin x + \sin^2 x}{\cos x(1 + \sin x)}$$

$$= \frac{(\sin^2 x + \cos^2 x) + 1 + 2\sin x}{\cos x(1 + \sin x)}$$

$$= \frac{1 + 1 + 2\sin x}{\cos x(1 + \sin x)}$$

$$= \frac{2(1 + \sin x)}{\cos x(1 + \sin x)}$$

$$= \frac{2}{\cos x} = 2\left(\frac{1}{\cos x}\right) = 2\sec x$$

59. Rewrite the following expression so that it is *not* in fractional form.

$$\frac{3}{\sec x - \tan x}$$

Solution:

$$\frac{3}{\sec x - \tan x} = \frac{3}{\sec x - \tan x} \cdot \frac{\sec x + \tan x}{\sec x + \tan x}$$

$$= \frac{3(\sec x + \tan x)}{\sec^2 x - \tan^2 x}$$

$$= \frac{3(\sec x + \tan x)}{(1 + \tan^2 x) - \tan^2 x}$$

$$= 3(\sec x + \tan x)$$

63. Use $x = 3 \sec \theta$ to write $\sqrt{x^2 - 9}$ as a trigonometric function of θ, where $0 < \theta < \pi/2$.

Solution:

Since $x = 3 \sec \theta$,

$$\sqrt{x^2 - 9} = \sqrt{(3 \sec \theta)^2 - 9}$$

$$= \sqrt{9 \sec^2 \theta - 9}$$

$$= \sqrt{9(\sec^2 \theta - 1)}$$

$$= \sqrt{9 \tan^2 \theta}$$

$$= 3 \tan \theta.$$

69. Use $x = 3 \tan \theta$ to write $\sqrt{(9 + x^2)^3}$ as a trigonometric function of θ, where $0 < \theta < \pi/2$.

Solution:

Since $x = 3 \tan \theta$,

$$\sqrt{(9 + x^2)^3} = \sqrt{[9 + (3 \tan \theta)^2]^3}$$

$$= \sqrt{(9 + 9 \tan^2 \theta)^3}$$

$$= \sqrt{[9(1 + \tan^2 \theta)]^3}$$

$$= \sqrt{(9 \sec^2 \theta)^3}$$

$$= (\sqrt{9 \sec^2 \theta})^3$$

$$= (3 \sec \theta)^3$$

$$= 27 \sec^3 \theta.$$

73. Determine whether the equation is an identity, and give a reason for your answer.

$$\frac{\sin k\theta}{\cos k\theta} = \tan \theta, \quad k \text{ is constant}$$

Solution:

$\dfrac{\sin k\theta}{\cos k\theta} = \tan \theta$ is not an identity, since $\dfrac{\sin k\theta}{\cos k\theta} = \tan k\theta.$

77. Use a calculator to demonstrate that $\csc^2 \theta - \cot^2 \theta = 1$ is true for the following.

(a) $\theta = 132°$

(b) $\theta = \dfrac{2\pi}{7}$

Solution:

(a) $\theta = 132°$
$\csc 132° \approx 1.34563$
$\cot 132° \approx -0.90040$
Therefore,
$\csc^2 132° - \cot^2 132° \approx 1.81072 - 0.81072$

$$= 1.$$

(b) $\theta = \dfrac{2\pi}{7}$

$\csc \dfrac{2\pi}{7} \approx 1.2790$

$\cot \dfrac{2\pi}{7} \approx 0.7975$

Therefore,

$$\csc^2 \dfrac{2\pi}{7} - \cot^2 \dfrac{2\pi}{7} \approx 1.6360 - 0.6360$$

$$= 1.$$

81. Express each of the other trigonometric functions of θ in terms of $\sin \theta$.

Solution:

Since $\sin^2 \theta + \cos^2 \theta = 1$ and $\cos^2 \theta = 1 - \sin^2 \theta$:

$$\cos \theta = \pm\sqrt{1 - \sin^2 \theta}$$

$$\tan \theta = \frac{\sin \theta}{\cos \theta} = \pm\frac{\sin \theta}{\sqrt{1 - \sin^2 \theta}}$$

$$\cot \theta = \frac{1}{\tan \theta} = \pm\frac{\sqrt{1 - \sin^2 \theta}}{\sin \theta}$$

$$\sec \theta = \frac{1}{\cos \theta} = \pm\frac{1}{\sqrt{1 - \sin^2 \theta}}$$

$$\csc \theta = \frac{1}{\sin \theta}$$

SECTION 3.2

Verifying Trigonometric Identities

- ■ You should know the difference between an expression, a conditional equation, and an identity.

- ■ You should be able to solve trigonometric identities, using the following techniques.

  (a) Work with *one* side at a time. Do not "cross" the equal sign.

  (b) Use algebraic techniques such as combining fractions, factoring expressions, rationalizing denominators, and squaring binomials.

  (c) Use the fundamental identities.

  (d) Convert all the terms into sines and cosines.

Solutions to Selected Exercises

5. Verify $\cos^2 \beta - \sin^2 \beta = 1 - 2\sin^2 \beta$.

Solution:

$$\cos^2 \beta - \sin^2 \beta = (1 - \sin^2 \beta) - \sin^2 \beta$$

$$= 1 - 2\sin^2 \beta$$

9. Verify $\sin^2 \alpha - \sin^4 \alpha = \cos^2 \alpha - \cos^4 \alpha$.

Solution:

$$\sin^2 \alpha - \sin^4 \alpha = \sin^2 \alpha(1 - \sin^2 \alpha)$$

$$= (1 - \cos^2 \alpha)(\cos^2 \alpha)$$

$$= \cos^2 \alpha - \cos^4 \alpha$$

13. Verify $\dfrac{\cot^2 t}{\csc t} = \csc t - \sin t$.

Solution:

$$\frac{\cot^2 t}{\csc t} = \frac{\csc^2 t - 1}{\csc t}$$

$$= \frac{\csc^2 t}{\csc t} - \frac{1}{\csc t}$$

$$= \csc t - \sin t$$

17. Verify $\dfrac{1}{\sec x \tan x} = \csc x - \sin x$.

Solution:

$$\frac{1}{\sec x \tan x} = \frac{1}{\sec x} \cdot \frac{1}{\tan x}$$

$$= \cos x \cot x$$

$$= \cos x \left(\frac{\cos x}{\sin x} \right)$$

$$= \frac{\cos^2 x}{\sin x} = \frac{1 - \sin^2 x}{\sin x}$$

$$= \frac{1}{\sin x} - \frac{\sin^2 x}{\sin x}$$

$$= \csc x - \sin x$$

19. Verify $\csc x - \sin x = \cos x \cot x$.

Solution:

$$\csc x - \sin x = \frac{1}{\sin x} - \frac{\sin^2 x}{\sin x}$$

$$= \frac{1 - \sin^2 x}{\sin x} = \frac{\cos^2 x}{\sin x} = \cos x \left(\frac{\cos x}{\sin x} \right) = \cos x \cot x$$

25. Verify $\dfrac{\cos \theta \cot \theta}{1 - \sin \theta} - 1 = \csc \theta$.

Solution:

$$\frac{\cos \theta \cot \theta}{1 - \sin \theta} - 1 = \frac{\cos \theta \left(\dfrac{\cos \theta}{\sin \theta} \right)}{1 - \sin \theta} \cdot \frac{1 + \sin \theta}{1 + \sin \theta} - 1$$

$$= \frac{\cos^2 \theta (1 + \sin \theta)}{\sin \theta (1 - \sin^2 \theta)} - 1$$

$$= \frac{\cos^2 \theta (1 + \sin \theta)}{\sin \theta \cos^2 \theta} - 1$$

$$= \frac{1 + \sin \theta}{\sin \theta} - 1$$

$$= \frac{1}{\sin \theta} + \frac{\sin \theta}{\sin \theta} - 1$$

$$= \csc \theta + 1 - 1$$

$$= \csc \theta$$

29. Verify $2 \sec^2 x - 2 \sec^2 x \sin^2 x - \sin^2 x - \cos^2 x = 1$.

Solution:

$$2 \sec^2 x - 2 \sec^2 x \sin^2 x - \sin^2 x - \cos^2 x = 2 \sec^2 x (1 - \sin^2 x) - (\sin^2 x + \cos^2 x)$$

$$= 2 \sec^2 x (\cos^2 x) - 1$$

$$= 2 \left(\frac{1}{\cos^2 x} \right) (\cos^2 x) - 1$$

$$= 2 - 1 = 1$$

33. Verify $\csc^4 x - 2 \csc^2 x + 1 = \cot^4 x$.

Solution:

$$\csc^4 x - 2 \csc^2 x + 1 = (\csc^2 x - 1)^2 = (\cot^2 x)^2 = \cot^4 x$$

37. Verify $\dfrac{\sin \beta}{1 - \cos \beta} = \dfrac{1 + \cos \beta}{\sin \beta}$.

Solution:

$$\dfrac{\sin \beta}{1 - \cos \beta} = \dfrac{\sin \beta}{1 - \cos \beta} \cdot \dfrac{1 + \cos \beta}{1 + \cos \beta} = \dfrac{\sin \beta(1 + \cos \beta)}{1 - \cos^2 \beta} = \dfrac{\sin \beta(1 + \cos \beta)}{\sin^2 \beta} = \dfrac{1 + \cos \beta}{\sin \beta}$$

41. Verify $\cos\left(\dfrac{\pi}{2} - x\right) \csc x = 1$.

Solution:

$$\cos\left(\dfrac{\pi}{2} - x\right) \csc x = \sin x \csc x = \sin x \left(\dfrac{1}{\sin x}\right) = 1$$

45. Verify $\dfrac{\cos(-\theta)}{1 + \sin(-\theta)} = \sec \theta + \tan \theta$.

Solution:

$$\dfrac{\cos(-\theta)}{1 + \sin(-\theta)} = \dfrac{\cos \theta}{1 - \sin \theta}$$

$$= \dfrac{\cos \theta}{1 - \sin \theta} \cdot \dfrac{1 + \sin \theta}{1 + \sin \theta}$$

$$= \dfrac{\cos \theta(1 + \sin \theta)}{1 - \sin^2 \theta}$$

$$= \dfrac{\cos \theta(1 + \sin \theta)}{\cos^2 \theta}$$

$$= \dfrac{1 + \sin \theta}{\cos \theta}$$

$$= \dfrac{1}{\cos \theta} + \dfrac{\sin \theta}{\cos \theta}$$

$$= \sec \theta + \tan \theta$$

49. Verify $\dfrac{\tan x + \cot y}{\tan x \cot y} = \tan y + \cot x$.

Solution:

$$\dfrac{\tan x + \cot y}{\tan x \cot y} = \dfrac{\tan x}{\tan x \cot y} + \dfrac{\cot y}{\tan x \cot y}$$

$$= \dfrac{1}{\cot y} + \dfrac{1}{\tan x}$$

$$= \tan y + \cot x$$

53. Verify $\sin^2 x + \sin^2\left(\dfrac{\pi}{2} - x\right) = 1$.

Solution:

$$\sin^2 x + \sin^2\left(\dfrac{\pi}{2} - x\right) = \sin^2 x + \cos^2 x$$

$$= 1$$

59. Explain why $\sqrt{\tan^2 x} = \tan x$ is *not* an identity and find one value of the variable for which the equation is not true.

Solution:

$$\sqrt{\tan^2 x} = |\tan x|$$

To show that $\sqrt{\tan^2 x} = \tan x$ is not true, pick any value of x whose tangent is negative. For example, $\sqrt{\tan^2 135°} = 1$, whereas, $\tan 135° = -1$.

SECTION 3.3

Solving Trigonometric Equations

- You should be able to identify and solve trigonometric equations.

- A trigonometric equation is a conditional equation. It is true for a specific set of values.

- To solve trigonometric equations, use algebraic techniques such as collecting like terms, taking square roots, factoring, squaring, converting to quadratic form, and using formulas.

Solutions to Selected Exercises

5. Verify that the given values of x are solutions of the equation $2\sin^2 x - \sin x - 1 = 0$.

   (a) $x = \dfrac{\pi}{2}$

   (b) $x = \dfrac{7\pi}{6}$

Solution:

(a)
$$x = \frac{\pi}{2}$$
$$\sin\frac{\pi}{2} = 1$$
$$2\sin^2\frac{\pi}{2} - \sin\frac{\pi}{2} - 1 = 2(1)^2 - 1 - 1 = 0$$

(b)
$$x = \frac{7\pi}{6}$$
$$\sin\frac{7\pi}{6} = -\frac{1}{2}$$
$$2\sin^2\frac{7\pi}{6} - \sin\frac{7\pi}{6} - 1 = 2\left(-\frac{1}{2}\right)^2 - \left(-\frac{1}{2}\right) - 1 = 2\left(\frac{1}{4}\right) + \frac{1}{2} - 1 = \frac{1}{2} + \frac{1}{2} - 1 = 0$$

9. Find all solutions of $\sqrt{3}\csc x - 2 = 0$. (Do not use a calculator.)

Solution:

$$\sqrt{3}\csc x - 2 = 0$$

$$\csc x = \frac{2}{\sqrt{3}}$$

$$x = \frac{\pi}{3} \quad \text{or} \quad \frac{2\pi}{3} \quad \text{in } [0,\ 2\pi)$$

In general form, $x = (\pi/3) + 2n\pi$ or $x = (2\pi/3) + 2n\pi$ where n is an integer.

13. Find all solutions of $3\sec^2 x - 4 = 0$. (Do not use a calculator.)

Solution:

$$3\sec^2 x - 4 = 0$$

$$\sec^2 x = \frac{4}{3}$$

$$\sec x = \pm\sqrt{\frac{4}{3}} = \pm\frac{2}{\sqrt{3}} = \pm\frac{2\sqrt{3}}{3}$$

$$\sec x = \frac{2\sqrt{3}}{3} \qquad \text{or} \quad \sec x = -\frac{2\sqrt{3}}{3}$$

$$x = \frac{\pi}{6},\ \frac{11\pi}{6} \qquad\qquad x = \frac{5\pi}{6},\ \frac{7\pi}{6} \quad \text{in } [0,\ 2\pi)$$

In general form, the solutions are $x = (\pi/6) + n\pi$ or $x = (5\pi/6) + n\pi$ where n is an integer.

17. Find all solutions of $\sin x(\sin x + 1) = 0$. (Do not use a calculator.)

Solution:

$$\sin x = 0 \qquad \text{or} \quad \sin x = -1$$

$$x = 0,\ \pi \qquad\qquad x = \frac{3\pi}{2} \quad \text{in } [0,\ 2\pi)$$

In general form, the solutions are $x = n\pi$ and $x = (3\pi/2) + 2n\pi$, where n is an integer.

21. Find all solutions of $\sec x \csc x - 2 \csc x = 0$ in the interval $[0, \, 2\pi)$. (Do not use a calculator.)

Solution:

$$\sec x \csc x - 2 \csc x = 0$$

$$\csc x (\sec x - 2) = 0$$

$\csc x = 0$ or $\sec x = 2$

Not possible $x = \dfrac{\pi}{3}, \, \dfrac{5\pi}{3}$

25. Find all solutions of $\cos^3 x = \cos x$ in the interval $[0, \, 2\pi)$. (Do not use a calculator.)

Solution:

$$\cos^3 x = \cos x$$

$$\cos^3 x - \cos x = 0$$

$$\cos x (\cos^2 x - 1) = 0$$

$\cos x = 0$ or $\cos^2 x - 1 = 0$

$x = \dfrac{\pi}{2}, \, \dfrac{3\pi}{2}$ $\cos x = \pm 1$

$x = 0, \, \dfrac{\pi}{2}, \, \pi, \, \dfrac{3\pi}{2}$ $x = 0, \, \pi$

29. Find all solutions of $2 \sec^2 x + \tan^2 x - 3 = 0$ in the interval $[0, \, 2\pi)$. (Do not use a calculator.)

Solution:

$$2 \sec^2 x + \tan^2 x - 3 = 0$$

$$2 \sec^2 x + (\sec^2 x - 1) - 3 = 0$$

$$3 \sec^2 x - 4 = 0$$

$$\sec^2 x = \dfrac{4}{3}$$

$$\sec x = \pm \dfrac{2}{\sqrt{3}}$$

$\sec x = \dfrac{2}{\sqrt{3}}$ or $\sec x = -\dfrac{2}{\sqrt{3}}$

$x = \dfrac{\pi}{6}, \, \dfrac{11\pi}{6}$ $x = \dfrac{5\pi}{6}, \, \dfrac{7\pi}{6}$

$x = \dfrac{\pi}{6}, \, \dfrac{5\pi}{6}, \, \dfrac{7\pi}{6}, \, \dfrac{11\pi}{6}$

33. Find all solutions of $\sin 2x = -\sqrt{3}/2$ in the interval $[0,\ 2\pi)$. (Do not use a calculator.)

Solution:

$$\sin 2x = -\frac{\sqrt{3}}{2}$$

$$2x = \frac{4\pi}{3}, \qquad 2x = \frac{5\pi}{3}, \qquad 2x = \frac{10\pi}{3}, \qquad 2x = \frac{11\pi}{3}$$

$$x = \frac{2\pi}{3}, \qquad x = \frac{5\pi}{6}, \qquad x = \frac{5\pi}{3}, \qquad x = \frac{11\pi}{6}$$

39. Find all solutions of

$$\frac{1+\sin x}{\cos x} + \frac{\cos x}{1+\sin x} = 4$$

in the interval $[0,\ 2\pi)$. (Do not use a calculator.)

Solution:

$$\frac{1+\sin x}{\cos x} + \frac{\cos x}{1+\sin x} = 4$$

$$(1+\sin x)^2 + (\cos x)^2 = 4\cos x(1+\sin x)$$

$$1 + 2\sin x + \sin^2 x + \cos^2 x = 4\cos x(1+\sin x)$$

$$1 + 2\sin x + 1 = 4\cos x(1+\sin x)$$

$$2(1+\sin x) - 4\cos(1+\sin x) = 0$$

$$2(1+\sin x)(1 - 2\cos x) = 0$$

$$\sin x = -1 \qquad\qquad\qquad \text{or} \quad \cos x = \frac{1}{2}$$

$$x = \frac{3\pi}{2}, \ \text{extraneous} \qquad\qquad\qquad x = \frac{\pi}{3}, \ \frac{5\pi}{3}$$

(Makes the denominator zero.)

The only solutions are $x = \pi/3,\ 5\pi/3$.

43. Solve $12y^2 - 13y + 3 = 0$ and $12\sin^2 x - 13\sin x + 3 = 0$. Restrict the solutions to the interval $[0, \, 2\pi)$.

Solution:

$12y^2 - 12y + 3 = 0$

$(4y - 3)(3y - 1) = 0$

$y = \frac{3}{4}$ or $y = \frac{1}{3}$

$12\sin^2 x - 13\sin x + 3 = 0$

$(4\sin x - 3)(3\sin x - 1) = 0$

$\sin x = \frac{3}{4}$ or $\sin x = \frac{1}{3}$

$x \approx 0.8481, \, 2.2935$ $\qquad$ $x \approx 0.3398, \, 2.8018$

47. Solve $y^2 - 8y + 13 = 0$ and $\tan^2 x - 8\tan x + 13 = 0$. Restrict the solutions to the interval $[0, \, 2\pi)$.

Solution:

$y^2 - 8y + 13 = 0$

$y = \dfrac{8 \pm \sqrt{64 - 52}}{2}$

$= \dfrac{8 \pm \sqrt{12}}{2}$

$= \dfrac{8 \pm 2\sqrt{3}}{2}$

$= 4 \pm \sqrt{3}$

$\tan^2 x - 8\tan x + 13 = 0$

$\tan x = \dfrac{8 \pm \sqrt{64 - 52}}{2}$

$= \dfrac{8 \pm 2\sqrt{3}}{2}$

$\tan x = 4 + \sqrt{3}$ $\qquad$ or $\quad \tan x = 4 - \sqrt{3}$

$x \approx 1.3981, \, 4.5397$ $\qquad$ $x \approx 1.1555, \, 4.2971$

53. A 5-pound weight is oscillating on the end of a spring, and the position of the weight relative to the point of equilibrium is given by $y = \frac{1}{4}(\cos 8t - 3\sin 8t)$ where t is the time in seconds. Find the times when the weight is at the point of equilibrium $[y = 0]$ for $0 \le t \le 1$.

Solution:

$\dfrac{1}{4}(\cos 8t - 3\sin 8t) = 0$

$\cos 8t = 3\sin 8t$

$\dfrac{1}{3} = \tan 8t$

$8t \approx 0.32175 + n\pi$

$t \approx 0.04 + \dfrac{n\pi}{8}$

In the interval $0 \le t \le 1$, we have $t = 0.04, \, 0.43$, and 0.83.

SECTION 3.4

Sum and Difference Formulas

- You should memorize the sum and difference formulas.

$$\sin(u \pm v) = \sin u \cos v \pm \cos u \sin v$$

$$\cos(u \pm v) = \cos u \cos v \mp \sin u \sin v$$

$$\tan(u \pm v) = \frac{\tan u \pm \tan v}{1 \mp \tan u \tan v}$$

- You should be able to use these formulas to find the values of the trigonometric functions of angles whose sums or differences are special angles.

- You should be able to use these formulas to solve trigonometric equations.

Solutions to Selected Exercises

5. Determine the exact value of the sine, cosine, and tangent of the angle $195° = 225° - 30°$.

Solution:

$$\sin 195° = \sin(225° - 30°) = \sin 225° \cos 30° - \cos 225° \sin 30°$$

$$= (-\sin 45°) \cos 30° - (-\cos 45°) \sin 30° = -\frac{\sqrt{2}}{2} \cdot \frac{\sqrt{3}}{2} + \frac{\sqrt{2}}{2} \cdot \frac{1}{2} = \frac{\sqrt{2}}{4}(1 - \sqrt{3})$$

$$\cos 195° = \cos(225° - 30°) = \cos 225° \cos 30° + \sin 225° \sin 30°$$

$$= (-\cos 45°) \cos 30° + (-\sin 45°) \sin 30° = -\frac{\sqrt{2}}{2} \cdot \frac{\sqrt{3}}{2} - \frac{\sqrt{2}}{2} \cdot \frac{1}{2} = -\frac{\sqrt{2}}{4}(1 + \sqrt{3})$$

$$\tan 195° = \tan(225° - 30°) = \frac{\tan 225° - \tan 30°}{1 + \tan 225° \tan 30°} = \frac{\tan 45° - \tan 30°}{1 + \tan 45° \tan 30°}$$

$$= \frac{1 - \sqrt{3}/3}{1 + (1)(\sqrt{3}/3)} \cdot \frac{3}{3} = \frac{3 - \sqrt{3}}{3 + \sqrt{3}} \cdot \frac{3 - \sqrt{3}}{3 - \sqrt{3}}$$

$$= \frac{(3 - \sqrt{3})^2}{9 - 3} = \frac{9 - 6\sqrt{3} + 3}{6}$$

$$= \frac{12 - 6\sqrt{3}}{6} = \frac{6(2 - \sqrt{3})}{6} = 2 - \sqrt{3}$$

11. Simplify $\cos 25° \cos 15° - \sin 25° \sin 15°$.

Solution:

$$\cos 25° \cos 15° - \sin 25° \sin 15° = \cos(25° + 15°) = \cos 40°$$

15. Simplify $\dfrac{\tan 325° - \tan 86°}{1 + \tan 325° \tan 86°}$.

Solution:

$$\frac{\tan 325° - \tan 86°}{1 + \tan 325° \tan 86°} = \tan(325° - 86°)$$
$$= \tan 239°$$

19. Simplify $\dfrac{\tan 2x + \tan x}{1 - \tan 2x \tan x}$.

Solution:

$$\frac{\tan 2x + \tan x}{1 - \tan 2x \tan x} = \tan(2x + x)$$
$$= \tan 3x$$

23. Find the exact value of $\cos(v + u)$ given that $\sin u = 5/13$, $0 < u < \pi/2$, and $\cos v = -3/5$, $\pi/2 < v < \pi$.

Solution:

$$\sin u = \frac{5}{13}, \ 0 < u < \frac{\pi}{2} \quad \Rightarrow \quad \cos u = \frac{12}{13}$$

$$\cos v = -\frac{3}{5}, \ \frac{\pi}{2} < v < \pi \quad \Rightarrow \quad \sin v = \frac{4}{5}$$

$$\cos(v + u) = \cos v \cos u - \sin v \sin u = \left(-\frac{3}{5}\right)\left(\frac{12}{13}\right) - \left(\frac{4}{5}\right)\left(\frac{5}{13}\right) = -\frac{56}{65}$$

27. Find the exact value of $\sin(v - u)$ given that $\sin u = 7/25$, $\pi/2 < u < \pi$ and $\cos v = 4/5$, $3\pi/2 < v < 2\pi$.

Solution:

$$\sin u = \frac{7}{25}, \ \frac{\pi}{2} < u < \pi \quad \Rightarrow \quad \cos u = -\frac{24}{25}$$

$$\cos v = \frac{4}{5}, \ \frac{3\pi}{2} < v < 2\pi \quad \Rightarrow \quad \sin v = -\frac{3}{5}$$

$$\sin(v - u) = \sin v \cos u - \cos v \sin u = \left(-\frac{3}{5}\right)\left(-\frac{24}{25}\right) - \left(\frac{4}{5}\right)\left(\frac{7}{25}\right) = \frac{44}{125}$$

31. Verify $\cos\left(\dfrac{3\pi}{2} - x\right) = -\sin x$.

Solution:

$$\cos\left(\frac{3\pi}{2} - x\right) = \cos\frac{3\pi}{2}\cos x + \sin\frac{3\pi}{2}\sin x = (0)(\cos x) + (-1)(\sin x) = -\sin x$$

35. Verify $\cos(\pi - \theta) + \sin\left(\dfrac{\pi}{2} + \theta\right) = 0$.

Solution:

$$\cos(\pi - \theta) + \sin\left(\frac{\pi}{2} + \theta\right) = (\cos\pi\cos\theta + \sin\pi\sin\theta) + \left(\sin\frac{\pi}{2}\cos\theta + \cos\frac{\pi}{2}\sin\theta\right)$$

$$= (-1)\cos\theta + (0)\sin\theta + (1)\cos\theta + (0)\sin\theta$$

$$= -\cos\theta + 0 + \cos\theta + 0$$

$$= 0$$

39. Verify $\cos(x + y)\cos(x - y) = \cos^2 x - \sin^2 y$.

Solution:

$$\cos(x + y)\cos(x - y) = (\cos x \cos y - \sin x \sin y)(\cos x \cos y + \sin x \sin y)$$

$$= \cos^2 x \cos^2 y - \sin^2 x \sin^2 y$$

$$= \cos^2 x(1 - \sin^2 y) - (1 - \cos^2 x)\sin^2 y$$

$$= \cos^2 x - \cos^2 x \sin^2 y - \sin^2 y + \cos^2 x \sin^2 y$$

$$= \cos^2 x - \sin^2 y$$

41. Verify $\sin(x + y) + \sin(x - y) = 2\sin x \cos y$.

Solution:

$$\sin(x + y) + \sin(x - y) = (\sin x \cos y + \cos x \sin y) + (\sin x \cos y - \cos x \sin y)$$

$$= 2\sin x \cos y$$

45. Verify $a\sin B\theta + b\cos B\theta = \sqrt{a^2 + b^2}\sin(B\theta + C)$, where $C = \arctan(b/a)$.

Solution:

$$\sqrt{a^2 + b^2}\sin(B\theta + C) = \sqrt{a^2 + b^2}(\sin B\theta \cos C + \cos B\theta \sin C)$$

$$= \sqrt{a^2 + b^2}\left[\sin B\theta\left(\frac{a}{\sqrt{a^2 + b^2}}\right) + \cos B\theta\left(\frac{b}{\sqrt{a^2 + b^2}}\right)\right]$$

$$= \frac{\sqrt{a^2 + b^2}}{\sqrt{a^2 + b^2}}(a\sin B\theta + b\cos B\theta)$$

$$= a\sin B\theta + b\cos B\theta$$

[43] $\cos\eta\pi + \cos\theta - \sin\eta\pi \sin\theta$

$\cos\eta\pi \cos\theta$

$(-1)^n \cos\theta$

49. Use the formulas given in Exercises 45 and 46 to write $12 \sin 3\theta + 5 \cos 3\theta$ in the following forms.

(a) $\sqrt{a^2 + b^2} \sin(B\theta + C)$ (b) $\sqrt{a^2 + b^2} \cos(B\theta - C)$

Solution:

$a = 12, \ b = 5, \ B = 3, \ C = \arctan \frac{5}{12} \approx 0.3948$

$\sqrt{12^2 + 5^2} = \sqrt{169} = 13$

(a) Thus, $\sqrt{a^2 + b^2} \sin(B\theta + C) = 13 \sin(3\theta + 0.3948)$, and

(b) $\sqrt{a^2 + b^2} \cos(B\theta - C) = 13 \cos(3\theta - 0.3948)$.

53. Write $\sin(\arcsin x + \arccos x)$ as an algebraic expression.

Solution:

$$\sin(\arcsin x + \arccos x) = \sin(\arcsin x)\cos(\arccos x) + \cos(\arcsin x)\sin(\arccos x)$$

$$= (x)(x) + \frac{\sqrt{1-x^2}}{1} \cdot \frac{\sqrt{1-x^2}}{1}$$

$$= x^2 + 1 - x^2 = 1$$

57. Find all solutions in the interval $[0, \ 2\pi)$ of $\cos\left(x + \frac{\pi}{4}\right) + \cos\left(x - \frac{\pi}{4}\right) = 1$.

Solution:

$$\cos\left(x + \frac{\pi}{4}\right) + \cos\left(x - \frac{\pi}{4}\right) = 1$$

$$\cos x \cos \frac{\pi}{4} - \sin x \sin \frac{\pi}{4} + \cos x \cos \frac{\pi}{4} + \sin x \sin \frac{\pi}{4} = 1$$

$$\frac{\sqrt{2}}{2} \cos x + \frac{\sqrt{2}}{2} \cos x = 1$$

$$\sqrt{2} \cos x = 1$$

$$\cos x = \frac{1}{\sqrt{2}}$$

$$x = \frac{\pi}{4}, \ \frac{7\pi}{4}$$

59.

$$\frac{\tan x + \tan \pi}{1 - \tan x \tan \pi} + 2\left[\sin x \cos \pi + \cos x \sin \pi \right]_{=0}$$

$$\tan x + 2\left[\sin x (-1) + \cos x (0) \right] = 0$$

$$\tan x - 2 \sin x = 0$$

$$\frac{\sin - 2 \sin x}{\cos} = 0$$

$$\sin(1 - 2\cos x) = 0 \qquad \sin x = 0$$

$$x = 0, \pi$$

$$1 = 2 \cos x$$

$$\frac{1}{2} = \cos x$$

$$x = \frac{\pi}{3}, \frac{5\pi}{3}$$

61. The equation of a standing wave is obtained by adding the displacements of two waves traveling in opposite directions (see figure). Assume that each of the waves has amplitude A, period T, and wavelength λ. If the models for these waves are

$$y_1 = A \cos 2\pi \left(\frac{t}{T} - \frac{x}{\lambda} \right) \quad \text{and}$$

$$y_2 = A \cos 2\pi \left(\frac{t}{T} + \frac{x}{\lambda} \right)$$

show that

$$y_1 + y_2 = 2A \cos \frac{2\pi t}{T} \cos \frac{2\pi x}{\lambda}.$$

Solution:

$$y_1 + y_2 = A \cos 2\pi \left(\frac{t}{T} - \frac{x}{\lambda} \right) + A \cos 2\pi \left(\frac{t}{T} + \frac{x}{\lambda} \right)$$

$$= A \left[\cos \left(\frac{2\pi t}{T} - \frac{2\pi x}{\lambda} \right) + \cos \left(\frac{2\pi t}{T} + \frac{2\pi x}{\lambda} \right) \right]$$

$$= A \left[\cos \frac{2\pi t}{T} \cos \frac{2\pi x}{\lambda} + \sin \frac{2\pi t}{T} \sin \frac{2\pi x}{\lambda} + \cos \frac{2\pi t}{T} \cos \frac{2\pi x}{\lambda} - \sin \frac{2\pi t}{T} \sin \frac{2\pi x}{\lambda} \right]$$

$$= 2A \cos \frac{2\pi t}{T} \cos \frac{2\pi x}{\lambda}$$

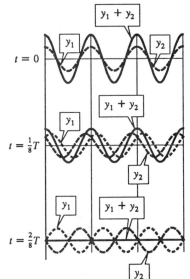

63. Verify that $\dfrac{\cos(x + h) - \cos x}{h} = \cos x \left(\dfrac{\cos h - 1}{h} \right) - \sin x \left(\dfrac{\sin h}{h} \right).$

Solution:

$$\frac{\cos(x + h) - \cos x}{h} = \frac{\cos x \cos h - \sin x \sin h - \cos x}{h}$$

$$= \frac{\cos x (\cos h - 1) - \sin x \sin h}{h}$$

$$= \frac{\cos x (\cos h - 1)}{h} - \frac{\sin x \sin h}{h}$$

$$= \cos x \left(\frac{\cos h - 1}{h} \right) - \sin x \left(\frac{\sin h}{h} \right)$$

SECTION 3.5

Multiple-Angle Formulas and Product-Sum Formulas

■ You should know the following double-angle formulas.

(a) $\sin 2u = 2 \sin u \cos u$

(b) $\cos 2u = \cos^2 u - \sin^2 u$

$\qquad = 2 \cos^2 u - 1$

$\qquad = 1 - 2 \sin^2 u$

(c) $\tan 2u = \dfrac{2 \tan u}{1 - \tan^2 u}$

■ You should be able to reduce the power of a trigonometric function.

(a) $\sin^2 u = \dfrac{1 - \cos 2u}{2}$

(b) $\cos^2 u = \dfrac{1 + \cos 2u}{2}$

(c) $\tan^2 u = \dfrac{1 - \cos 2u}{1 + \cos 2u}$

■ You should be able to use the half-angle formulas.

(a) $\sin \dfrac{u}{2} = \pm\sqrt{\dfrac{1 - \cos u}{2}}$

(b) $\cos \dfrac{u}{2} = \pm\sqrt{\dfrac{1 + \cos u}{2}}$

(c) $\tan \dfrac{u}{2} = \dfrac{1 - \cos u}{\sin u} = \dfrac{\sin u}{1 + \cos u}$

■ You should be able to use the product-sum formulas.

(a) $\sin u \sin v = \dfrac{1}{2}[\cos(u - v) - \cos(u + v)]$

(b) $\cos u \cos v = \dfrac{1}{2}[\cos(u - v) + \cos(u + v)]$

(c) $\sin u \cos v = \dfrac{1}{2}[\sin(u + v) + \sin(u - v)]$

(d) $\cos u \sin v = \dfrac{1}{2}[\sin(u + v) - \sin(u - v)]$

You should be able to use the sum-product formulas.

(a) $\sin x + \sin y = 2\sin\left(\dfrac{x+y}{2}\right)\cos\left(\dfrac{x-y}{2}\right)$

(b) $\sin x - \sin y = 2\cos\left(\dfrac{x+y}{2}\right)\sin\left(\dfrac{x-y}{2}\right)$

(c) $\cos x + \cos y = 2\cos\left(\dfrac{x+y}{2}\right)\cos\left(\dfrac{x-y}{2}\right)$

(d) $\cos x - \cos y = -2\sin\left(\dfrac{x+y}{2}\right)\sin\left(\dfrac{x-y}{2}\right)$

Solutions to Selected Exercises

3. Find all the solutions of $4\sin x \cos x = 1$ in the interval $[0,\ 2\pi)$.

Solution:

$$4\sin x \cos x = 1$$
$$2[2\sin x \cos x] = 1$$
$$2\sin 2x = 1$$
$$\sin 2x = \frac{1}{2}$$

$$2x = \frac{\pi}{6}, \qquad 2x = \frac{5\pi}{6}, \qquad 2x = \frac{13\pi}{6}, \qquad 2x = \frac{17\pi}{6}$$

$$x = \frac{\pi}{12}, \qquad x = \frac{5\pi}{12}, \qquad x = \frac{13\pi}{12}, \qquad x = \frac{17\pi}{12}$$

9. Find all solutions of $\sin 4x + 2\sin 2x = 0$ in the interval $[0,\ 2\pi)$.

Solution:

$$\sin 4x + 2\sin 2x = 0$$
$$2\sin 2x \cos 2x + 2\sin 2x = 0$$
$$2\sin 2x(\cos 2x + 1) = 0$$

$$\sin 2x = 0 \qquad\qquad \text{or} \qquad \cos 2x = -1$$
$$2x = 0,\ \pi,\ 2\pi,\ 3\pi \qquad\qquad 2x = \pi,\ 3\pi$$
$$x = 0,\ \frac{\pi}{2},\ \pi,\ \frac{3\pi}{2} \qquad\qquad x = \frac{\pi}{2},\ \frac{3\pi}{2}$$

13. Use a double-angle identity to rewrite $g(x) = 4 - 8\sin^2 x$ and sketch its graph.

Solution:

$$g(x) = 4 - 8\sin^2 x$$
$$= 4(1 - 2\sin^2 x)$$
$$= 4\cos 2x$$

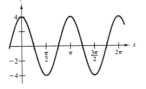

17. Find the exact values of $\sin 2u$, $\cos 2u$, and $\tan 2u$, given $\tan u = 1/2$, $\pi < u < 3\pi/2$.

Solution:

$$\tan u = \frac{1}{2}, \quad u \text{ lies in Quadrant III.}$$

$$\sin u = -\frac{1}{\sqrt{5}} \text{ and } \cos u = -\frac{2}{\sqrt{5}}$$

$$\sin 2u = 2\left(-\frac{1}{\sqrt{5}}\right)\left(-\frac{2}{\sqrt{5}}\right) = \frac{4}{5}$$

$$\cos 2u = \left(-\frac{2}{\sqrt{5}}\right)^2 - \left(-\frac{1}{\sqrt{5}}\right)^2 = \frac{3}{5}$$

$$\tan 2u = \frac{\sin 2u}{\cos 2u} = \frac{4}{3}$$

21. Use the power-reducing formulas to write $\cos^4 x$ in terms of the first power of the cosine.

Solution:

$$\cos^4 x = (\cos^2 x)^2$$
$$= \left(\frac{1 + \cos 2x}{2}\right)^2$$
$$= \frac{1}{4}(1 + 2\cos 2x + \cos^2 2x)$$
$$= \frac{1}{4}\left(1 + 2\cos 2x + \frac{1 + \cos 4x}{2}\right)$$
$$= \frac{1}{4}\left(\frac{3}{2} + 2\cos 2x + \frac{1}{2}\cos 4x\right)$$
$$= \frac{1}{8}(3 + 4\cos 2x + \cos 4x)$$

25. Use the power-reducing formulas to write $\sin^2 x \cos^4 x$ in terms of the first power of the cosine.

Solution:

$$\sin^2 x \cos^4 x = \left(\frac{1 - \cos 2x}{2} \right) \cos^4 x$$

$$= \frac{1}{2}(1 - \cos 2x)\frac{1}{8}(3 + 4\cos 2x + \cos 4x) \quad \text{from Exercise 21}$$

$$= \frac{1}{16}(3 + 4\cos 2x + \cos 4x - 3\cos 2x - 4\cos^2 2x - \cos 4x \cos 2x)$$

$$= \frac{1}{16}\left[3 + \cos 2x + \cos 4x - 4\left(\frac{1 + \cos 4x}{2} \right) - \frac{1}{2}(\cos 2x + \cos 6x) \right]$$

$$= \frac{1}{16}\left(3 + \cos 2x + \cos 4x - 2 - 2\cos 4x - \frac{1}{2}\cos 2x - \frac{1}{2}\cos 6x \right)$$

$$= \frac{1}{16}\left(1 + \frac{1}{2}\cos 2x - \cos 4x - \frac{1}{2}\cos 6x \right)$$

$$= \frac{1}{32}(2 + \cos 2x - 2\cos 4x - \cos 6x)$$

29. Use half-angle formulas to determine the exact values of the sine, cosine, and tangent of the angle $112°30'$.

Solution:

$$\sin 112°30' = +\sqrt{\frac{1 - \cos 225°}{2}} = \sqrt{\frac{1 - (-\sqrt{2}/2)}{2}} = \sqrt{\frac{2 + \sqrt{2}}{4}} = \frac{\sqrt{2 + \sqrt{2}}}{2}$$

$$\cos 112°30' = -\sqrt{\frac{1 + \cos 225°}{2}} = -\sqrt{\frac{1 + (-\sqrt{2}/2)}{2}} = -\sqrt{\frac{2 - \sqrt{2}}{4}} = -\frac{\sqrt{2 - \sqrt{2}}}{2}$$

$$\tan 112°30' = -\sqrt{\frac{1 - \cos 225°}{1 + \cos 225°}} = -\sqrt{\frac{1 + \sqrt{2}/2}{1 - \sqrt{2}/2}} = -\sqrt{\frac{2 + \sqrt{2}}{2 - \sqrt{2}} \cdot \frac{2 + \sqrt{2}}{2 + \sqrt{2}}}$$

$$= -\sqrt{\frac{(2 + \sqrt{2})^2}{4 - 2}} = -\frac{2 + \sqrt{2}}{\sqrt{2}} = -(\sqrt{2} + 1) = -1 - \sqrt{2}$$

35. Find the exact values of $\sin(u/2)$, $\cos(u/2)$, and $\tan(u/2)$ by using the half-angle formulas, given $\tan u = -5/8$, $3\pi/2 < u < 2\pi$.

Solution:

$\tan u = -\dfrac{5}{8}$, u lies in Quadrant IV; $\sin u = -\dfrac{5}{\sqrt{89}}$ and $\cos u = \dfrac{8}{\sqrt{89}}$

$$\sin\frac{u}{2} = \sqrt{\frac{1 - 8/\sqrt{89}}{2}} = \sqrt{\frac{\sqrt{89} - 8}{2\sqrt{89}}} = \sqrt{\frac{89 - 8\sqrt{89}}{178}}$$

$$\cos\frac{u}{2} = -\sqrt{\frac{1 + 8/\sqrt{89}}{2}} = -\sqrt{\frac{\sqrt{89} + 8}{2\sqrt{89}}} = \sqrt{\frac{89 + 8\sqrt{89}}{178}}$$

$$\tan\frac{u}{2} = -\sqrt{\frac{1 - 8/\sqrt{89}}{1 + 8/\sqrt{89}}} = -\sqrt{\frac{\sqrt{89} - 8}{\sqrt{89} + 8} \cdot \frac{\sqrt{89} - 8}{\sqrt{89} - 8}} = \sqrt{\frac{(\sqrt{89} - 8)^2}{89 - 64}} = -\left(\frac{\sqrt{89} - 8}{5}\right)$$

$$= \frac{1}{5}(8 - \sqrt{89})$$

39. Use the half-angle formulas to simplify $\sqrt{\dfrac{1 - \cos 6x}{2}}$.

Solution:

$$\sqrt{\frac{1 - \cos 6x}{2}} = \sqrt{\frac{1 - \cos 2(3x)}{2}} = \sin 3x$$

43. Find all the solutions of $\sin(x/2) + \cos x = 0$ in the interval $[0, \, 2\pi)$.

Solution:

$$\sin\frac{x}{2} + \cos x = 0$$

$$\pm\sqrt{\frac{1 - \cos x}{2}} = -\cos x$$

$$\frac{1 - \cos x}{2} = \cos^2 x$$

$$0 = 2\cos^2 x + \cos x - 1 = (2\cos x - 1)(\cos x + 1)$$

$\cos x = \dfrac{1}{2}$ \qquad or \qquad $\cos x = -1$

$x = \dfrac{\pi}{3}, \dfrac{5\pi}{3}$ \qquad\qquad $x = \pi$

By checking these values in the original equation, we see that $x = \pi/3$ and $x = 5\pi/3$ are extraneous, and $x = \pi$ is the only solution.

49. Rewrite $\sin 5\theta \cos 3\theta$ as a sum.

Solution:

$$\sin 5\theta \cos 3\theta = \tfrac{1}{2}[\sin(5\theta + 3\theta) + \sin(5\theta - 3\theta)] = \tfrac{1}{2}(\sin 8\theta + \sin 2\theta)$$

53. Rewrite $\sin(x + y)\sin(x - y)$ as a sum.

Solution:

$$\sin(x + y)\sin(x - y) = \tfrac{1}{2}\{\cos[(x + y) - (x - y)] - \cos[(x + y) + (x - y)]\}$$
$$= \tfrac{1}{2}\{\cos 2y - \cos 2x\}$$

57. Express $\sin 60° + \sin 30°$ as a product.

Solution:

$$\sin 60° + \sin 30° = 2\sin\left(\frac{60° + 30°}{2}\right)\cos\left(\frac{60° - 30°}{2}\right) = 2\sin 45° \cos 15°$$

61. Express $\cos 6x + \cos 2x$ as a product.

Solution:

$$\cos 6x + \cos 2x = 2\cos\left(\frac{6x + 2x}{2}\right)\cos\left(\frac{6x - 2x}{2}\right) = 2\cos 4x \cos 2x$$

65. Express $\cos(\phi + 2\pi) + \cos\phi$ as a product.

Solution:

$$\cos(\phi + 2\pi) + \cos\phi = 2\cos\left(\frac{\phi + 2\pi + \phi}{2}\right)\cos\left(\frac{\phi + 2\pi - \phi}{2}\right) = 2\cos(\phi + \pi)\cos\pi$$

67. Find all solutions of $\sin 6x + \sin 2x = 0$ in the interval $[0,\ 2\pi)$.

Solution:

$$\sin 6x + \sin 2x = 0$$

$$2\sin\left(\frac{6x + 2x}{2}\right)\cos\left(\frac{6x - 2x}{2}\right) = 0$$

$$2(\sin 4x)\cos 2x = 0$$

$\sin 4x = 0$ $\qquad$ or $\qquad$ $\cos 2x = 0$

$\qquad 4x = n\pi$ $\qquad\qquad\qquad 2x = \dfrac{\pi}{2} + n\pi$

$\qquad x = \dfrac{n\pi}{4}$ $\qquad\qquad\qquad x = \dfrac{\pi}{4} + \dfrac{n\pi}{2}$

In the interval $[0,\ 2\pi)$, we have

$$x = 0,\ \frac{\pi}{4},\ \frac{\pi}{2},\ \frac{3\pi}{4},\ \pi,\ \frac{5\pi}{4},\ \frac{3\pi}{2},\ \frac{7\pi}{4}.$$

71. Verify $\csc 2\theta = \dfrac{\csc \theta}{2\cos \theta}$.

Solution:

$$\csc 2\theta = \frac{1}{\sin 2\theta} = \frac{1}{2\sin\theta(\cos\theta)} = \frac{1}{\sin\theta}\cdot\frac{1}{2\cos\theta} = \frac{\csc\theta}{2\cos\theta}$$

75. Verify $(\sin x + \cos x)^2 = 1 + \sin 2x$.

Solution:

$$(\sin x + \cos x)^2 = \sin^2 x + 2\sin x \cos x + \cos^2 x$$

$$= (\sin^2 x + \cos^2 x) + 2\sin x \cos x$$

$$= 1 + \sin 2x$$

79. Verify $1 + \cos 10y = 2\cos^2 5y$.

Solution:

$$2\cos^2 5y = 2\left[\frac{1 + \cos 10y}{2}\right] = 1 + \cos 10y$$

85. Verify $\dfrac{\cos 4x - \cos 2x}{2 \sin 3x} = -\sin x.$

Solution:

$$\frac{\cos 4x - \cos 2x}{2 \sin 3x} = \frac{-2 \sin\left(\dfrac{4x + 2x}{2}\right) \sin\left(\dfrac{4x - 2x}{2}\right)}{2 \sin 3x} = \frac{-2 \sin 3x \sin x}{2 \sin 3x} = -\sin x$$

87. Verify $\dfrac{\cos t + \cos 3t}{\sin 3t - \sin t} = \cot t.$

Solution:

$$\frac{\cos t + \cos 3t}{\sin 3t - \sin t} = \frac{2 \cos\left(\dfrac{t + 3t}{2}\right) \cos\left(\dfrac{t - 3t}{2}\right)}{2 \cos\left(\dfrac{3t + t}{2}\right) \sin\left(\dfrac{3t - t}{2}\right)} = \frac{2 \cos 2t \cos(-t)}{2 \cos 2t \sin t} = \frac{\cos t}{\sin t} = \cot t$$

89. Sketch the graph of $f(x) = \sin^2 x$ by using the power-reducing formulas.

Solution:

$$f(x) = \sin^2 x$$
$$= \frac{1 - \cos 2x}{2}$$
$$= \frac{1}{2} - \frac{1}{2} \cos 2x$$

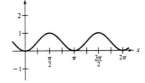

Period: π

x	$-\pi$	$-\dfrac{3\pi}{4}$	$-\dfrac{\pi}{2}$	$-\dfrac{\pi}{4}$	0	$\dfrac{\pi}{4}$	$\dfrac{\pi}{2}$	$\dfrac{3\pi}{4}$	π
$f(x)$	0	$\dfrac{1}{2}$	1	$\dfrac{1}{2}$	0	$\dfrac{1}{2}$	1	$\dfrac{1}{2}$	0

93. Prove $\cos u \sin v = \frac{1}{2}[\sin(u + v) - \sin(u - v)].$

Solution:

$$\frac{1}{2}[\sin(u + v) - \sin(u - v)] = \frac{1}{2}\{(\sin u \cos v + \cos u \sin v) - (\sin u \cos v - \cos u \sin v)\}$$
$$= \frac{1}{2}\{2 \cos u \sin v\}$$
$$= \cos u \sin v$$

REVIEW EXERCISES FOR CHAPTER 3

Solutions to Selected Exercises

3. Simplify $\dfrac{\sin^2\alpha - \cos^2\alpha}{\sin^2\alpha - \sin\alpha\cos\alpha}$.

Solution:

$$\frac{\sin^2\alpha - \cos^2\alpha}{\sin^2\alpha - \sin\alpha\cos\alpha} = \frac{(\sin\alpha + \cos\alpha)(\sin\alpha - \cos\alpha)}{\sin\alpha(\sin\alpha - \cos\alpha)}$$

$$= \frac{\sin\alpha + \cos\alpha}{\sin\alpha} = \frac{\sin\alpha}{\sin\alpha} + \frac{\cos\alpha}{\sin\alpha} = 1 + \cot\alpha$$

7. Simplify $\tan^2\theta(\csc^2\theta - 1)$.

Solution:

$$\tan^2\theta(\csc^2\theta - 1) = \tan^2\theta(\cot^2\theta)$$

$$= \tan^2\theta\left(\frac{1}{\tan^2\theta}\right)$$

$$= 1$$

11. Verify $\tan x(1 - \sin^2 x) = \frac{1}{2}\sin 2x$.

Solution:

$$\tan x(1 - \sin^2 x) = \frac{\sin x}{\cos x}(\cos^2 x)$$

$$= (\sin x)\cos x$$

$$= \frac{1}{2}(2(\sin x)\cos x)$$

$$= \frac{1}{2}\sin 2x$$

15. Verify $\sin^5 x\cos^2 x = (\cos^2 x - 2\cos^4 x + \cos^6 x)\sin x$.

Solution:

$$(\cos^2 x - 2\cos^4 x + \cos^6 x)\sin x = \cos^2 x(1 - 2\cos^2 x + \cos^4 x)\sin x$$

$$= \cos^2 x(1 - \cos^2 x)^2\sin x$$

$$= \cos^2 x(\sin^2 x)^2\sin x$$

$$= \cos^2 x\sin^4 x\sin x$$

$$= \cos^2 x\sin^5 x$$

$$= \sin^5 x\cos^2 x$$

19. Verify $\sqrt{\dfrac{1 - \sin\theta}{1 + \sin\theta}} = \dfrac{1 - \sin\theta}{|\cos\theta|}$.

Solution:

$$\sqrt{\dfrac{1 - \sin\theta}{1 + \sin\theta}} = \sqrt{\dfrac{1 - \sin\theta}{1 + \sin\theta} \cdot \dfrac{1 - \sin\theta}{1 - \sin\theta}}$$

$$= \sqrt{\dfrac{(1 - \sin\theta)^2}{1 - \sin^2\theta}} = \sqrt{\dfrac{(1 - \sin\theta)^2}{\cos^2\theta}} = \dfrac{|1 - \sin\theta|}{|\cos\theta|} = \dfrac{1 - \sin\theta}{|\cos\theta|}$$

Note: We can drop the absolute value on $1 - \sin\theta$ since it is always nonnegative.

23. Verify $\sin\left(x - \dfrac{3\pi}{2}\right) = \cos x$.

Solution:

$$\sin\left(x - \dfrac{3\pi}{2}\right) = (\sin x)\cos\dfrac{3\pi}{2} - (\cos x)\sin\dfrac{3\pi}{2} = (\sin x)(0) - \cos x(-1) = \cos x$$

29. Verify $\dfrac{\cos 3x - \cos x}{\sin 3x - \sin x} = -\tan 2x$.

Solution:

$$\dfrac{\cos 3x - \cos x}{\sin 3x - \sin x} = \dfrac{-2\sin\left(\dfrac{3x + x}{2}\right)\sin\left(\dfrac{3x - x}{2}\right)}{2\cos\left(\dfrac{3x + x}{2}\right)\sin\left(\dfrac{3x - x}{2}\right)}$$

$$= \dfrac{-2(\sin 2x)\sin x}{2(\cos 2x)\sin x} = -\dfrac{\sin 2x}{\cos 2x} = -\tan 2x$$

31. Verify $2\sin y \cos y \sec 2y = \tan 2y$.

Solution:

$$2\sin y \cos y \sec 2y = \sin 2y \sec 2y = \sin 2y\left(\dfrac{1}{\cos 2y}\right) = \dfrac{\sin 2y}{\cos 2y} = \tan 2y$$

33. Verify $\tan^2 x = \dfrac{1 - \cos 2x}{1 + \cos 2x}$.

Solution:

$$\dfrac{1 - \cos 2x}{1 + \cos 2x} = \dfrac{1 - (1 - 2\sin^2 x)}{1 + (2\cos^2 x - 1)} = \dfrac{2\sin^2 x}{2\cos^2 x} = \tan^2 x$$

35. Verify $1 + \cos 2x + \cos 4x + \cos 6x = 4 \cos x \cos 2x \cos 3x$.

Solution:

$$4 \cos x \cos 2x \cos 3x = 4 \cos x \left[\tfrac{1}{2}(\cos(-x) + \cos(5x))\right] = 2 \cos x (\cos x + \cos 5x)$$
$$= 2 \cos^2 x + 2 \cos x \cos 5x = 2 \cos^2 x + 2\left[\tfrac{1}{2}(\cos(-4x) + \cos 6x)\right]$$
$$= 2 \cos^2 x + \cos(-4x) + \cos 6x = 1 + \cos 2x + \cos 4x + \cos 6x$$

39. Using the sum, difference, or half-angle formulas, find the exact value of

$$\cos(157°30') = \cos \frac{315°}{2}.$$

Solution:

$$\cos(157°30') = \cos \frac{315°}{2} = -\sqrt{\frac{1 + \cos 315°}{2}} = -\sqrt{\frac{1 + \cos 45°}{2}}$$

$$= -\sqrt{\frac{1 + \frac{\sqrt{2}}{2}}{2}} = -\sqrt{\frac{2 + \sqrt{2}}{4}} = -\frac{\sqrt{2 + \sqrt{2}}}{2}$$

43. Find the exact value of $\cos(u - v)$, given that $\sin u = 3/4$, $\cos v = -5/13$, and u and v are in Quadrant II.

Solution:

Since u and v are in Quadrant II,

$$\sin u = \frac{3}{4} \quad \Rightarrow \quad \cos u = -\frac{\sqrt{7}}{4}$$

$$\cos v = -\frac{5}{13} \quad \Rightarrow \quad \sin v = \frac{12}{13}.$$

$$\cos(u - v) = \cos u \cos v + \sin u \sin v = \left(-\frac{\sqrt{7}}{4}\right)\left(-\frac{5}{13}\right) + \left(\frac{3}{4}\right)\left(\frac{12}{13}\right) = \frac{5\sqrt{7} + 36}{52}$$

47. Determine if the statement is true or false. If it is false, make the necessary correction.

If $\dfrac{\pi}{2} < \theta < \pi$, then $\cos \dfrac{\theta}{2} < 0$.

Solution:

False; if $\pi/2 < \theta < \pi$, then $\pi/4 < \theta/2 < \pi/2$ and $\cos(\theta/2) > 0$ since $\theta/2$ is in Quadrant I.

51. Find all solutions of

$$\sin x - \tan x = 0$$

in the interval $[0,\ 2\pi)$.

Solution:

$$\sin x - \tan x = 0$$

$$\sin x - \frac{\sin x}{\cos x} = 0$$

$$(\sin x)\cos x - \sin x = 0$$

$$\sin x(\cos x - 1) = 0$$

$$\sin x = 0 \qquad \text{or} \qquad \cos x = 1$$

$$x = 0,\ \pi \qquad\qquad x = 0$$

55. Find all solutions of

$$\sin 2x + \sqrt{2}\sin x = 0$$

in the interval $[0,\ 2\pi)$.

Solution:

$$\sin 2x + \sqrt{2}\sin x = 0$$

$$2(\sin x)\cos x + \sqrt{2}\sin x = 0$$

$$\sin x(2\cos x + \sqrt{2}) = 0$$

$$\sin x = 0 \qquad \text{or} \qquad \cos x = -\frac{\sqrt{2}}{2}$$

$$x = 0,\ \pi \qquad\qquad x = \frac{3\pi}{4},\ \frac{5\pi}{4}$$

59. Find all solutions of $\tan^3 x - \tan^2 x + 3\tan x - 3 = 0$ in the interval $[0,\ 2\pi)$.

Solution:

$$\tan^3 x - \tan^2 x + 3\tan x - 3 = 0$$

$$(\tan x - 1)(\tan^2 x + 3) = 0$$

$$\tan x = 1 \qquad \text{or} \qquad \tan^2 x = -3$$

$$x = \frac{\pi}{4},\ \frac{5\pi}{4} \qquad\qquad \text{No real solutions}$$

63. Write $\sin 3\alpha \sin 2\alpha$ as a sum or difference.

Solution:

$$\sin 3\alpha \sin 2\alpha = \tfrac{1}{2}[\cos(3\alpha - 2\alpha) - \cos(3\alpha + 2\alpha)] = \tfrac{1}{2}[\cos \alpha - \cos 5\alpha]$$

67. The rate of change of the function $f(x) = 2\sqrt{\sin x}$ with respect to change in the variable x is given by the expression $\sin^{-1/2} x \cos x$. Show that the expression for the rate of change can also be given by $\cot x\sqrt{\sin x}$.

Solution:

$$\sin^{-1/2} x \cos x = \frac{\cos x}{\sqrt{\sin x}}$$

$$= \frac{\cos x}{\sqrt{\sin x}} \cdot \frac{\sqrt{\sin x}}{\sqrt{\sin x}} = \frac{\cos x\sqrt{\sin x}}{\sin x} = \frac{\cos x}{\sin x}\sqrt{\sin x} = \cot x\sqrt{\sin x}$$

Practice Test for Chapter 3

1. Find the value of the other five trigonometric functions, given $\tan x = \frac{4}{11}$, $\sec x < 0$.

2. Simplify $\dfrac{\sec^2 x + \csc^2 x}{\csc^2 x(1 + \tan^2 x)}$.

3. Rewrite as a single logarithm and simplify $\ln|\tan\theta| - \ln|\cot\theta|$.

4. True or false:
$$\cos\left(\frac{\pi}{2} - x\right) = \frac{1}{\csc x}$$

5. Factor and simplify :
$$\sin^4 x + (\sin^2 x)\cos^2 x$$

6. Multiply and simplify:
$$(\csc x + 1)(\csc x - 1)$$

7. Rationalize the denominator and simplify:
$$\frac{\cos^2 x}{1 - \sin x}$$

8. Verify:
$$\frac{1 + \cos\theta}{\sin\theta} + \frac{\sin\theta}{1 + \cos\theta} = 2\csc\theta$$

9. Verify:
$$\tan^4 x + 2\tan^2 x + 1 = \sec^4 x$$

10. Use the sum or difference formulas to determine:
   (a) $\sin 105°$ (b) $\tan 15°$

11. Simplify:
$$(\sin 42°)\cos 38° - (\cos 42°)\sin 38°$$

12. Verify $\tan\left(\theta + \dfrac{\pi}{4}\right) = \dfrac{1 + \tan\theta}{1 - \tan\theta}$.

13. Write $\sin(\arcsin x - \arccos x)$ as an algebraic expression in x.

14. Use the double-angle formulas to determine:
   (a) $\cos 120°$ (b) $\tan 300°$

15. Use the half-angle formulas to determine:
   (a) $\sin 22.5°$ (b) $\tan \dfrac{\pi}{12}$

16. Given $\sin = 4/5$, θ lies in Quadrant II, find $\cos\theta/2$.

17. Use the power-reducing identities to write $(\sin^2 x)\cos^2 x$ in terms of the first power of cosine.

18. Rewrite as a sum:
$$6(\sin 5\theta)\cos 2\theta.$$

19. Rewrite as a product:

$\sin(x + \pi) + \sin(x - \pi)$.

20. Verify $\dfrac{\sin 9x + \sin 5x}{\cos 9x - \cos 5x} = -\cot 2x$.

21. Verify:

$(\cos u) \sin v = \frac{1}{2}[\sin(u+v) - \sin(u-v)]$.

22. Find all solutions in the interval $[0, \ 2\pi)$:

$4 \sin^2 x = 1$

23. Find all solutions in the interval $[0, \ 2\pi)$:

$\tan^2 \theta + (\sqrt{3} - 1) \tan \theta - \sqrt{3} = 0$

24. Find all solutions in the interval $[0, \ 2\pi)$:

$\sin 2x = \cos x$

25. Use the quadratic formula to find all solutions in the interval $[0, \ 2\pi)$:

$\tan^2 x - 6 \tan x + 4 = 0$

CHAPTER 4

Additional Topics in Trigonometry

SECTION 4.1

Law of Sines

- If ABC is any oblique triangle with sides a, b, and c, then

$$\frac{a}{\sin A} = \frac{b}{\sin B} = \frac{c}{\sin C}.$$

- You should be able to use the Law of Sines to solve an oblique triangle for the remaining three parts, given:
  - (a) Two angles and any side (AAS or ASA)
  - (b) Two sides and an angle opposite one of them (SSA)
    1. If A is acute and:
       - (a) $a < h$, no triangle is possible.
       - (b) $a = h$ or $a > b$, one triangle is possible.
       - (c) $h < a < b$, two triangles are possible.
    2. If A is obtuse and:
       - (a) $a \le b$, no triangle is possible.
       - (b) $a > b$, one triangle is possible.

- The area of any triangle equals one-half the product of the lengths of two sides times the sine of their included angle.

$$A = \tfrac{1}{2}ab \sin C = \tfrac{1}{2}ac \sin B = \tfrac{1}{2}bc \sin A$$

Solutions to Selected Exercises

3. Find the remaining sides and angles of the triangle.

Solution:

$A = 10°$, $B = 60°$, $a = 4.5$

$C = 180° - (10° + 60°) = 110°$

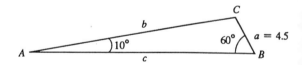

$$\frac{4.5}{\sin 10°} = \frac{b}{\sin 60°}$$

$$b = \sin 60° \left(\frac{4.5}{\sin 10°} \right) \approx 22.44$$

$$\frac{4.5}{\sin 10°} = \frac{c}{\sin 110°}$$

$$c = \sin 110° \left(\frac{4.5}{\sin 10°} \right) \approx 24.35$$

7. Find the remaining sides and angles of the triangle, given $A = 150°$, $C = 20°$, $a = 200$.

Solution:

$A = 150°$, $C = 20°$, $a = 200$

$B = 180° - (150° + 20°) = 10°$

$$\frac{200}{\sin 150°} = \frac{b}{\sin 10°}$$

$$b = \sin 10° \left(\frac{200}{\sin 150°} \right) \approx 69.46$$

$$\frac{200}{\sin 150°} = \frac{c}{\sin 20°}$$

$$c = \sin 20° \left(\frac{200}{\sin 150°} \right) \approx 136.81$$

11. Find the remaining sides and angles of the triangle, given $B = 15°30'$, $a = 4.5$, $b = 6.8$.

Solution:

$B = 15°30'$, $a = 4.5$, $b = 6.8$

$B = 15°30' = 15.5°$

$$\frac{6.8}{\sin 15.5°} = \frac{4.5}{\sin A}$$

$$\sin A = \frac{4.5 \sin 15.5}{6.8} \approx 0.17684$$

$$A \approx 10.19° \approx 10°11'$$

$$C = 180° - (10°11' + 15°30')$$

$$= 154°19'$$

$$\frac{6.8}{\sin 15.5°} = \frac{c}{\sin 154.32°}$$

$$c \approx 11.03$$

15. Find the remaining sides and angles of the triangle, given $A = 110°15'$, $a = 48$, $b = 16$.

Solution:

$A = 110°15'$, $a = 48$, $b = 16$

$$\frac{48}{\sin 110.25°} = \frac{16}{\sin B}$$

$$\sin B \approx 0.3127$$

$$B \approx 18.22° \approx 18°13'$$

$$C = 180° - (110°15' + 18°13') = 51°32'$$

$$\frac{48}{\sin 110.25°} = \frac{c}{\sin 51.53°}$$

$$c \approx 40.06$$

19. Solve the triangle: $A = 58°$, $a = 4.5$, $b = 5$, (if possible). If two solutions exist, find both.

Solution:

$A = 58°$, $a = 4.5$, $b = 5$

$h = b \sin A = 5 \sin 58° = 4.24$

A is acute and $h < a < b$, so there are two possible solutions.

$$\frac{4.5}{\sin 58°} = \frac{5}{\sin B}$$

$$\sin B \approx 0.9423$$

$B \approx 70.4°$	or	$B \approx 109.6°$
$C = 51.6°$		$C = 12.4°$

$$\frac{4.5}{\sin 58°} = \frac{c}{\sin 51.6°} \qquad\qquad \frac{4.5}{\sin 58°} = \frac{c}{\sin 12.4°}$$

$$c \approx 4.16 \qquad\qquad\qquad\qquad c \approx 1.14$$

25. Find the area of the triangle with $C = 120°$, $a = 4$, and $b = 6$.

Solution:

$$\text{Area} = \tfrac{1}{2}ab \sin C = \tfrac{1}{2}(4)(6)\sin 120° \approx 10.4 \text{ square units}$$

31. Find the length d of the brace required to support the streetlight shown in the figure.

Solution:

$$\frac{3}{\sin 30°} = \frac{5}{\sin \alpha}$$

$$\sin \alpha \approx 0.8333$$

$$\alpha \approx 56.44°$$

$$\beta = 93.56°$$

$$\frac{3}{\sin 30°} = \frac{d}{\sin 93.56°}$$

$$d \approx 6 \text{ feet}$$

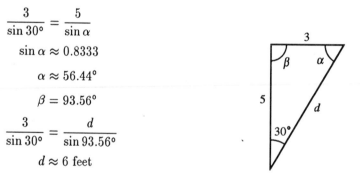

37. Two fire towers A and B are 18.5 miles apart. The bearing from A to B is N 65° E. A fire is spotted by the ranger in each tower, and its bearings from A and B are N 28° E and N 16.5° W, respectively (see figure). Find the distance of the fire from each tower.

Solution:

$A = 37°$, $B = 98.5°$, $C = 44.5°$, $c = 18.5$

$$\frac{b}{\sin 98.5°} = \frac{18.5}{\sin 44.5°}$$

$$b \approx 26.1 \text{ mi}$$

$$\frac{a}{\sin 37°} = \frac{18.5}{\sin 44.5°}$$

$$a \approx 15.9 \text{ mi}$$

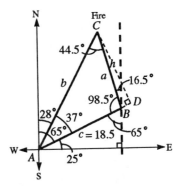

41. The following information about a triangular parcel of land is given at a zoning board meeting: "One side is 450 feet long and another is 120 feet long. The angle opposite the shorter side is 30°." Could this information be correct?

Solution:

$$h = b \sin A = 450 \sin 30° = 225$$

$$a = 120$$

Since $a < h$, no such triangle is possible.

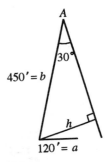

$$\frac{\sin 30°}{120} = \frac{\sin X}{450}$$

$$\sin X = 1.875$$

$$\text{Sin}^{-1}(1.875) = \text{Error!!}$$

SECTION 4.2

Law of Cosines

- If ABC is any oblique triangle with sides a, b, and c, the following equations are valid.

  (a) $a^2 = b^2 + c^2 - 2bc \cos A$ or $\cos A = \dfrac{b^2 + c^2 - a^2}{2bc}$

  (b) $b^2 = a^2 + c^2 - 2ac \cos B$ or $\cos B = \dfrac{a^2 + c^2 - b^2}{2ac}$

  (c) $c^2 = a^2 + b^2 - 2ab \cos C$ or $\cos C = \dfrac{a^2 + b^2 - c^2}{2ab}$

- You should be able to use the Law of Cosines to solve an oblique triangle for the remaining three parts, given:
  (a) Three sides (SSS)
  (b) Two sides and their included angle (SAS)

- Given any triangle with sides of length a, b, and c, then the area of the triangle is

$$\text{Area} = \sqrt{s(s-a)(s-b)(s-c)}, \text{ where } s = \frac{a+b+c}{2}. \quad \text{(Heron's Formula)}$$

Solutions to Selected Exercises

5. Use the Law of Cosines to solve the triangle: $a = 9$, $b = 12$, $c = 15$.

   Solution:

   $$\cos A = \frac{144 + 225 - 81}{360} = 0.8$$

   $$A \approx 36.9°$$

   $$\cos B = \frac{81 + 225 - 144}{270} = 0.6$$

   $$B \approx 53.1°$$

   $$C \approx 180° - (36.9° + 53.1°) \approx 90°$$

7. Use the Law of Cosines to solve the triangle: $a = 75.4$, $b = 52$, $c = 52$.

Solution:

$$\cos A = \frac{(52)^2 + (52)^2 - (75.4)^2}{2(52)(52)} = -0.05125$$

$$A \approx 92.9°$$

Since $b = c$, the triangle is isosceles and $B = C$.

$$2B \approx 180° - 92.9°$$

$$B = C \approx 43.55°$$

13. Use the Law of Cosines to solve the triangle: $C = 125°40'$, $a = 32$, $b = 32$.

Solution:

Since $a = b$, the triangle is isosceles and $A = B$.

$$2A = 180° - 125°40'$$

$$A = B = 27°10'$$

$$c^2 = (32)^2 + (32)^2 - 2(32)(32) \cos 125°40'$$

$$c \approx 56.9$$

17. Solve the parallelogram shown in the figure, given $a = 10$, $b = 14$, and $c = 20$.

Solution:

$a = 10$, $b = 14$, $c = 20$

$$\cos \phi = \frac{a^2 + b^2 - c^2}{2ab}$$

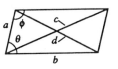

$$= \frac{100 + 196 - 400}{2(10)(14)} = -\frac{104}{280}$$

$$\phi \approx 111.8°$$

$$2\theta = 360° - 2\phi$$

$$\theta = \frac{360° - 2(11.8°)}{2} \approx 68.2°$$

$$d^2 = a^2 + b^2 - 2ab \cos \theta$$

$$= 100 + 196 - 280 \cos 68.2°$$

$$d \approx 13.86$$

23. Use Heron's Formula to find the area of the triangle: $a = 12$, $b = 15$, $c = 9$.

Solution:

$$s = \tfrac{1}{2}(12 + 15 + 9) = 18$$

$$\text{Area} = \sqrt{18(18 - 12)(18 - 15)(18 - 9)} = \sqrt{2916} = 54 \text{ square units}$$

27. The lengths of the sides of a triangular parcel of land are approximately 400 feet, 500 feet, and 700 feet. Approximate the area of the parcel.

Solution:

$a = 400$, $b = 500$, $c = 700$

$$s = \tfrac{1}{2}(400 + 500 + 700) = 800$$

$$\text{Area} = \sqrt{800(800 - 400)(800 - 500)(800 - 700)}$$

$$= \sqrt{9{,}600{,}000{,}000} = 40{,}000\sqrt{6} \approx 97{,}979.6 \text{ square feet}$$

31. Two ships leave a port at 9 A. M. One travels at a bearing of N 53° W at 12 miles per hour and the other at a bearing of S 67° W at 16 miles per hour. Approximately how far apart are they at noon of that day?

Solution:

By noon, the first ship has traveled $3(12) = 36$ miles, and the second ship has traveled $3(16) = 48$ miles.

$$d^2 = 36^2 + 48^2 - 2(36)(48) \cos 60°$$

$$d^2 = 1872$$

$$d \approx 43.3 \text{ miles}$$

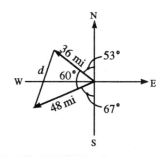

35. Determine the angle θ as shown on the streetlight in the figure.

Solution:

$$\cos \theta = \frac{3^2 + 2^2 - 4.25^2}{2(3)(2)} = -0.421875$$

$$\theta \approx 114.95°$$

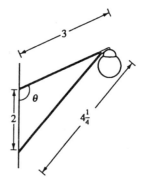

39. On a certain map, Orlando is 7 inches due south of Niagara Falls, Denver is 10.75 inches from Orlando, and Denver is 9.25 inches from Niagara Falls (see figure).

(a) Find the bearing of Denver from Orlando.

(b) Find the bearing of Denver from Niagara Falls.

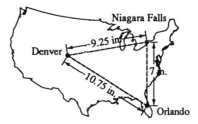

Solution:

(a) $\cos\theta = \dfrac{(10.75)^2 + 7^2 - (9.25)^2}{2(10.75)(7)} = \dfrac{79}{150.5}$

$\theta \approx 58.3°$

Bearing: N 58.3° W

(b) $\cos\phi = \dfrac{(9.25)^2 + 7^2 - (10.75)^2}{2(9.25)(7)} = \dfrac{19}{129.5}$

$\phi \approx 81.6°$

Bearing: S 81.6° W

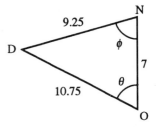

41. In a (square) baseball diamond with 90-foot sides the pitcher's mound is 60 feet from home plate.

(a) How far is it from the pitcher's mound to third base?

(b) When a runner is halfway from second to third, how far is the runner from the pitcher's mound?

Solution:

(a) $x^2 = 90^2 + 60^2 - 2(90)(60)\cos 45°$

$x \approx 63.7$ feet

(b) $\dfrac{60}{\sin\alpha} = \dfrac{63.7}{\sin 45°}$

$\sin\alpha = \dfrac{60\sin 45°}{63.7}$

$\alpha \approx 41.76°$

$\beta = 90° - \alpha = 48.24°$

$y^2 = 45^2 + 63.7^2 - 2(45)(63.7)\cos 48.24°$

$y \approx 47.6$ feet

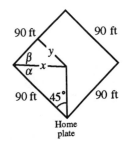

47. Use the Law of Cosines to prove that

$$\frac{1}{2}bc(1 + \cos A) = \frac{a+b+c}{2} \cdot \frac{-a+b+c}{2}.$$

Solution:

$$\frac{1}{2}bc(1 + \cos A) = \frac{1}{2}bc\left[1 + \frac{b^2 + c^2 - a^2}{2bc}\right]$$

$$= \frac{1}{2}bc\left[\frac{2bc + b^2 + c^2 - a^2}{2bc}\right]$$

$$= \frac{1}{4}[(b+c)^2 - a^2]$$

$$= \frac{1}{4}[(b+c) + a][(b+c) - a]$$

$$= \frac{b+c+a}{2} \cdot \frac{b+c-a}{2}$$

$$= \frac{a+b+c}{2} \cdot \frac{-a+b+c}{2}$$

SECTION 4.3

Vectors in the Plane

■ A vector **v** is the collection of all directed line segments that are equivalent to a given directed line segment $\overrightarrow{PQ}$.

■ You should be able to *geometrically* perform the operations of vector addition and scalar multiplication.

■ The component form of the vector with initial point $P = (p_1, p_2)$ and terminal point $Q = (q_1, q_2)$ is

$$\overrightarrow{PQ} = \langle q_1 - p_1, q_2 - p_2 \rangle = \langle v_1, v_2 \rangle = \mathbf{v}.$$

■ The magnitude of $\mathbf{v} = \langle v_1, v_2 \rangle$ is given by $\|\mathbf{v}\| = \sqrt{v_1{}^2 + v_2{}^2}$.

■ You should be able to perform the operations of scalar multiplication and vector addition in component form.

■ You should know the following properties of vector addition and scalar multiplication.

(a) $\mathbf{u} + \mathbf{v} = \mathbf{v} + \mathbf{u}$
(b) $(\mathbf{u} + \mathbf{v}) + \mathbf{w} = \mathbf{u} + (\mathbf{v} + \mathbf{w})$
(c) $\mathbf{u} + \mathbf{0} = \mathbf{u}$
(d) $\mathbf{u} + (-\mathbf{u}) = \mathbf{0}$
(e) $c(d\mathbf{u}) = (cd)\mathbf{u}$
(f) $(c + d)\mathbf{u} = c\mathbf{u} + d\mathbf{u}$
(g) $c(\mathbf{u} + \mathbf{v}) = c\mathbf{u} + c\mathbf{v}$
(h) $1(\mathbf{u}) = \mathbf{u}$, $0\mathbf{u} = \mathbf{0}$
(i) $\|c\mathbf{v}\| = |c|\,\|\mathbf{v}\|$

■ A unit vector in the direction of **v** is given by $\mathbf{u} = \dfrac{\mathbf{v}}{\|\mathbf{v}\|}$.

■ The standard unit vectors are $\mathbf{i} = \langle 1, 0 \rangle$ and $\mathbf{j} = \langle 0, 1 \rangle$. $\mathbf{v} = \langle v_1, v_2 \rangle$ can be written as $\mathbf{v} = v_1\mathbf{i} + v_2\mathbf{j}$.

■ A vector **v** with magnitude $\|\mathbf{v}\|$ and direction θ can be written as $\mathbf{v} = a\mathbf{i} + b\mathbf{j} = \|\mathbf{v}\|(\cos\theta)\mathbf{i} + \|\mathbf{v}\|(\sin\theta)\mathbf{j}$ where $\tan\theta = b/a$.

Solutions to Selected Exercises

3. Use the figure to sketch a graph of $\mathbf{u} + \mathbf{v}$.

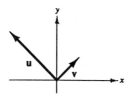

Solution:

Move the initial point of $\mathbf{v}$ to the terminal point of $\mathbf{u}$.

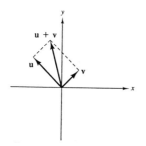

9. Find the component form and the magnitude of the vector $\mathbf{v}$.

Solution:

$$\mathbf{v} = \langle -1 - 2,\ 3 - 1 \rangle = \langle -3,\ 2 \rangle$$
$$\|\mathbf{v}\| = \sqrt{(-3)^2 + (2)^2} = \sqrt{13}$$

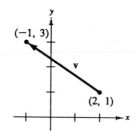

13. Find the component form and the magnitude of the vector $\mathbf{v}$ with initial point $(-1,\ 5)$ and terminal point $(15,\ 2)$.

Solution:

$$\mathbf{v} = \langle 15 - (-1),\ 2 - 5 \rangle = \langle 16,\ -3 \rangle$$
$$\|\mathbf{v}\| = \sqrt{(16)^2 + (-3)^2} = \sqrt{265}$$

19. Find (a) $\mathbf{u} + \mathbf{v}$, (b) $\mathbf{u} - \mathbf{v}$, and (c) $2\mathbf{u} - 3\mathbf{v}$ for $\mathbf{u} = \langle -2,\ 3 \rangle$, $\mathbf{v} = \langle -2,\ 1 \rangle$.

Solution:

(a) $\mathbf{u} + \mathbf{v} = \langle -2 + (-2),\ 3 + 1 \rangle = \langle -4,\ 4 \rangle$

(b) $\mathbf{u} - \mathbf{v} = \langle -2 - (-2),\ 3 - 1 \rangle = \langle 0,\ 2 \rangle$

(c) $2\mathbf{u} - 3\mathbf{v} = \langle 2(-2) - 3(-2),\ 2(3) - 3(1) \rangle = \langle 2,\ 3 \rangle$

25. Find (a) $\mathbf{u} + \mathbf{v}$, (b) $\mathbf{u} - \mathbf{v}$, and (c) $2\mathbf{u} - 3\mathbf{v}$ for $\mathbf{u} = 2\mathbf{i}$, $\mathbf{v} = \mathbf{j}$.

Solution:

(a) $\mathbf{u} + \mathbf{v} = 2\mathbf{i} + \mathbf{j}$

(b) $\mathbf{u} - \mathbf{v} = 2\mathbf{i} - \mathbf{j}$

(c) $2\mathbf{u} - 3\mathbf{v} = 4\mathbf{i} - 3\mathbf{j}$

29. Find the magnitude and direction angle for $\mathbf{v} = 6\mathbf{i} - 6\mathbf{j}$.

Solution:

$$\mathbf{v} = 6\mathbf{i} - 6\mathbf{j}$$

$$\|\mathbf{v}\| = \sqrt{6^2 + (-6)^2} = \sqrt{72} = 6\sqrt{2}$$

$$\tan \theta = -\tfrac{6}{6} = -1$$

Since $\mathbf{v}$ lies in Quadrant IV, $\theta = 315°$.

33. Sketch $\mathbf{v}$ and find its component form given $\|\mathbf{v}\| = 1$, $\theta = 150°$. (Assume θ is measured counterclockwise from the x-axis to the vector.)

Solution:

$$\mathbf{v} = 1\cos 150°\mathbf{i} + 1\sin 150°\mathbf{j}$$

$$= -\frac{\sqrt{3}}{2}\mathbf{i} + \frac{1}{2}\mathbf{j}$$

$$= \left\langle -\frac{\sqrt{3}}{2},\ \frac{1}{2} \right\rangle$$

37. Sketch **v** and find its component form given $\|\mathbf{v}\| = 2$, and **v** is in the direction of $\mathbf{i} + 3\mathbf{j}$. (Assume θ is measured counterclockwise from the x-axis to the vector.)

Solution:

$$\tan \theta = \frac{3}{1} \Rightarrow \sin \theta = \frac{3\sqrt{10}}{10} \text{ and } \cos \theta = \frac{\sqrt{10}}{10}$$

$$\mathbf{v} = 2 \left(\frac{\sqrt{10}}{10} \right) \mathbf{i} + 2 \left(\frac{3\sqrt{10}}{10} \right) \mathbf{j}$$

$$= \left\langle \frac{\sqrt{10}}{5}, \frac{3\sqrt{10}}{5} \right\rangle$$

41. Find the component form of $\mathbf{v} = \mathbf{u} + 2\mathbf{w}$ and sketch the indicated vector operations geometrically, where $\mathbf{u} = 2\mathbf{i} - \mathbf{j}$ and $\mathbf{w} = \mathbf{i} + 2\mathbf{j}$.

Solution:

$$\mathbf{v} = \mathbf{u} + 2\mathbf{w}$$

$$= 4\mathbf{i} + 3\mathbf{j}$$

$$= \langle 4, \ 3 \rangle$$

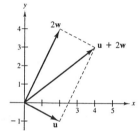

45. Find the component form of the sum of the vectors **u** and **v** with direction angles $\theta_\mathbf{u}$ and $\theta_\mathbf{v}$, respectively, given $\|\mathbf{u}\| = 5$, $\theta_\mathbf{u} = 0°$, and $\|\mathbf{v}\| = 5$, $\theta_\mathbf{v} = 90°$.

Solution:

$$\|\mathbf{u}\| = 5, \ \theta_\mathbf{u} = 0° \Rightarrow \mathbf{u} = 5\mathbf{i}$$

$$\|\mathbf{v}\| = 5, \ \theta_\mathbf{v} = 90° \Rightarrow \mathbf{v} = 5\mathbf{j}$$

$$\mathbf{u} + \mathbf{v} = 5\mathbf{i} + 5\mathbf{j} = \langle 5, \ 5 \rangle$$

49. Find a unit vector in the direction of $\mathbf{v} = 4\mathbf{i} - 3\mathbf{j}$.

Solution:

$$\|\mathbf{v}\| = \sqrt{(4)^2 + (-3)^2} = 5$$

$$\frac{\mathbf{v}}{\|\mathbf{v}\|} = \frac{4\mathbf{i} - 3\mathbf{j}}{5} = \left\langle \frac{4}{5}, \ -\frac{3}{5} \right\rangle$$

53. Use the Law of Cosines to find the angle α between the vectors $\mathbf{v} = \mathbf{i} + \mathbf{j}$ and $\mathbf{w} = 2(\mathbf{i} - \mathbf{j})$. (Assume $0° \le \alpha \le 180°$.)

Solution:

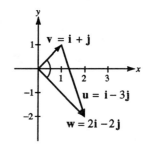

$\mathbf{v} = \mathbf{i} + \mathbf{j}, \quad \mathbf{w} = 2(\mathbf{i} - \mathbf{j})$

$\mathbf{u} = \mathbf{w} - \mathbf{v} = \mathbf{i} - 3\mathbf{j}$

$\|\mathbf{v}\| = \sqrt{2}$

$\|\mathbf{w}\| = 2\sqrt{2}$

$\|\mathbf{u}\| = \sqrt{10}$

$\cos \alpha = \dfrac{2 + 8 - 10}{2(\sqrt{2})(2\sqrt{2})} = 0$

$\alpha = 90°$

59. Forces with magnitudes of 35 pounds and 50 pounds act on a hook. The angle between the two forces is 30°. Find the direction and magnitude of the resultant (vector sum) of these two forces.

Solution:

$\mathbf{u} = 50\mathbf{i}$

$\mathbf{v} = 35(\cos 30°\mathbf{i} + \sin 30°\mathbf{j}) = 35\left(\dfrac{\sqrt{3}}{2}\mathbf{i} + \dfrac{1}{2}\mathbf{j}\right)$

$\mathbf{r} = \mathbf{u} + \mathbf{v} = \left(50 + \dfrac{35\sqrt{3}}{2}\right)\mathbf{i} + \dfrac{35}{2}\mathbf{j}$

$\|\mathbf{r}\| \approx 82.2 \text{ lb}$

$\tan \theta = \dfrac{35/2}{50 + (35\sqrt{3}/2)}$

$\theta \approx 12.3°$

63. A ball is thrown with an initial velocity of 80 feet per second at an angle of 50° with the horizontal (see figure). Find the vertical and horizontal components of the velocity.

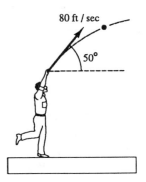

Solution:

Vertical component: $80 \sin 50° \approx 61.28$ ft/sec
Horizontal component: $80 \cos 50° \approx 51.42$ ft/sec

69. An airplane is flying in the direction S 32° E, with an airspeed of 540 miles per hour. Because of the wind, its groundspeed and direction are 500 miles per hour and S 40° E, respectively. Find the direction and speed of the wind.

Solution:

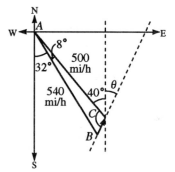

$$a = \|\overrightarrow{BC}\| = \text{speed of wind}$$

$$a^2 = 500^2 + 540^2 - 2(500)(540) \cos 8°$$

$$a \approx 82.8 \text{ mi/hr}$$

$$\cos C \approx \frac{82.8^2 + 500^2 - 540^2}{2(82.8)(500)}$$

$$C \approx 114.8°$$

$$C + \theta + 40 \approx 180°$$

$$\theta \approx \text{N } 25.2° \text{ E}$$

71. A heavy implement is pulled 10 feet across the floor, using a force of 85 pounds. Find the work done if the direction of the force is 60° above the horizontal (see figure). (Use the formula for work, $W = FD$, where F is the component of the force in the direction of motion and D is the distance.)

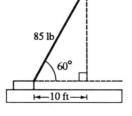

Solution:

The horizontal component of the force is $85 \cos 60° = \frac{85}{2}$.

$$W = FD = \frac{85}{2}(10) = 425 \text{ ft-lb}$$

SECTION 4.4

The Dot Product

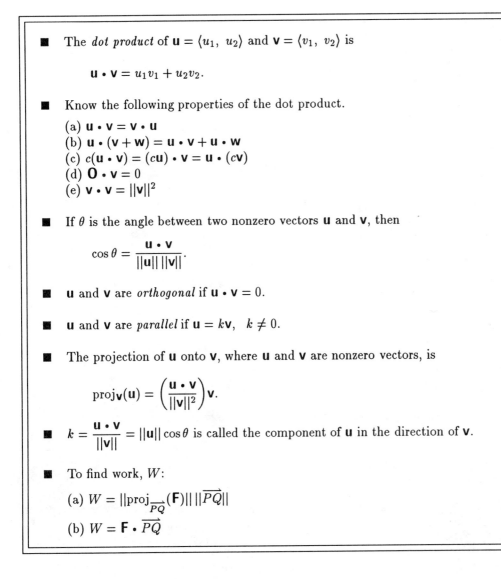

- The *dot product* of $\mathbf{u} = \langle u_1,\ u_2 \rangle$ and $\mathbf{v} = \langle v_1,\ v_2 \rangle$ is

  $$\mathbf{u} \cdot \mathbf{v} = u_1 v_1 + u_2 v_2.$$

- Know the following properties of the dot product.
  (a) $\mathbf{u} \cdot \mathbf{v} = \mathbf{v} \cdot \mathbf{u}$
  (b) $\mathbf{u} \cdot (\mathbf{v} + \mathbf{w}) = \mathbf{u} \cdot \mathbf{v} + \mathbf{u} \cdot \mathbf{w}$
  (c) $c(\mathbf{u} \cdot \mathbf{v}) = (c\mathbf{u}) \cdot \mathbf{v} = \mathbf{u} \cdot (c\mathbf{v})$
  (d) $\mathbf{O} \cdot \mathbf{v} = 0$
  (e) $\mathbf{v} \cdot \mathbf{v} = \|\mathbf{v}\|^2$

- If θ is the angle between two nonzero vectors $\mathbf{u}$ and $\mathbf{v}$, then

  $$\cos \theta = \frac{\mathbf{u} \cdot \mathbf{v}}{\|\mathbf{u}\| \, \|\mathbf{v}\|}.$$

- $\mathbf{u}$ and $\mathbf{v}$ are *orthogonal* if $\mathbf{u} \cdot \mathbf{v} = 0$.

- $\mathbf{u}$ and $\mathbf{v}$ are *parallel* if $\mathbf{u} = k\mathbf{v}, \quad k \neq 0$.

- The projection of $\mathbf{u}$ onto $\mathbf{v}$, where $\mathbf{u}$ and $\mathbf{v}$ are nonzero vectors, is

  $$\text{proj}_{\mathbf{v}}(\mathbf{u}) = \left(\frac{\mathbf{u} \cdot \mathbf{v}}{\|\mathbf{v}\|^2} \right) \mathbf{v}.$$

- $k = \dfrac{\mathbf{u} \cdot \mathbf{v}}{\|\mathbf{v}\|} = \|\mathbf{u}\| \cos \theta$ is called the component of $\mathbf{u}$ in the direction of $\mathbf{v}$.

- To find work, W:
  (a) $W = \|\text{proj}_{\overrightarrow{PQ}}(\mathbf{F})\| \, \|\overrightarrow{PQ}\|$
  (b) $W = \mathbf{F} \cdot \overrightarrow{PQ}$

Solutions to Selected Exercises

3. Find (a) $\mathbf{u} \cdot \mathbf{v}$, (b) $\mathbf{u} \cdot \mathbf{u}$, (c) $||\mathbf{u}||^2$, (d) $(\mathbf{u} \cdot \mathbf{v})\mathbf{v}$, and (e) $\mathbf{u} \cdot (2\mathbf{v})$ for $\mathbf{u} = \langle 2, -3 \rangle$ and $\mathbf{v} = \langle 0, 6 \rangle$.

Solution:

(a) $\mathbf{u} \cdot \mathbf{v} = 2(0) + (-3)(6) = -18$

(b) $\mathbf{u} \cdot \mathbf{u} = 2(2) + (-3)(-3) = 13$

(c) $||\mathbf{u}||^2 = (2)^2 + (-3)^2 = 13$

(d) $(\mathbf{u} \cdot \mathbf{v})\mathbf{v} = -18\mathbf{v} = \langle 0, -108 \rangle$

(e) $\mathbf{u} \cdot (2\mathbf{v}) = 2((2)(0)) + (-3)(2(6)) = -36$

9. Find the angle θ between the vectors $\mathbf{u} = 3\mathbf{i} + \mathbf{j}$ and $\mathbf{v} = -2\mathbf{i} + 4\mathbf{j}$.

Solution:

$$\cos\theta = \frac{\mathbf{u} \cdot \mathbf{v}}{||\mathbf{u}||\,||\mathbf{v}||} = \frac{3(-2) + (1)(4)}{\sqrt{(3)^2 + (1)^2}\sqrt{(-2)^2 + (4)^2}} = \frac{-2}{\sqrt{10}\sqrt{20}} = \frac{-2}{10\sqrt{2}} = -\frac{\sqrt{2}}{10}$$

$$\theta = \arccos\left(-\frac{\sqrt{2}}{10}\right) \approx 98.1°$$

13. Find the angle θ between the vectors $\mathbf{u} = \cos(\pi/4)\mathbf{i} + \sin(\pi/4)\mathbf{j}$ and $\mathbf{v} = \cos(\pi/2)\mathbf{i} + \sin(\pi/2)\mathbf{j}$.

Solution:

$$\mathbf{u} = \cos\left(\frac{\pi}{4}\right)\mathbf{i} + \sin\left(\frac{\pi}{4}\right)\mathbf{j} = \frac{\sqrt{2}}{2}\mathbf{i} + \frac{\sqrt{2}}{2}\mathbf{j}$$

$$\mathbf{v} = \cos\left(\frac{\pi}{2}\right)\mathbf{i} + \sin\left(\frac{\pi}{2}\right)\mathbf{j} = \mathbf{j}$$

$$\cos\theta = \frac{\mathbf{u} \cdot \mathbf{v}}{||\mathbf{u}||\,||\mathbf{v}||} = \frac{(\sqrt{2}/2)(0) + (\sqrt{2}/2)(1)}{\sqrt{(\sqrt{2}/2)^2 + (\sqrt{2}/2)^2}\sqrt{(0)^2 + (1)^2}} = \frac{\sqrt{2}/2}{\sqrt{1}\sqrt{1}} = \frac{\sqrt{2}}{2}$$

$$\theta = \arccos\frac{\sqrt{2}}{2} = 45°$$

15. Determine whether $\mathbf{u}$ and $\mathbf{v}$ are orthogonal, parallel, or neither.

$$\mathbf{u} = \langle 4, 0 \rangle, \quad \mathbf{v} = \langle 1, 1 \rangle$$

Solution:

$\mathbf{u} \cdot \mathbf{v} = 4 \neq 0$. Therefore, $\mathbf{u}$ and $\mathbf{v}$ are not orthogonal. $k\mathbf{v} = \langle k, k \rangle \neq \mathbf{u}$ for any real number k. Therefore, $\mathbf{u}$ and $\mathbf{v}$ are not parallel. Neither

21. Determine whether $\mathbf{u}$ and $\mathbf{v}$ are orthogonal, parallel, or neither.

$$\mathbf{u} = \langle 2, -2 \rangle, \quad \mathbf{v} = \langle -1, -1 \rangle$$

Solution:

$\mathbf{u} \cdot \mathbf{v} = 0$. Therefore, $\mathbf{u}$ and $\mathbf{v}$ are orthogonal.

23. (a) Find the projection of **u** onto **v**, and (b) the vector component of **u** orthogonal to **v**.

$$\mathbf{u} = \langle 2,\ 3 \rangle, \quad \mathbf{v} = \langle 5,\ 1 \rangle$$

Solution:

(a) $\text{proj}_{\mathbf{v}}(\mathbf{u}) = \left(\dfrac{\mathbf{u} \cdot \mathbf{v}}{\|\mathbf{v}\|^2} \right) \mathbf{v} = \dfrac{13}{26}\mathbf{v} = \dfrac{1}{2}\langle 5,\ 1 \rangle = \left\langle \dfrac{5}{2},\ \dfrac{1}{2} \right\rangle$

(b) $\mathbf{u} - \text{proj}_{\mathbf{v}}(\mathbf{u}) = \langle 2,\ 3 \rangle - \left\langle \dfrac{5}{2},\ \dfrac{1}{2} \right\rangle = \left\langle -\dfrac{1}{2},\ \dfrac{5}{2} \right\rangle$

27. (a) Find the projection of **u** onto **v**, and (b) the vector component of **u** orthogonal to **v**.

$$\mathbf{u} = \langle 1,\ 1 \rangle, \quad \mathbf{v} = \langle -2,\ -1 \rangle$$

Solution:

(a) $\text{proj}_{\mathbf{v}}(\mathbf{u}) = \left(\dfrac{\mathbf{u} \cdot \mathbf{v}}{\|\mathbf{v}\|^2} \right) \mathbf{v} = \dfrac{-3}{5}\mathbf{v} = -\dfrac{3}{5}\langle -2,\ -1 \rangle = \left\langle \dfrac{6}{5},\ \dfrac{3}{5} \right\rangle$

(b) $\mathbf{u} - \text{proj}_{\mathbf{v}}(\mathbf{u}) = \langle 1,\ 1 \rangle - \left\langle \dfrac{6}{5},\ \dfrac{3}{5} \right\rangle = \left\langle -\dfrac{1}{5},\ \dfrac{2}{5} \right\rangle$

31. Find two vectors in opposite directions that are orthogonal to the vector $\mathbf{u} = \langle 3,\ 5 \rangle$.

Solution:

$$\mathbf{u} = \langle 3,\ 5 \rangle$$

Let $\mathbf{v} = \langle a,\ b \rangle$. If **u** and **v** are orthogonal, then $\mathbf{u} \cdot \mathbf{v} = 0$.

$$\mathbf{u} \cdot \mathbf{v} = 3a + 5b = 0$$

Any vector $\mathbf{v} = \langle a,\ b \rangle$ that satisfies this equation is orthogonal to **u**. One possible solution is $\mathbf{v} = \langle 5,\ -3 \rangle$. A vector in the opposite direction is $\mathbf{w} = \langle -5,\ 3 \rangle$.

37. Determine the work done in lifting a 100-pound bag of sugar 10 feet.

Solution:

$$W = (\text{magnitude of force})(\text{distance})$$
$$= (100 \text{ pounds})(10 \text{ feet})$$
$$= 1000 \text{ ft-lb}$$

39. A force of 85 pounds in the direction of 60° above the horizontal is required to slide an implement across a floor (see figure). Find the work done if the implement is dragged 10 feet.

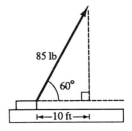

85 lb

60°

←—10 ft—→

Solution:

$$W = \mathbf{F} \cdot \overrightarrow{PQ}$$

$$= (\cos \theta) \|\mathbf{F}\| \, \|\overrightarrow{PQ}\|$$

$$= (\cos 60°)(85)(10)$$

$$= \left(\tfrac{1}{2}\right)(85)(10)$$

$$= 425 \text{ ft-lb}$$

41. Find the work done in moving a particle from P to Q if the magnitude and direction of the force is given by $\mathbf{v}$.

$$P = (0,\ 0), \quad Q = (4,\ 7), \quad \mathbf{v} = \langle 1,\ 4 \rangle$$

Solution:

$$\overrightarrow{PQ} = \langle 4,\ 7 \rangle$$

$$W = \mathbf{v} \cdot \overrightarrow{PQ} = 4 + 28 = 32$$

45. What is known about θ, the angle between two nonzero vectors $\mathbf{u}$ and $\mathbf{v}$, if the following are true?

(a) $\mathbf{u} \cdot \mathbf{v} = 0$ (b) $\mathbf{u} \cdot \mathbf{v} > 0$ (c) $\mathbf{u} \cdot \mathbf{v} < 0$

Solution:

Since $\cos \theta = \dfrac{\mathbf{u} \cdot \mathbf{v}}{\|\mathbf{u}\| \, \|\mathbf{v}\|}$, we know the following about θ.

(a) If $\mathbf{u} \cdot \mathbf{v} = 0$, then $\cos \theta = 0$ which tells us that $\theta = \pi/2$.

(b) If $\mathbf{u} \cdot \mathbf{v} > 0$, then $\cos \theta > 0$ which tells us that $0 \le \theta < \pi/2$; i.e., θ is acute.

(c) If $\mathbf{u} \cdot \mathbf{v} < 0$, then $\cos \theta < 0$ which tells us that $\pi/2 < \theta \le \pi$; i.e., θ is obtuse.

REVIEW EXERCISES FOR CHAPTER 4

Solutions to Selected Exercises

5. Solve the triangle, given
$B = 110°$, $a = 4$, $c = 4$.

Solution:

Since the triangle is isosceles,

$$A = C = \frac{1}{2}(180 - 110) = 35°.$$

By the Law of Sines:

$$\frac{4}{\sin 35°} = \frac{b}{\sin 110°}$$

$$b \approx 6.6$$

9. Solve the triangle, given
$B = 115°$, $a = 7$, $b = 14.5$.

Solution:

By the Law of Sines:

$$\frac{\sin A}{7} = \frac{\sin 115°}{14.5}$$

$$\sin A \approx 0.4375$$

$$A \approx 25.9°$$

$$C \approx 180 - (115 + 25.9) \approx 39.1°$$

$$\frac{c}{\sin 39.1°} = \frac{14.5}{\sin 115°}$$

$$c \approx 10.1$$

13. Solve the triangle, given
$B = 150°$, $a = 10$, $c = 20$.

Solution:

By the Law of Cosines:

$$b^2 = 10^2 + 20^2 - 2(10)(20)\cos 150°$$

$$b \approx 29.1$$

By the Law of Sines:

$$\frac{\sin A}{10} = \frac{\sin 150°}{29.1}$$

$$\sin A \approx 0.1718$$

$$A \approx 9.9°$$

$$C \approx 180 - (150 + 9.9) \approx 20.1°$$

17. Find the area of the triangle with
$a = 4$, $b = 5$, and $c = 7$.

Solution:

$$s = \frac{4 + 5 + 7}{2} = 8$$

$$A = \sqrt{8(8 - 4)(8 - 5)(8 - 7)}$$

$$= \sqrt{96}$$

$$= 4\sqrt{6}$$

$$\approx 9.798 \text{ square units}$$

21. Find the height of a tree that stands on a hillside of slope 32° (from the horizontal) if from a point 75 feet downhill the angle of elevation to the top of the tree is 48° (see figure).

Solution:

Let x = the height of the hillside.

$$\sin 32° = \frac{x}{75}$$

$$x = 75 \sin 32° \approx 39.7439 \text{ feet}$$

Let y = the horizontal distance.

$$y = \sqrt{75^2 - x^2} = \sqrt{75^2 - 39.7439^2} \approx 63.6036 \text{ feet}$$

Let h = the height of the tree.

$$\tan 48° = \frac{x+h}{y} = \frac{39.7439 + h}{63.6036}$$

$$h = 63.6036 \tan 48° - 39.7439 \approx 31 \text{ feet}$$

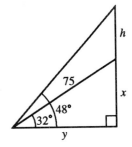

23. From a certain distance, the angle of elevation of the top of a building is 17°. At a point 50 meters closer to the building, the angle of elevation is 31°. Approximate the height of the building.

Solution:

$$\tan 17° = \frac{h}{50+y} \Rightarrow h = (50+y)\tan 17°$$

$$\tan 31° = \frac{h}{y} \Rightarrow h = y \tan 31°$$

$$(50+y)\tan 17° = y\tan 31°$$

$$50\tan 17° + y\tan 17° = y\tan 31°$$

$$y(\tan 17° - \tan 31°) = -50\tan 17°$$

$$y = \frac{-50\tan 17°}{\tan 17° - \tan 31°} \approx 51.7959 \text{ m}$$

$$h = y\tan 31° \approx 51.7959 \tan 31° \approx 31.1 \text{ m}$$

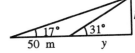

27. Find the component form of the vector **v** with initial point $(0, 10)$, and terminal point $(7, 3)$.

Solution:

$$\mathbf{v} = \langle 7 - 0,\ 3 - 10 \rangle = \langle 7,\ -7 \rangle$$

33. Find the component form of $4\mathbf{u} - 5\mathbf{v}$ and sketch its graph given that $\mathbf{u} = 6\mathbf{i} - 5\mathbf{j}$ and $\mathbf{v} = 10\mathbf{i} + 3\mathbf{j}$.

Solution:

$$4\mathbf{u} - 5\mathbf{v} = (24\mathbf{i} - 20\mathbf{j}) - (50\mathbf{i} + 15\mathbf{j})$$

$$= -26\mathbf{i} - 35\mathbf{j}$$

$$= \langle -26, -35 \rangle$$

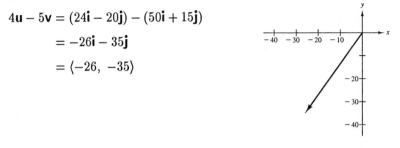

35. Find the direction and magnitude of the resultant of the three forces shown in the figure.

Solution:

$$\tan\alpha = \tfrac{12}{5} \;\Rightarrow\; \sin\alpha = \tfrac{12}{13} \text{ and } \cos\alpha = \tfrac{5}{13}$$

$$\tan\beta = \tfrac{3}{4} \;\Rightarrow\; \sin(180° - \beta) = \tfrac{3}{5} \text{ and } \cos(180° - \beta) = -\tfrac{4}{5}$$

$$\mathbf{u} = 300\left(\tfrac{5}{13}\mathbf{i} + \tfrac{12}{13}\mathbf{j}\right)$$

$$\mathbf{v} = 150\left(-\tfrac{4}{5}\mathbf{i} + \tfrac{3}{5}\mathbf{j}\right)$$

$$\mathbf{w} = 250(0\mathbf{i} - \mathbf{j})$$

$$\mathbf{r} = \mathbf{u} + \mathbf{v} + \mathbf{w}$$

$$= \left(\tfrac{1500}{13} - 120 + 0\right)\mathbf{i} + \left(\tfrac{3600}{13} + 90 - 250\right)\mathbf{j}$$

$$= \tfrac{-60}{13}\mathbf{i} + \tfrac{1520}{13}\mathbf{j}$$

$$\|\mathbf{r}\| = \sqrt{\left(-\tfrac{60}{13}\right)^2 + \left(\tfrac{1520}{13}\right)^2} \approx 117.0 \text{ lb}$$

$$\theta = 180° - \arctan\tfrac{1520}{60} \approx 92.3°$$

41. Let $\mathbf{u} = \overrightarrow{PQ}$ and $\mathbf{v} = \overrightarrow{PR}$, and find (a) the component forms of $\mathbf{u}$ and $\mathbf{v}$, (b) the magnitude of $\mathbf{v}$, (c) $\mathbf{u} \cdot \mathbf{v}$, (d) $2\mathbf{u} + \mathbf{v}$, (e) the projection of $\mathbf{u}$ onto $\mathbf{v}$, and (f) the component of $\mathbf{u}$ orthogonal to $\mathbf{v}$.

$$P = (1, \, 2), \quad Q = (4, \, 1), \quad R = (5, \, 4)$$

Solution:

(a) $\mathbf{u} = \overrightarrow{PQ} = \langle 4 - 1, \, 1 - 2 \rangle$

$\qquad = \langle 3, \, -1 \rangle = 3\mathbf{i} - \mathbf{j}$

$\mathbf{v} = \overrightarrow{PR} = \langle 5 - 1, \, 4 - 2 \rangle$

$\qquad = \langle 4, \, 2 \rangle = 4\mathbf{i} + 2\mathbf{j}$

(b) $\|\mathbf{v}\| = \sqrt{4^2 + 2^2}$

$\qquad = \sqrt{20} = 2\sqrt{5}$

(c) $\mathbf{u} \cdot \mathbf{v} = 3(4) + (-1)(2) = 10$

(d) $2\mathbf{u} + \mathbf{v} = 2\langle 3, \, -1 \rangle + \langle 4, \, 2 \rangle$

$\qquad = \langle 6, \, -2 \rangle + \langle 4, \, 2 \rangle$

$\qquad = \langle 10, \, 0 \rangle = 10\mathbf{i}$

(e) $\text{proj}_{\mathbf{v}}(\mathbf{u}) = \left(\dfrac{\mathbf{u} \cdot \mathbf{v}}{\|\mathbf{v}\|^2} \right) \mathbf{v}$

$\qquad = \dfrac{10}{(\sqrt{20}\,)^2} \mathbf{v}$

$\qquad = \dfrac{1}{2} \langle 4, \, 2 \rangle$

$\qquad = \langle 2, \, 1 \rangle = 2\mathbf{i} + \mathbf{j}$

(f) $\mathbf{w} = \mathbf{u} - \text{proj}_{\mathbf{v}}(\mathbf{u})$

$\qquad = \langle 3, \, -1 \rangle - \langle 2, \, 1 \rangle$

$\qquad = \langle 1, \, -2 \rangle = \mathbf{i} - 2\mathbf{j}$

45. Find the angle θ between the vectors $\mathbf{u} = \langle 1, \, 0 \rangle$ and $\mathbf{v} = \langle -2, \, 2 \rangle$.

Solution:

$\mathbf{u} = \langle 1, \, 0 \rangle, \quad \mathbf{v} = \langle -2, \, 2 \rangle$

$$\cos \theta = \frac{\mathbf{u} \cdot \mathbf{v}}{\|\mathbf{u}\| \, \|\mathbf{v}\|} = \frac{(1)(-2) + (0)(2)}{\sqrt{1^2 + 0^2}\sqrt{(-2)^2 + 2^2}} = \frac{-2}{2\sqrt{2}} = -\frac{1}{\sqrt{2}}$$

$$\theta = \arccos\left(-\frac{1}{\sqrt{2}} \right) = 135° = \frac{3\pi}{4}$$

51. Prove that $\mathbf{w} = (\mathbf{w} \cdot \mathbf{u})\mathbf{u} + (\mathbf{w} \cdot \mathbf{v})\mathbf{v}$ for any vector $\mathbf{w}$ if $\mathbf{u}$ and $\mathbf{v}$ are orthogonal unit vectors.

Solution:

Since $||\mathbf{u}|| = 1$ and $||\mathbf{v}|| = 1$, we have

$$(\mathbf{w} \cdot \mathbf{u})\mathbf{u} + (\mathbf{w} \cdot \mathbf{v})\mathbf{v} = \left(\frac{\mathbf{w} \cdot \mathbf{u}}{||\mathbf{u}||^2}\right)\mathbf{u} + \left(\frac{\mathbf{w} \cdot \mathbf{v}}{||\mathbf{v}||^2}\right)\mathbf{v}$$

$$= \text{proj}_{\mathbf{u}}\mathbf{w} + \text{proj}_{\mathbf{v}}\mathbf{w}.$$

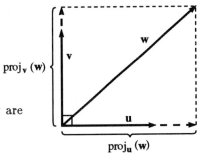

Since each of these is a component of $\mathbf{w}$ and since they are orthogonal, their sum yields $\mathbf{w}$.

Practice Test for Chapter 4

For Exercises 1 and 2, use the Law of Sines to find the remaining sides and angles of the triangle.

1. $A = 40°$, $B = 12°$, $b = 100$

2. $C = 150°$, $a = 5$, $c = 20$

3. Find the area of the triangle: $a = 3$, $b = 5$, $C = 130°$.

4. Determine the number of solutions to the triangle: $a = 10$, $b = 35$, $A = 22.5°$.

For Exercises 5 and 6, use the Law of Cosines to find the remaining sides and angles of the triangle.

5. $a = 49$, $b = 53$, $c = 38$

6. $C = 29°$, $a = 100$, $b = 300$

7. Use Heron's Formula to find the area of the triangle: $a = 4.1$, $b = 6.8$, $c = 5.5$.

8. A ship travels 40 miles due east, then adjusts its course 12° southward. After traveling 70 miles in that direction, how far is the ship from its point of departure?

9. $\mathbf{w}$ is $4\mathbf{u} - 7\mathbf{v}$ where $\mathbf{u} = 3\mathbf{i} + \mathbf{j}$ and $\mathbf{v} = -\mathbf{i} + 2\mathbf{j}$. Find $\mathbf{w}$.

10. Find a unit vector in the direction of $\mathbf{v} = 5\mathbf{i} - 3\mathbf{j}$.

11. Find the angle between $\mathbf{u} = 6\mathbf{i} + 5\mathbf{j}$ and $\mathbf{v} = 2\mathbf{i} - 3\mathbf{j}$.

12. Find $\mathbf{v}$, a vector of magnitude 4 making an angle of 30° with the positive x-axis.

For Exercises 13–19, use the vectors $\mathbf{u} = \langle 3, -5 \rangle$ and $\mathbf{v} = \langle -2, 1 \rangle$.

13. Find $\mathbf{u} \cdot \mathbf{v}$.

14. Find $\|\mathbf{u}\|$.

15. Find the angle θ between $\mathbf{u}$ and $\mathbf{v}$.

16. Find $(\mathbf{v} \cdot \mathbf{u})\mathbf{u}$.

17. Determine if $\mathbf{u}$ and $\mathbf{v}$ are orthogonal, parallel, or neither.

18. Find the projection of $\mathbf{u}$ onto $\mathbf{v}$.

19. Find the vector component of $\mathbf{u}$ orthogonal to $\mathbf{v}$.

20. An implement is dragged 20 feet across a floor, using a force of 70 pounds. Find the work done if the direction of the force is 40° above the horizontal.

CHAPTER 5

Complex Numbers

SECTION 5.1

Complex Numbers

■ You should know how to work with complex numbers.

■ Operations on Complex Numbers
   (a) Addition: $(a + bi) + (c + di) = (a + c) + (b + d)i$
   (b) Subtraction: $(a + bi) - (c + di) = (a - c) + (b - d)i$
   (c) Multiplication: $(a + bi)(c + di) = (ac - bd) + (ad + bc)i$
   (d) Division: $\dfrac{a + bi}{c + di} = \dfrac{a + bi}{c + di} \cdot \dfrac{c - di}{c - di} = \dfrac{ac + bd}{c^2 + d^2} + \dfrac{bc - ad}{c^2 + d^2}i$

■ The complex conjugate of $a + bi$ is $a - bi$:

$$(a + bi)(a - bi) = a^2 + b^2$$

■ The additive inverse of $a + bi$ is $-a - bi$.

■ The multiplicative inverse of $a + bi$ is

$$\frac{a - bi}{a^2 + b^2}.$$

■ $\sqrt{-a} = \sqrt{a}\, i$ for $a > 0$.

Solutions to Selected Exercises

3. Find real numbers a and b so that the equation $(a - 1) + (b + 3)i = 5 + 8i$ is true.
   Solution:

$$(a - 1) + (b + 3)i = 5 + 8i$$
$$a - 1 = 5 \quad \Rightarrow \quad a = 6$$
$$b + 3 = 8 \quad \Rightarrow \quad b = 5$$

7. Write $2 - \sqrt{-27}$ in standard form.
   Solution:

$$2 - \sqrt{-27} = 2 - \sqrt{27}\, i = 2 - 3\sqrt{3}\, i$$

11. Write $-6i + i^2$ in standard form.
   Solution:

$$-6i + i^2 = -6i + (-1) = -1 - 6i$$

15. Write $\sqrt{-0.09}$ in standard form.

Solution:

$$\sqrt{-0.09} = \sqrt{0.09}\,i = 0.3i$$

19. Perform the indicated operation and write the result in standard form.

$$(8 - i) - (4 - i)$$

Solution:

$$(8 - i) - (4 - i) = 8 - i - 4 + i = 4$$

21. Perform the indicated operation and write the result in standard form.

$$(-2 + \sqrt{-8}) + (5 - \sqrt{-50})$$

Solution:

$$(-2 + \sqrt{-8}) + (5 - \sqrt{-50}) = -2 + 2\sqrt{2}\,i + 5 - 5\sqrt{2}\,i = 3 - 3\sqrt{2}\,i$$

25. Perform the indicated operations and write the result in standard form.

$$-\left(\tfrac{3}{2} + \tfrac{5}{2}i\right) + \left(\tfrac{5}{3} + \tfrac{11}{3}i\right)$$

Solution:

$$-\left(\tfrac{3}{2} + \tfrac{5}{2}i\right) + \left(\tfrac{5}{3} + \tfrac{11}{3}i\right) = -\tfrac{3}{2} - \tfrac{5}{2}i + \tfrac{5}{3} + \tfrac{11}{3}i$$
$$= -\tfrac{9}{6} - \tfrac{15}{6}i + \tfrac{10}{6} + \tfrac{22}{6}i$$
$$= \tfrac{1}{6} + \tfrac{7}{6}i$$

29. Write the conjugate of $-2 - \sqrt{5}\,i$ and find the product of the number and its conjugate.

Solution:

The complex conjugate of $-2 - \sqrt{5}\,i$ is $-2 + \sqrt{5}\,i$.

$$(-2 - \sqrt{5}\,i)(-2 + \sqrt{5}\,i) = 4 - 5i^2 = 4 + 5 = 9.$$

31. Write the conjugate of $20i$ and find the product of the number and its conjugate.

Solution:

The complex conjugate of $20i$ is $-20i$.

$$(20i)(-20i) = -400i^2 = 400.$$

35. Perform the specified operation and write the result in standard form.

$$\sqrt{-6}\sqrt{-2}$$

Solution:

$$\sqrt{-6}\sqrt{-2} = (\sqrt{6}\,i)(\sqrt{2}\,i) = \sqrt{12}\,i^2 = 2\sqrt{3}(-1) = -2\sqrt{3}$$

Note: $\sqrt{-6}\sqrt{-2} \neq \sqrt{12}$

39. Perform the specified operation and write the result in standard form.

$$(1+i)(3-2i)$$

Solution:

$$(1+i)(3-2i) = 3 - 2i + 3i - 2i^2 = 3 + i + 2 = 5 + i$$

41. Perform the specified operation and write the result in standard form.

$$6i(5-2i)$$

Solution:

$$6i(5-2i) = 30i - 12i^2 = 12 + 30i$$

43. Perform the specified operation and write the result in standard form.

$$(\sqrt{14} + \sqrt{10}\,i)(\sqrt{14} - \sqrt{10}\,i)$$

Solution:

$$(\sqrt{14} + \sqrt{10}\,i)(\sqrt{14} - \sqrt{10}\,i) = 14 - 10i^2 = 14 + 10 = 24$$

47. Perform the specified operation and write the result in standard form.

$$(2+3i)^2 + (2-3i)^2$$

Solution:

$$(2+3i)^2 + (2-3i)^2 = (4 + 12i + 9i^2) + (4 - 12i + 9i^2)$$
$$= 8 + 18i^2$$
$$= 8 - 18$$
$$= -10$$

51. Perform the specified operation and write the result in standard form.

$$\frac{2+i}{2-i}$$

Solution:

$$\frac{2+i}{2-i} = \frac{2+i}{2-i} \cdot \frac{2+i}{2+i} = \frac{4 + 4i + i^2}{4+1} = \frac{3+4i}{5} = \frac{3}{5} + \frac{4}{5}i$$

55. Perform the specified operation and write the result in standard form.

$$\frac{1}{(4-5i)^2}$$

Solution:

$$\frac{1}{(4-5i)^2} = \frac{1}{16 - 40i + 25i^2} = \frac{1}{-9 - 40i} \cdot \frac{-9+40i}{-9+40i}$$

$$= \frac{-9+40i}{81+1600} = \frac{-9+40i}{1681} = -\frac{9}{1681} + \frac{40}{1681}i$$

59. Use the Quadratic Formula to solve $4x^2 + 16x + 17 = 0$.

Solution:

$4x^2 + 16x + 17 = 0;\ a = 4,\ b = 16,\ c = 17$

$$x = \frac{-16 \pm \sqrt{(16)^2 - 4(4)(17)}}{2(4)}$$

$$= \frac{-16 \pm \sqrt{-16}}{8} = \frac{-16 \pm 4i}{8}$$

$$= -2 \pm \frac{1}{2}i$$

63. Use the Quadratic Formula to solve $16t^2 - 4t + 3 = 0$.

Solution:

$16t^2 - 4t + 3 = 0;\ a = 16,\ b = -4,\ c = 3$

$$t = \frac{-(-4) \pm \sqrt{(-4)^2 - 4(16)(3)}}{2(16)}$$

$$= \frac{4 \pm \sqrt{-176}}{32} = \frac{4 \pm 4\sqrt{11}i}{32}$$

$$= \frac{1}{8} \pm \frac{\sqrt{11}}{8}i$$

65. Write out the first 16 positive powers of i and express each as i, $-i$, 1, or -1.

Solution:

$$
\begin{array}{llll}
i = i & i^5 = i & i^9 = i & i^{13} = i \\
i^2 = -1 & i^6 = -1 & i^{10} = -1 & i^{14} = -1 \\
i^3 = -i & i^7 = -i & i^{11} = -i & i^{15} = -i \\
i^4 = 1 & i^8 = 1 & i^{12} = 1 & i^{16} = 1
\end{array}
$$

69. Simplify $-5i^5$ and write it in standard form.

Solution:

$$-5i^5 = -5i$$

73. Simplify $\dfrac{1}{i^3}$ and write it in standard form.

Solution:

$$\frac{1}{i^3} = \frac{1}{-i} = \frac{1}{-i} \cdot \frac{i}{i} = \frac{i}{-i^2} = \frac{i}{1} = i$$

77. Prove that the sum of a complex number $a + bi$ and its conjugate is a real number.

Solution:

$$(a + bi) + (a - bi) = (a + a) + (b - b)i$$
$$= 2a + 0i = 2a \qquad \text{which is a real number.}$$

81. Prove that the conjugate of the sum of two complex numbers $a_1 + b_1 i$ and $a_2 + b_2 i$ is the sum of their conjugates.

Solution:

$$(a_1 + b_1 i) + (a_2 + b_2 i) = (a_1 + a_2) + (b_1 + b_2)i$$

The complex conjugate of the sum is $(a_1 + a_2) - (b_1 + b_2)i$, and the sum of the conjugates is

$$(a_1 - b_1 i) + (a_2 - b_2 i) = (a_1 + a_2) + (-b_1 - b_2)i$$
$$= (a_1 + a_2) - (b_1 + b_2)i$$

Thus, the conjugate of the sum is the sum of the conjugates.

SECTION 5.2

Complex Solutions of Equations

> ■ A polynomial of degree n has exactly n solutions in the complex number system. These solutions may be real or complex and may be repeated.
>
> ■ If $a + bi$, $(b \neq 0)$ is a zero of a polynomial function with real coefficients, then so is its conjugate, $a - bi$.

Solutions to Selected Exercises

1. Determine the number of solutions of the equation $x^3 - 4x + 5 = 0$ in the complex number system.

Solution:

Since $x^3 - 4x + 5 = 0$ is a third degree polynomial, it has exactly **three** solutions in the complex number system.

7. Use the discriminant to determine the number of real solutions of the quadratic equation $3x^2 + 4x + 1 = 0$.

Solution:

$a = 3$, $b = 4$, $c = 1$
$b^2 - 4ac = (4)^2 - 4(3)(1) = 4 > 0$
There are *two* real solutions.

11. Use the discriminant to determine the number of real solutions of the quadratic equation $\frac{1}{5}x^2 + \frac{6}{5}x - 8 = 0$.

Solution:

$a = \frac{1}{5}$, $b = \frac{6}{5}$, $c = -8$
$b^2 - 4ac = \left(\frac{6}{5}\right)^2 - 4\left(\frac{1}{5}\right)(-8)$
$\qquad\qquad = \frac{36}{25} + \frac{32}{5} = \frac{196}{25} > 0$

There are *two* real solutions.

13. Solve the equation $x^2 - 5 = 0$. List any complex solutions in $a + bi$ form.

Solution:

$$x^2 - 5 = 0$$
$$x^2 = 5$$
$$x = \pm\sqrt{5}$$

17. Solve the equation $x^2 - 8x + 16 = 0$. List any complex solutions in $a + bi$ form.

Solution:

$$x^2 - 8x + 16 = 0$$
$$(x - 4)^2 = 0$$
$$x = 4$$

23. Solve the equation $230 + 20x - 0.5x^2 = 0$. List any complex solutions in $a + bi$ form.

Solution:

$$230 + 20x - 0.5x^2 = 0$$

$$-0.5x^2 + 20x + 230 = 0$$

Multiply by -2 and complete the square.

$$x^2 - 40x - 460 = 0$$

$$x^2 - 40x = 460$$

$$x^2 - 40x + 400 = 460 + 400$$

$$(x - 20)^2 = 860$$

$$x - 20 = \pm\sqrt{860}$$

$$x - 20 = \pm 2\sqrt{215}$$

$$x = 20 \pm 2\sqrt{215}$$

27. Find all the zeros of $h(x) = x^2 - 4x + 1$ and write the polynomial as a product of linear factors.

Solution:

h has no rational zeros. By the Quadratic Formula, the zeros are

$$x = \frac{4 \pm \sqrt{16 - 4}}{2} = 2 \pm \sqrt{3}.$$

$$h(x) = [x - (2 + \sqrt{3})][x - (2 - \sqrt{3})]$$

$$= (x - 2 - \sqrt{3})(x - 2 + \sqrt{3})$$

31. Use the zero $x = 2$ as an aid in finding all the zeros of $g(x) = x^3 - 6x^2 + 13x - 10$. Write the polynomial as a product of linear factors.

Solution:

Since $g(2) = 0$, $x - 2$ is a factor. By long division we have:

$$
\begin{array}{r}
x^2 - 4x + 5 \\
x - 2 \overline{)\, x^3 - 6x^2 + 13x - 10} \\
\underline{x^3 - 2x^2} \\
-4x^2 + 13x \\
\underline{-4x^2 + 8x} \\
5x - 10 \\
\underline{5x - 10} \\
0
\end{array}
$$

Thus, $g(x) = (x - 2)(x^2 - 4x + 5)$ and by the Quadratic Formula, $x = \dfrac{4 \pm \sqrt{16 - 20}}{2} = 2 \pm i$ are also zeros.

$$g(x) = (x - 2)[x - (2 + i)][x - (2 - i)] = (x - 2)(x - 2 - i)(x - 2 + i)$$

37. Use the zero $x = 1 - \frac{1}{2}i$ as an aid in finding all the zeros of $f(x) = 16x^3 - 20x^2 - 4x + 15$. Write the polynomial as a product of linear factors.

Solution:

Since $x = 1 - \frac{1}{2}i$ is a zero, so is $x = 1 + \frac{1}{2}i$.

$$\left[x - \left(1 - \tfrac{1}{2}i\right)\right]\left[x - \left(1 + \tfrac{1}{2}i\right)\right] = \left[(x-1) + \tfrac{1}{2}i\right]\left[(x-1) - \tfrac{1}{2}i\right]$$

$$= (x-1)^2 + \tfrac{1}{4}i^2$$

$$= x^2 - 2x + 1 + \tfrac{1}{4}$$

$$= x^2 - 2x + \tfrac{5}{4} \quad \text{is a factor of the polynomial.}$$

By long division we have:

$$
\begin{array}{r}
16x + 12 \\
x^2 - 2x + \tfrac{5}{4} \enclose{longdiv}{16x^3 - 20x^2 - 4x + 15} \\
\underline{16x^3 - 32x^2 + 20x} \\
12x^2 - 24x + 15 \\
\underline{12x^2 - 24x + 15} \\
0
\end{array}
$$

$$f(x) = (16x + 12)\left(x^2 - 2x + \tfrac{5}{4}\right)$$

$$= (4x + 3)(4)\left(x^2 - 2x + \tfrac{5}{4}\right)$$

The zeros of f are $x = -\frac{3}{4}$ and $x = 1 \pm \frac{1}{2}i$.

$$f(x) = (4x + 3)4\left[x - \left(1 - \tfrac{1}{2}i\right)\right]\left[x - \left(1 + \tfrac{1}{2}i\right)\right]$$

$$= (4x + 3)2\left(x - 1 + \tfrac{1}{2}i\right) 2\left(x - 1 - \tfrac{1}{2}i\right)$$

$$= (4x + 3)(2x - 2 + i)(2x - 2 - i)$$

43. Use the zero $x = 2i$ as an aid in finding all the zeros of $g(x) = x^4 - 4x^3 + 8x^2 - 16x + 16$. Write the polynomial as a product of linear factors.

Solution:

Since $x = 2i$ is a zero, so is $x = -2i$. $(x - 2i)(x + 2i) = x^2 + 4$ is a factor of the polynomial. By long division we have:

$$
\begin{array}{r}
x^2 - 4x\ + 4 \\
x^2 + 4 \overline{)\ x^4 - 4x^3 + 8x^2 - 16x + 16} \\
\underline{x^4\qquad\ + 4x^2} \\
-4x^3 + 4x^2 - 16x \\
\underline{-4x^3\qquad\quad - 16x} \\
4x^2\qquad + 16 \\
\underline{4x^2\qquad + 16} \\
0
\end{array}
$$

$$g(x) = (x^2 + 4)(x^2 - 4x + 4)$$
$$= (x - 2i)(x + 2i)(x - 2)^2$$

The zeros of g are $x = \pm 2i$ and $x = 2$.

49. Use the zero $r = 2i$, to find all the zeros of $f(x) = 2x^4 - x^3 + 7x^2 - 4x - 4$.

Solution:

Since $2i$ is a zero of f, so is $-2i$. Thus, $(x - 2i)(x + 2i) = x^2 + 4$ is a factor of $f(x)$. By long division we have

$$
\begin{array}{r}
2x^2 - x\ - 1 \\
x^2 + 4 \overline{)\ 2x^4 - x^3 + 7x^2 - 4x - 4} \\
\underline{2x^4\qquad\ + 8x^2} \\
-x^3 - x^2 - 4x \\
\underline{-x^3\qquad - 4x} \\
-x^2\qquad - 4 \\
\underline{-x^2\qquad - 4} \\
0
\end{array}
$$

$$f(x) = (x^2 + 4)(2x^2 - x - 1)$$
$$= (x - 2i)(x + 2i)(2x + 1)(x - 1)$$

The zeros of f are $\pm 2i$, $-\frac{1}{2}$, and 1.

53. Use the zero $r = -3 + \sqrt{2}\,i$, to find all the zeros of $f(x) = x^4 + 3x^3 - 5x^2 - 21x + 22$.

Solution:

Since $-3 + \sqrt{2}\,i$ is a zero of f, so is $-3 - \sqrt{2}\,i$. Thus,

$$[x - (-3 + \sqrt{2}\,i)][x - (-3 - \sqrt{2}\,i)] = [(x + 3) - \sqrt{2}\,i)][(x + 3) + \sqrt{2}\,i] \quad \text{is a factor of } x.$$
$$= (x + 3)^2 - 2i^2$$
$$= x^2 + 6x + 11$$

Now, by long division we have

$$
\begin{array}{r}
x^2 - 3x + 2 \\
x^2 + 6x + 11 \overline{\smash{)}\ x^4 + 3x^3 - 5x^2 - 21x + 22} \\
x^4 + 6x^3 + 11x^2 \\
\hline
-3x^3 - 16x^2 - 21x \\
-3x^3 - 18x^2 - 33x \\
\hline
2x^2 + 12x + 22 \\
2x^2 + 12x + 22 \\
\hline
0
\end{array}
$$

$$
\begin{aligned}
f(x) &= [x - (-3 + \sqrt{2}\,i)][x - (-3 - \sqrt{2}\,i)](x^2 - 3x + 2) \\
&= [x - (-3 + \sqrt{2}\,i)][x - (-3 - \sqrt{2}\,i)](x - 1)(x - 2) \\
&= (x - 1)(x - 2)(x + 3 - \sqrt{2}\,i)(x + 3 + \sqrt{2}\,i)
\end{aligned}
$$

The zeros of f are $-3 + \sqrt{2}\,i$, $-3 - \sqrt{2}\,i$, 1, and 2.

59. Write $f(x) = x^4 - 4x^3 + 5x^2 - 2x - 6$ in completely factored form. [*Hint:* One factor is $x^2 - 2x - 2$.]

Solution:

$$
\begin{array}{r}
x^2 - 2x + 3 \\
x^2 - 2x - 2 \overline{)\; x^4 - 4x^3 + 5x^2 - 2x - 6} \\
\underline{x^4 - 2x^3 - 2x^2} \\
-2x^3 + 7x^2 - 2x \\
\underline{-2x^3 + 4x^2 + 4x} \\
3x^2 - 6x - 6 \\
\underline{3x^2 - 6x - 6} \\
0
\end{array}
$$

$$f(x) = (x^2 - 2x + 3)(x^2 - 2x - 2)$$
$$f(x) = (x - 1 + \sqrt{2}\,i)(x - 1 - \sqrt{2}\,i)(x - 1 + \sqrt{3})(x - 1 - \sqrt{3})$$

Note: Use the Quadratic Formula on each factor.

61. Find a polynomial with integer coefficients that has the zeros 1, $5i$, and $-5i$.

Solution:

$$
\begin{aligned}
f(x) &= (x - 1)(x - 5i)(x + 5i) \\
&= (x - 1)(x^2 + 25) \\
&= x^3 - x^2 + 25x - 25
\end{aligned}
$$

65. Find a polynomial with integer coefficients that has the zeros i, $-i$, $6i$, and $-6i$.

Solution:

$$
\begin{aligned}
f(x) &= (x - i)(x + i)(x - 6i)(x + 6i) \\
&= (x^2 + 1)(x^2 + 36) \\
&= x^4 + 37x^2 + 36
\end{aligned}
$$

69. Find a polynomial with integer coefficients that has the zeros $\frac{3}{4}$, -2, and $-\frac{1}{2} + i$.

Solution:

Since $-\frac{1}{2} + i$ is a zero, so is $-\frac{1}{2} - i$.

$$f(x) = 16(x - \tfrac{3}{4})(x + 2)\left[x - (-\tfrac{1}{2} + i)\right]\left[x - (-\tfrac{1}{2} - i)\right] \qquad \text{Multiply by 16 to clear fractions.}$$

$$= 4(4x - 3)(x + 2)\left[x^2 + x + (\tfrac{1}{4} + 1)\right]$$

$$= (4x^2 + 5x - 6)(4x^2 + 4x + 5)$$

$$= 16x^4 + 36x^3 + 16x^2 + x - 30$$

73. Find a quadratic function f (with integer coefficients) that has $\pm\sqrt{b}\,i$ as zeros. Assume that b is a positive integer.

Solution:

$$f(x) = (x - \sqrt{b}\,i)(x + \sqrt{b}\,i) = x^2 + b$$

SECTION 5.3

Trigonometric Form of a Complex Number

■ You should be able to graphically represent complex numbers and know the following facts about them.

■ The absolute value of the complex number $z = a + bi$ is $|z| = \sqrt{a^2 + b^2}$.

■ The trigonometric form of the complex number $z = a + bi$ is $z = r(\cos\theta + i\sin\theta)$ where
   (a) $a = r\cos\theta$
   (b) $b = r\sin\theta$
   (c) $r = \sqrt{a^2 + b^2}$; r is called the modulus of z.
   (d) $\tan\theta = b/a$; θ is called the argument of z.

■ Given $z_1 = r_1(\cos\theta_1 + i\sin\theta_1)$ and $z_2 = r_2(\cos\theta_2 + i\sin\theta_2)$:
   (a) $z_1 z_2 = r_1 r_2[\cos(\theta_1 + \theta_2) + i\sin(\theta_1 + \theta_2)]$
   (b) $\dfrac{z_1}{z_2} = \dfrac{r_1}{r_2}[\cos(\theta_1 - \theta_2) + i\sin(\theta_1 - \theta_2)]$, $z_2 \neq 0$

Solutions to Selected Exercises

5. Represent the complex number $6 - 7i$ graphically and find its absolute value.

   Solution:

   $$|6 - 7i| = \sqrt{(6)^2 + (-7)^2}$$
   $$= \sqrt{36 + 49}$$
   $$= \sqrt{85}$$

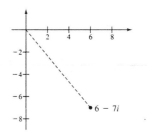

9. Express the complex number $-3 - 3i$ in trigonometric form.

   Solution:

   $$z = -3 - 3i$$

   $$r = \sqrt{(-3)^2 + (-3)^2} = \sqrt{18} = 3\sqrt{2}$$

   $$\tan \theta = \frac{-3}{-3} = 1, \ \theta \text{ is in Quadrant III}$$

   $$\theta = 225° \text{ or } \frac{5\pi}{4}$$

   $$z = 3\sqrt{2}\left(\cos \frac{5\pi}{4} + i \sin \frac{5\pi}{4}\right)$$

13. Represent $\sqrt{3} + i$ graphically, and find the trigonometric form of the number.

    Solution:

    $$z = \sqrt{3} + i$$

    $$r = \sqrt{(\sqrt{3})^2 + 1^2} = 2$$

    $$\tan \theta = \frac{1}{\sqrt{3}}$$

    $$\theta = 30° \text{ or } \frac{\pi}{6}$$

    $$z = 2\left(\cos \frac{\pi}{6} + i \sin \frac{\pi}{6}\right)$$

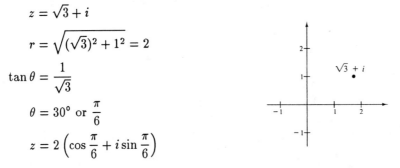

17. Represent $6i$ graphically, and find the trigonometric form of the number.

    Solution:

    $$z = 6i$$

    $$r = \sqrt{0^2 + 6^2} = 6$$

    $$\tan \theta = \frac{6}{0}, \text{ undefined}$$

    $$\theta = \frac{\pi}{2}$$

    $$z = 6\left(\cos \frac{\pi}{2} + i \sin \frac{\pi}{2}\right)$$

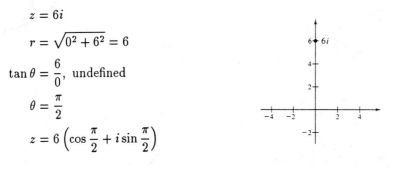

23. Represent $1 + 6i$ graphically, and find the trigonometric form of the number.

Solution:

$$z = 1 + 6i$$

$$r = \sqrt{37}$$

$$\tan \theta = 6$$

$$\theta \approx 1.41 \text{ rad}$$

$$z = \sqrt{37}[\cos(1.41) + i\sin(1.41)]$$

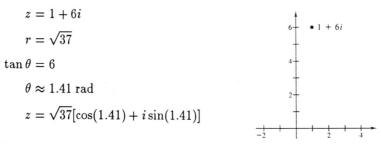

27. Represent $2(\cos 150° + i\sin 150°)$ graphically, and find the standard form of the number.

Solution:

$$z = 2(\cos 150° + i\sin 150°)$$

$$= 2\left(-\frac{\sqrt{3}}{2} + \frac{1}{2}i\right)$$

$$= -\sqrt{3} + i$$

31. Represent $3.75\left(\cos(3\pi/4) + i\sin(3\pi/4)\right)$ graphically, and find the standard form of the number.

Solution:

$$z = 3.75\left(\cos\frac{3\pi}{4} + i\sin\frac{3\pi}{4}\right)$$

$$= \frac{15}{4}\left(-\frac{\sqrt{2}}{2} + \frac{\sqrt{2}}{2}i\right)$$

$$= \frac{-15\sqrt{2}}{8} + \frac{15\sqrt{2}}{8}i$$

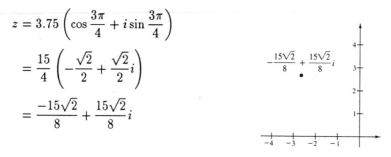

35. Represent $3[\cos(18°45') + i\sin(18°45')]$ graphically, and find the standard form of the number.

Solution:

$$z = 3(\cos 18°45' + i\sin 18°45')$$
$$= 3\cos 18°45' + 3i\sin 18°45'$$
$$\approx 2.8408 + 0.9643i$$

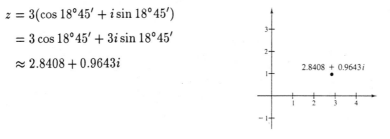

39. Perform the indicated operation and leave the result in trigonometric form.

$$\left[\tfrac{5}{3}(\cos 140° + i\sin 140°)\right]\left[\tfrac{2}{3}(\cos 60° + i\sin 60°)\right]$$

Solution:

$$\left[\tfrac{5}{3}(\cos 140° + i\sin 140°)\right]\left[\tfrac{2}{3}(\cos 60° + i\sin 60°)\right]$$
$$= \left(\tfrac{5}{3}\right)\left(\tfrac{2}{3}\right)[\cos(140° + 60°) + i\sin(140° + 60°)]$$
$$= \tfrac{10}{9}[\cos 200° + i\sin 200°]$$

45. Perform the indicated operation and leave the result in trigonometric form.

$$\frac{\cos(5\pi/3) + i\sin(5\pi/3)}{\cos \pi + i\sin \pi}$$

Solution:

$$\frac{\cos(5\pi/3) + i\sin(5\pi/3)}{\cos \pi + i\sin \pi} = \cos\left(\frac{5\pi}{3} - \pi\right) + i\sin\left(\frac{5\pi}{3} - \pi\right) = \cos\frac{2\pi}{3} + i\sin\frac{2\pi}{3}$$

49. For $(2 + 2i)(1 - i)$, (a) give the trigonometric form of the complex numbers, (b) perform the indicated operation using the trigonometric form, and (c) perform the indicated operation using the standard form and check your result with the answer in part (b).

Solution:

(a) Trigonometric form: $\left[2\sqrt{2}\,(\cos 45° + i\sin 45°)\right]\left[\sqrt{2}\,(\cos 315° + i\sin 315°)\right]$

(b) Operation in trigonometric form:

$$(2\sqrt{2})(\sqrt{2})\,[\cos(45° + 315°) + i\sin(45° + 315°)] = \cos 360° + i\sin 360°$$
$$= 4[\cos(360°) + i\sin(360°)] = 4$$

(c) $(2 + 2i)(1 - i) = 2 - 2i + 2i - 2i^2 = 4$

53. For $5/(2 + 3i)$, (a) give the trigonometric form of the complex numbers, (b) perform the indicated operation using the trigonometric form, and (c) perform the indicated operation using the standard form and check your result with the answer in part (b).

Solution:

(a) Trigonometric form: $\dfrac{5[\cos 0° + i \sin 0°]}{\sqrt{13}[\cos 56.31° + i \sin 56.31°]}$

(b) Operation in trigonometric form:

$$\frac{5}{\sqrt{13}}[\cos(-56.31°) + i\sin(-56.31°)] = \frac{5\sqrt{13}}{13}[\cos(-56.31°) + i\sin(-56.31°)] \approx \frac{5}{13}(2 - 3i)$$

(c) $\dfrac{5}{2 + 3i} \cdot \dfrac{2 - 3i}{2 - 3i} = \dfrac{5(2 - 3i)}{13} = \dfrac{5}{13}(2 - 3i)$

57. Use the trigonometric form $z = r(\cos\theta + i\sin\theta)$ and $\overline{z} = r[\cos(-\theta) + i\sin(-\theta)]$ to find (a) $z\overline{z}$ and (b) $z/\overline{z}$, $z \neq 0$.

Solution:

(a) $z\overline{z} = [r(\cos\theta + i\sin\theta)][r\cos(-\theta) + i\sin(-\theta)]$

$= r^2[\cos(\theta - \theta) + i\sin(\theta - \theta)]$

$= r^2$

(b) $\dfrac{z}{\overline{z}} = \dfrac{r}{r}[\cos(\theta - (-\theta)) + i\sin(\theta - (-\theta))]$

$= \cos 2\theta + i\sin 2\theta$

SECTION 5.4

DeMoivre's Theorem and nth Roots

■ You should know DeMoivre's Theorem: If $z = r(\cos\theta + i\sin\theta)$, then for any positive integer n,

$$z^n = r^n(\cos n\theta + i\sin n\theta).$$

■ You should know that for any positive integer n, $z = r(\cos\theta + i\sin\theta)$ has n distinct nth roots given by

$$\sqrt[n]{r}\left[\cos\left(\frac{\theta + 2\pi k}{n}\right) + i\sin\left(\frac{\theta + 2\pi k}{n}\right)\right]$$

where $k = 0, 1, 2, \ldots, n-1$.

Solutions to Selected Exercises

3. Use DeMoivre's Theorem to find $(-1 + i)^{10}$. Express the result in standard form.

Solution:

$$(-1 + i)^{10} = \left[\sqrt{2}\left(\cos\frac{3\pi}{4} + i\sin\frac{3\pi}{4}\right)\right]^{10}$$

$$= (\sqrt{2})^{10}\left[\cos 10\left(\frac{3\pi}{4}\right) + i\sin 10\left(\frac{3\pi}{4}\right)\right]$$

$$= 32\left[\cos\frac{15\pi}{2} + i\sin\frac{15\pi}{2}\right]$$

$$= 32[0 - i]$$

$$= -32i$$

7. Use DeMoivre's Theorem to find $[5(\cos 20° + i\sin 20°)]^3$. Express the result in standard form.

Solution:

$$[5(\cos 20° + i\sin 20°)]^3 = 5^3[\cos 60° + i\sin 60°]$$

$$= 125\left(\frac{1}{2} + \frac{\sqrt{3}}{2}i\right)$$

$$= \frac{125}{2} + \frac{125\sqrt{3}}{2}i$$

11. Use DeMoivre's Theorem to find $[5(\cos 3.2 + i\sin 3.2)]^4$. Express the result in standard form.

Solution:

$$[5(\cos 3.2 + i\sin 3.2)]^4 = 5^4[\cos 12.8 + i\sin 12.8]$$

$$\approx 625(0.97283 + 0.2315i)$$

$$\approx 608.02 + 144.69i$$

15. (a) Use DeMoivre's Theorem to find the fourth roots of

$$16\left(\cos\frac{4\pi}{3} + i\sin\frac{4\pi}{3}\right),$$

(b) represent each of the roots graphically, and (c) express each of the roots in standard form.

Solution:

(a) & (c) $n = 4$

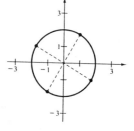

$$k = 0: \ 2\left(\cos\frac{\pi}{3} + i\sin\frac{\pi}{3}\right) = 1 + \sqrt{3}i$$

$$k = 1: \ 2\left(\cos\frac{5\pi}{6} + i\sin\frac{5\pi}{6}\right) = -\sqrt{3} + i$$

$$k = 2: \ 2\left(\cos\frac{4\pi}{3} + i\sin\frac{4\pi}{3}\right) = -1 - \sqrt{3}i$$

$$k = 3: \ 2\left(\cos\frac{11\pi}{6} + i\sin\frac{11\pi}{6}\right) = \sqrt{3} - i$$

19. (a) Use DeMoivre's Theorem to find the cube roots of $-\frac{125}{2}(1 + \sqrt{3}i)$, (b) represent each of the roots graphically, and (c) express each of the roots in standard form.

Solution:

$$-\frac{125}{2}(1 + \sqrt{3}i) = 125\left(\cos\frac{4\pi}{3} + i\sin\frac{4\pi}{3}\right)$$

(a) & (c) $n = 3$

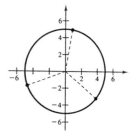

$$k = 0: \ 5\left(\cos\frac{4\pi}{9} + i\sin\frac{4\pi}{9}\right) \approx 0.868 + 4.924i$$

$$k = 1: \ 5\left(\cos\frac{10\pi}{9} + i\sin\frac{10\pi}{9}\right) \approx -4.698 - 1.710i$$

$$k = 2: \ 5\left(\cos\frac{16\pi}{9} + i\sin\frac{16\pi}{9}\right) \approx 3.830 - 3.214i$$

25. Find all the solutions of $x^4 - i = 0$ and represent your solutions graphically.

Solution:

$$x^4 - i = 0$$
$$x^4 = i$$

Find the fourth roots of $i = \cos\dfrac{\pi}{2} + i\sin\dfrac{\pi}{2}$.

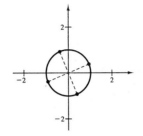

$n = 4$

$k = 0: \quad \cos\dfrac{\pi}{8} + i\sin\dfrac{\pi}{8}$

$k = 1: \quad \cos\dfrac{5\pi}{8} + i\sin\dfrac{5\pi}{8}$

$k = 2: \quad \cos\dfrac{9\pi}{8} + i\sin\dfrac{9\pi}{8}$

$k = 3: \quad \cos\dfrac{13\pi}{8} + i\sin\dfrac{13\pi}{8}$

29. Find all the solutions of $x^3 + 64i = 0$ and represent your solutions graphically.

Solution:

$$x^3 + 64i = 0$$
$$x^3 = -64i$$

Find the cube roots of $-64i = 64\left(\cos\dfrac{3\pi}{2} + i\sin\dfrac{3\pi}{2}\right)$.

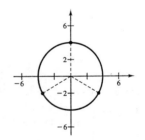

$n = 3$

$k = 0: \quad 4\left(\cos\dfrac{\pi}{2} + i\sin\dfrac{\pi}{2}\right)$

$k = 1: \quad 4\left(\cos\dfrac{7\pi}{6} + i\sin\dfrac{7\pi}{6}\right)$

$k = 2: \quad 4\left(\cos\dfrac{11\pi}{6} + i\sin\dfrac{11\pi}{6}\right)$

REVIEW EXERCISES FOR CHAPTER 5

Solutions to Selected Exercises

3. Perform the indicated operations and write the result in standard form.

$$\left(\frac{\sqrt{2}}{2} - \frac{\sqrt{2}}{2}i\right) - \left(\frac{\sqrt{2}}{2} + \frac{\sqrt{2}}{2}i\right)$$

Solution:

$$\left(\frac{\sqrt{2}}{2} - \frac{\sqrt{2}}{2}i\right) - \left(\frac{\sqrt{2}}{2} + \frac{\sqrt{2}}{2}i\right) = \left(\frac{\sqrt{2}}{2} - \frac{\sqrt{2}}{2}\right) + \left(-\frac{\sqrt{2}}{2} - \frac{\sqrt{2}}{2}\right)i = 0 - \sqrt{2}i = -\sqrt{2}i$$

7. Perform the indicated operations and write the result in standard form.

$$(10 - 8i)(2 - 3i)$$

Solution:

$$(10 - 8i)(2 - 3i) = 20 - 30i - 16i + 24i^2 = -4 - 46i$$

11. Perform the indicated operations and write the result in standard form.

$$\frac{4}{-3i}$$

Solution:

$$\frac{4}{-3i} = \frac{4}{-3i} \cdot \frac{3i}{3i} = \frac{12i}{9} = \frac{4}{3}i$$

13. Use the discriminant to determine the number of real solutions of $6x^2 + x - 2 = 0$.

Solution:

$$a = 6, \quad b = 1, \quad c = -2$$
$$b^2 - 4ac = (1)^2 - 4(6)(-2) = 49 > 0$$

There are *two* real solutions.

17. Use the discriminant to determine the number of real solutions of $0.13x^2 - 0.45x + 0.65 = 0$.

Solution:

$$a = 0.13, \quad b = -0.45, \quad c = 0.65$$
$$b^2 - 4ac = (-0.45)^2 - 4(0.13)(0.65)$$
$$= -0.1355 < 0$$

There are *no* real solutions.

21. Find all the zeros of $g(x) = x^2 - 2x$.

Solution:

$$g(x) = x^2 - 2x = x(x - 2)$$

The zeros of g are 0 and 2.

27. Use the zero $x = 1$ as an aid in finding all the zeros of $f(x) = 4x^3 - 11x^2 + 10x - 3$. Write the polynomial as a product of linear factors.

Solution:

Since 1 is a zero, $x - 1$ is a factor. Now, by long division we have:

$$
\begin{array}{r}
4x^2 - 7x + 3 \\
x - 1 \overline{)\ 4x^3 - 11x^2 + 10x - 3} \\
\underline{4x^3 - 4x^2} \\
-7x^2 + 10x \\
\underline{-7x^2 + 7x} \\
3x - 3 \\
\underline{3x - 3} \\
0
\end{array}
$$

$$f(x) = (x - 1)(4x^2 - 7x + 3) = (x - 1)(4x - 3)(x - 1) = (x - 1)^2(4x - 3)$$

The zeros of f are $x = 1$ and $x = \frac{3}{4}$.

31. Use the zero $x = 7 + i$ as an aid in finding all the zeros of $h(x) = x^3 - 18x^2 + 106x - 200$. Write the polynomial as a product of linear factors.

Solution:

Since $7 + i$ is a zero, so is $7 - i$. Thus, $[x - (7 + i)]$ and $[x - (7 - i)]$ are factors of $f(x)$.

$$
\begin{aligned}
[x - (7 + i)][x - (7 - i)] &= [(x - 7) - i][(x - 7) + i] \\
&= (x - 7)^2 - i^2 \\
&= x^2 - 14x + 50
\end{aligned}
$$

Now by long division, we have:

$$
\begin{array}{r}
x - 4 \\
x^2 - 14x + 50 \overline{)\ x^3 - 18x^2 + 106x - 200} \\
\underline{x^3 - 14x^2 + 50x} \\
-4x^2 + 56x - 200 \\
\underline{-4x^2 + 56x - 200} \\
0
\end{array}
$$

$$h(x) = (x^2 - 14x + 50)(x - 4) = (x - 4)(x - 7 - i)(x - 7 + i)$$

The zeros of h are $x = 7 + i$, $7 - i$, and 4.

33. Use the zero $x = -3 + \sqrt{5}\,i$ as an aid in finding all the zeros of $f(x) = x^4 + 5x^3 + 2x^2 - 50x - 84$. Write the polynomial as a product of linear factors.

Solution:

Since $x = -3 + \sqrt{5}\,i$ is a zero, so is $-3 - \sqrt{5}\,i$. Thus, $[x - (-3 + \sqrt{5}\,i)]$ and $[x - (-3 - \sqrt{5}\,i)]$ are factors of $f(x)$.

$$[x - (-3 + \sqrt{5}\,i)][x - (-3 - \sqrt{5}\,i)] = [(x + 3) - \sqrt{5}\,i][(x + 3) + \sqrt{5}\,i]$$
$$= (x + 3)^2 - 5i^2$$
$$= x^2 + 6x + 14$$

Now by long division, we have:

$$
\begin{array}{r}
x^2 - x - 6 \\
x^2 + 6x + 14 \,\overline{)\, x^4 + 5x^3 + 2x^2 - 50x - 84} \\
\underline{x^4 + 6x^3 + 14x^2} \\
- x^3 - 12x^2 - 50x \\
\underline{- x^3 - 6x^2 - 14x} \\
- 6x^2 - 36x - 84 \\
\underline{- 6x^2 - 36x - 84} \\
0
\end{array}
$$

$$f(x) = (x^2 + 6x + 14)(x^2 - x - 6) = (x + 3 - \sqrt{5}\,i)(x + 3 + \sqrt{5}\,i)(x - 3)(x + 2)$$

The zeros of f are $x = -3 + \sqrt{5}\,i,\ -3 - \sqrt{5}\,i,\ 3,$ and -2.

35. Find a polynomial with integer coefficients that has the zeros -1, -1, $\frac{1}{3}$, and $-\frac{1}{2}$.

Solution:

$$
\begin{aligned}
f(x) &= 6(x + 1)^2\left(x - \tfrac{1}{3}\right)\left(x + \tfrac{1}{2}\right) & \text{Multiply by 6 to clear the fractions.} \\
&= (x + 1)^2 3\left(x - \tfrac{1}{3}\right) 2\left(x + \tfrac{1}{2}\right) \\
&= (x^2 + 2x + 1)(3x - 1)(2x + 1) \\
&= (x^2 + 2x + 1)(6x^2 + x - 1) \\
&= 6x^4 + 13x^3 + 7x^2 - x - 1
\end{aligned}
$$

39. Find the trigonometric form of $5 - 5i$.

Solution:

$$z = 5 - 5i$$

$$|z| = \sqrt{5^2 + (-5)^2} = 5\sqrt{2}$$

$$\tan\theta = -\tfrac{5}{5} = -1, \ \theta \text{ is in Quadrant IV}$$

$$\theta = 315°$$

$$z = 5\sqrt{2}(\cos 315° + i\sin 315°)$$

43. Write $100(\cos 240° + i\sin 240°)$ in standard form.

Solution:

$$z = 100(\cos 240° + i\sin 240°)$$

$$= 100\left(-\frac{1}{2} - \frac{\sqrt{3}}{2}i\right)$$

$$= -50 - 50\sqrt{3}i$$

47. $z_1 = -6, \ z_2 = 5i$

(a) Express the two complex numbers in trigonometric form and (b) use the trigonometric form to find $z_1 z_2$ and z_1/z_2.

Solution:

(a) $z_1 = -6 = 6(\cos\pi + i\sin\pi)$

$$z_2 = 5i = 5\left(\cos\frac{\pi}{2} + i\sin\frac{\pi}{2}\right)$$

(b) $z_1 z_2 = 6(5)\left[\cos\left(\pi + \frac{\pi}{2}\right) + i\sin\left(\pi + \frac{\pi}{2}\right)\right] = 30\left(\cos\frac{3\pi}{2} + i\sin\frac{3\pi}{2}\right) = -30i$

$$\frac{z_1}{z_2} = \frac{6}{5}\left[\cos\left(\pi - \frac{\pi}{2}\right) + i\sin\left(\pi - \frac{\pi}{2}\right)\right] = \frac{6}{5}\left[\cos\frac{\pi}{2} + i\sin\frac{\pi}{2}\right] = \frac{6}{5}i$$

51. Use DeMoivre's Theorem to find the indicated power of the following complex number. Express the result in standard form.

$$\left[5\left(\cos\frac{\pi}{12} + i\sin\frac{\pi}{12}\right)\right]^4$$

Solution:

$$\left[5\left(\cos\frac{\pi}{12} + i\sin\frac{\pi}{12}\right)\right]^4 = 5^4\left[\cos 4\left(\frac{\pi}{12}\right) + i\sin 4\left(\frac{\pi}{12}\right)\right]$$

$$= 625\left(\cos\frac{\pi}{3} + i\sin\frac{\pi}{3}\right) = \frac{625}{2} + \frac{625\sqrt{3}}{2}i$$

55. Use DeMoivre's Theorem to find the sixth roots of $-729i$.

Solution:

Find the sixth roots of $-729i = 729\left(\cos\dfrac{3\pi}{2} + i\sin\dfrac{3\pi}{2}\right)$.

$$\sqrt[6]{729}\left[\cos\dfrac{(3\pi/2) + 2\pi k}{6} + i\sin\dfrac{(3\pi/2) + 2\pi k}{6}\right] = 3\left[\cos\dfrac{3\pi + 4\pi k}{12} + i\sin\dfrac{3\pi + 4\pi k}{12}\right]$$

$$k = 0,\ 1,\ 2,\ 3,\ 4,\ 5$$

$k = 0:\ 3\left(\cos\dfrac{\pi}{4} + i\sin\dfrac{\pi}{4}\right)$ $k = 3:\ 3\left(\cos\dfrac{5\pi}{4} + i\sin\dfrac{5\pi}{4}\right)$

$k = 1:\ 3\left(\cos\dfrac{7\pi}{12} + i\sin\dfrac{7\pi}{12}\right)$ $k = 4:\ 3\left(\cos\dfrac{19\pi}{12} + i\sin\dfrac{19\pi}{12}\right)$

$k = 2:\ 3\left(\cos\dfrac{11\pi}{12} + i\sin\dfrac{11\pi}{12}\right)$ $k = 5:\ 3\left(\cos\dfrac{23\pi}{12} + i\sin\dfrac{23\pi}{12}\right)$

59. Find all solutions to $x^4 + 81 = 0$ and represent the solutions graphically.

Solution:

$$x^4 + 81 = 0$$

$$x^4 = -81 \qquad \text{Find the fourth roots of } -81.$$

$$-81 = 81(\cos\pi + i\sin\pi)$$

By DeMoivre's Theorem we have:

$$\sqrt[4]{-81} = \sqrt[4]{81}\left[\cos\left(\dfrac{\pi + 2\pi k}{4}\right) + i\sin\left(\dfrac{\pi + 2\pi k}{4}\right)\right], \quad k = 0,\ 1,\ 2,\ 3$$

$k = 0:\ 3\left(\cos\dfrac{\pi}{4} + i\sin\dfrac{\pi}{4}\right) = \dfrac{3\sqrt{2}}{2} + \dfrac{3\sqrt{2}}{2}i$

$k = 1:\ 3\left(\cos\dfrac{3\pi}{4} + i\sin\dfrac{3\pi}{4}\right) = -\dfrac{3\sqrt{2}}{2} + \dfrac{3\sqrt{2}}{2}i$

$k = 2:\ 3\left(\cos\dfrac{5\pi}{4} + i\sin\dfrac{5\pi}{4}\right) = -\dfrac{3\sqrt{2}}{2} - \dfrac{3\sqrt{2}}{2}i$

$k = 3:\ 3\left(\cos\dfrac{7\pi}{4} + i\sin\dfrac{7\pi}{4}\right) = \dfrac{3\sqrt{2}}{2} - \dfrac{3\sqrt{2}}{2}i$

Practice Test for Chapter 5

1. Express i^{38} as i, $-i$, 1, or -1.

In Exercises 2–5, perform the indicated operation and write the result in standard form.

2. $(8 + \sqrt{-64}) + (6 + \sqrt{-25})$

3. $-(4 + 4i) - (-3i)$

4. $(-8 + 2i)(-8 - 2i)$

5. $\dfrac{12 + 16i}{4 - 2i}$

6. Use the quadratic equation to solve $3x^2 + 2x + 2 = 0$.

In Exercises 7–10, find all the zeros of the given equation. List any complex solutions in $a + bi$ form.

7. $3x^2 + 1 = -47$

8. $x^4 - 1296 = 0$

9. $x^4 - 7x^2 - 60 = 0$

10. $x^3 + 2x^2 + 9x + 18 = 0$

11. Find a polynomial with integer coefficients that has the zeros 0, $-2i$, 3.

12. Find all the zeros of $f(x) = x^3 + 4x^2 - 7x + 30$ given that $r = 1 + 2i$ is a zero.

13. Give the trigonometric form of $z = 5 - 5i$.

14. Give the standard form of $z = 6(\cos 225° + i \sin 225°)$.

15. Multiply $[7(\cos 23° + i \sin 23°)][4(\cos 7° + i \sin 7°)]$.

16. Divide $\dfrac{9\left(\cos \dfrac{5\pi}{4} + i \sin \dfrac{5\pi}{4}\right)}{3(\cos \pi + i \sin \pi)}$.

17. Find $(2 + 2i)^8$.

18. Find the cube roots of $8\left(\cos \dfrac{\pi}{3} + i \sin \dfrac{\pi}{3}\right)$.

19. Find all the solutions to $x^3 + 125 = 0$.

20. Find all the solutions to $x^4 + i = 0$.

CHAPTER 6

Exponential and Logarithmic Functions

SECTION 6.1

Exponential Functions

- You should know that a function of the form $y = a^x$, where $a > 0$, $a \neq 1$, is called an exponential function with base a.

- You should be able to graph exponential functions.

- You should know some properties of exponential functions where $a > 0$ and $a \neq 1$.

   (a) If $a^x = a^y$, then $x = y$.

   (b) If $a^x = b^x$ and $x \neq 0$, then $a = b$.

- You should know formulas for compound interest.

   (a) For n compoundings per year: $A = P\left(1 + \dfrac{r}{n}\right)^{nt}$.

   (b) For continuous compoundings: $A = Pe^{rt}$.

Solutions to Selected Exercises

3. Use a calculator to evaluate $1000(1.06)^{-5}$. Round your answer to three decimal places.

Solution:

$$1000(1.06)^{-5} \approx 747.258$$

$1.06 \boxed{y^x}\, 5 \boxed{+/-} \boxed{\times}\, 1000 \boxed{=}$

7. Use a calculator to evaluate $8^{2\pi}$. Round your answer to three decimal places.

Solution:

$$8^{2\pi} \approx 472{,}369.379$$

$8 \boxed{y^x} \boxed{(}\, 2 \boxed{x}\, \pi \boxed{)} \boxed{=}$

11. Use a calculator to evaluate e^2. Round your answer to three decimal places.

Solution:

$$e^2 \approx 7.389$$

2 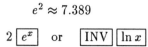 or $\boxed{\text{INV}}\,\boxed{\ln x}$

15. Match $f(x) = 3^x$ with its graph.

Solution:

$f(x) = 3^x$

y-intercept: $(0, 1)$

3^x increases as x increases

Matches graph (g)

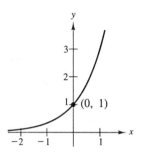

19. Match $f(x) = 3^x - 4$ with its graph.

Solution:

$f(x) = 3^x - 4$

y-intercept: $(0, -3)$

$3^x - 4$ increases as x increases

Matches graph (d)

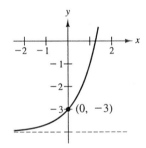

23. Sketch the graph of $g(x) = 5^x$.

Solution:

$g(x) = 5^x$

x	-2	-1	0	1	2
$g(x)$	$\frac{1}{25}$	$\frac{1}{5}$	1	5	25

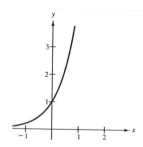

27. Sketch the graph of $h(x) = 5^{x-2}$.

Solution:

$h(x) = 5^{x-2}$

x	-1	0	1	2	3
$h(x)$	$\frac{1}{125}$	$\frac{1}{25}$	$\frac{1}{5}$	1	5

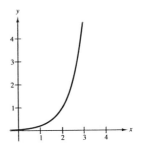

31. Sketch the graph of $f(x) = 3^{x-2} + 1$.

Solution:

$f(x) = 3^{x-2} + 1$

x	-1	0	1	2	3	4
y	$1\frac{1}{27}$	$1\frac{1}{9}$	$1\frac{1}{3}$	2	4	10

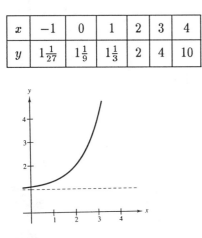

37. Sketch the graph of $f(x) = e^{2x}$.

Solution:

$f(x) = e^{2x}$

x	0	1	2	-1	-2
$f(x)$	1	7.39	54.60	0.135	0.02

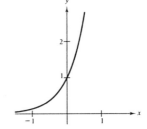

43. Use the table in the textbook to determine the balance A for \$2500 invested at 12% for 20 years and compounded n times per year.

Solution:

$$A = P\left(1 + \frac{r}{n}\right)^{nt}$$

$P = 2500, \quad r = 0.12, \quad t = 20$

–CONTINUED ON NEXT PAGE–

43. –CONTINUED–

When $n = 1$, $\quad A = 2500\left(1 + \dfrac{0.12}{1}\right)^{(1)(20)} \quad \approx \$24{,}115.73$

When $n = 2$, $\quad A = 2500\left(1 + \dfrac{0.12}{2}\right)^{(2)(20)} \quad \approx \$25{,}714.29$

When $n = 4$, $\quad A = 2500\left(1 + \dfrac{0.12}{4}\right)^{(4)(20)} \quad \approx \$26{,}602.23$

When $n = 12$, $\quad A = 2500\left(1 + \dfrac{0.12}{12}\right)^{(12)(20)} \quad \approx \$27{,}231.38$

When $n = 365$, $A = 2500\left(1 + \dfrac{0.12}{365}\right)^{(365)(20)} \quad \approx \$27{,}547.07$

For continuous compounding, $A = Pe^{rt}$, $\quad A = 2500e^{(0.12)(20)} \approx \$27{,}557.94$

n	1	2	4	12	365	Continuous compounding
A	\$24,115.73	\$25,714.29	\$26,602.23	\$27,231.38	\$27,547.07	\$27,557.94

45. Use the table in the textbook to determine the amount of money P that should be invested at 9% compounded continuously to produce a balance of \$100,000 in t years.

Solution:

$$A = Pe^{rt}$$
$$100{,}000 = Pe^{0.09t}$$
$$\dfrac{100{,}000}{e^{0.09t}} = P$$
$$P = 100{,}000e^{-0.09t}$$

–CONTINUED ON NEXT PAGE–

45. –CONTINUED–

When $t = 1$, $P = 100,000e^{-0.09(1)} \approx \$91,393.12$

When $t = 10$, $P = 100,000e^{-0.09(10)} \approx \$40,656.97$

When $t = 20$, $P = 100,000e^{-0.09(20)} \approx \$16,529.89$

When $t = 30$, $P = 100,000e^{-0.09(30)} \approx \$6,720.55$

When $t = 40$, $P = 100,000e^{-0.09(40)} \approx \$2,732.37$

When $t = 50$, $P = 100,000e^{-0.09(50)} \approx \$1,110.90$

t	1	10	20	30	40	50
P	\$91,393.12	\$40,656.97	\$16,529.89	\$6,720.55	\$2,732.37	\$1,110.90

49. On the day of your grandchild's birth, you deposited \$25,000 in a trust fund that pays 8.75% interest, compounded continuously. Determine the balance in this account on your grandchild's 25th birthday.

Solution:

$$A = 25,000e^{(0.0875)(25)} \approx \$222,822.57$$

51. The demand equation for a certain product is given by $p = 500 - 0.5e^{0.004x}$. Find the price p for a demand of (a) $x = 1000$ units and (b) $x = 1500$ units.

Solution:

(a) $x = 1000$

$p = 500 - 0.5e^4 \approx \$472.70$

(b) $x = 1500$

$p = 500 - 0.5e^6 \approx \$298.29$

55. Let Q represent the mass of radium (Ra^{226}) whose half-life is 1620 years. The quantity of radium present after t years is given by

$$Q = 25 \left(\frac{1}{2}\right)^{t/1620}.$$

(a) Determine the initial quantity (when $t = 0$).

(b) Determine the quantity present after 1000 years.

(c) Sketch the graph of this function over the interval $t = 0$ to $t = 5000$.

–CONTINUED ON NEXT PAGE–

55. –CONTINUED–

Solution:

(a) When $t = 0$, $Q = 25\left(\dfrac{1}{2}\right)^{0/1620} = 25(1) = 25$ units

(b) When $t = 1000$, $Q = 25\left(\dfrac{1}{2}\right)^{1000/1620} \approx 16.297$ units

(c)

t	0	1000	2000	3000	4000	5000
Q	25	16.297	10.624	6.926	4.515	2.943

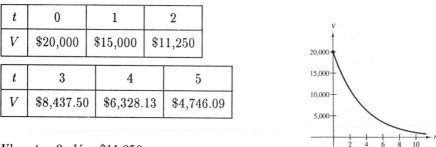

59. After t years, the value of a car that cost you $20,000 is given by

$$V(t) = 20{,}000 \left(\frac{3}{4}\right)^t.$$

Sketch a graph of the function and determine the value of the car two years after it was purchased.

Solution:

t	0	1	2
V	$20,000	$15,000	$11,250

t	3	4	5
V	$8,437.50	$6,328.13	$4,746.09

When $t = 2$, $V = \$11{,}250$.

61. Given the exponential function $f(x) = a^x$, show that (a) $f(u + v) = f(u) \cdot f(v)$ and (b) $f(2x) = [f(x)]^2$.

Solution:

(a) $f(u + v) = a^{u+v}$
$\qquad\qquad = a^u \cdot a^v = f(u) \cdot f(v)$

(b) $f(2x) = a^{2x}$
$\qquad\qquad = (a^x)^2 = [f(x)]^2$

SECTION 6.2

Logarithmic Functions

■ You should know that a function of the form $y = \log_b M$, where $b > 0$, $b \neq 1$, and $M > 0$, is called a logarithm of M to base b.

■ You should be able to convert from logarithmic form to exponential form and vice versa.
$$y = \log_b M \iff b^y = M$$

■ You should know the following properties of logarithms.

(a) $\log_a 1 = 0$ (b) $\log_a a = 1$ (c) $\log_a a^x = x$

■ You should know the definition of the natural logarithmic function.
$$\log_e x = \ln x, \quad x > 0$$

■ You should know the properties of the natural logarithmic function.

(a) $\ln 1 = 0$ (b) $\ln e = 1$ (c) $\ln e^x = x$

■ You should be able to graph logarithmic functions.

Solutions to Selected Exercises

5. Evaluate $\log_{16} 4$ without using a calculator.

Solution:
$$\log_{16} 4 = \log_{16} \sqrt{16}$$
$$= \log_{16} 16^{1/2} = \tfrac{1}{2}$$

9. Evaluate $\log_{10} 0.01$ without using a calculator.

Solution:
$$\log_{10} 0.01 = \log_{10} \tfrac{1}{100}$$
$$= \log_{10} 10^{-2} = -2$$

13. Evaluate $\ln e^{-2}$ without using a calculator.

Solution:
$$\ln e^{-2} = -2$$

17. Use the definition of a logarithm to write $5^3 = 125$ in logarithmic form.

Solution:
$$5^3 = 125$$
$$\log_5 125 = 3$$

23. Use the definition of a logarithm to write $e^3 = 20.0855\ldots$ in logarithmic form.

Solution:

$$e^3 = 20.0855\ldots$$

$$\log_e 20.0855\ldots = 3$$

$$\ln 20.0855\ldots = 3$$

27. Use a calculator to evaluate $\log_{10} 345$. Round your answer to three decimal places.

Solution:

$$\log_{10} 345 = 2.537819095\ldots \approx 2.538$$

33. Use a calculator to evaluate $\ln(1 + \sqrt{3})$. Round your answer to three decimal places.

Solution:

$$\ln(1 + \sqrt{3}) = 1.005052539\ldots \approx 1.005$$

37. Demonstrate that $f(x) = e^x$ and $g(x) = \ln x$ are inverses of each other by sketching their graphs on the same coordinate plane.

Solution:

x	-2	-1	0	1	2	3
$f(x)$	0.135	0.368	1	2.718	7.389	20.086
$g(x)$	—	—	—	0	0.693	1.097

The graph of g is obtained by reflecting the graph of f about the line $y = x$.

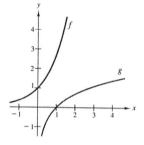

41. Use the graph of $y = \ln x$ to match $f(x) = -\ln(x + 2)$ to its graph.

Solution:

$$f(x) = -\ln(x + 2)$$

Reflection and horizontal shift two units to the left
Vertical asymptote: $x = -2$
x-intercept: $(-1, 0)$
Matches graph (a)

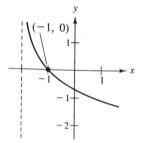

47. Find the domain, vertical asymptote, and x-intercept of $h(x) = \log_4(x - 3)$, and sketch its graph.

Solution:

$h(x) = \log_4(x - 3)$

Domain: $x - 3 > 0 \Rightarrow x > 3$
The domain is $(3, \infty)$.
Vertical asymptote: $x - 3 = 0 \Rightarrow x = 3$
The vertical asymptote is the line $x = 3$.
x-intercept: $\log_4(x - 3) = 0$
$x - 3 = 4^0$
$x - 3 = 1 \Rightarrow x = 4$
The x-intercept is $(4, 0)$.

x	3.5	4	5	7
$h(x)$	-0.5	0	0.5	1

51. Find the domain, vertical asymptote, and x-intercept of $y = \log_{10}(x/5)$, and sketch its graph.

Solution:

$y = \log_{10}\left(\dfrac{x}{5}\right)$

Domain: $\dfrac{x}{5} > 0 \Rightarrow x > 0$

The domain is $(0, \infty)$.

Vertical asymptote: $\dfrac{x}{5} = 0 \Rightarrow x = 0$

The vertical asymptote is the y-axis.

x-intercept: $\log_{10}\left(\dfrac{x}{5}\right) = 0$

$\dfrac{x}{5} = 10^0$

$\dfrac{x}{5} = 1 \Rightarrow x = 5$

The x-intercept is $(5, 0)$.

x	1	2	3	4
y	-0.699	-0.398	-0.222	-0.097

x	5	6	7
y	0	0.079	0.146

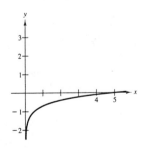

57. Students in a mathematics class were given an exam and then retested monthly with an equivalent exam. The average score for the class was given by the human memory model $f(t) = 80 - 17 \log_{10}(t + 1)$, $0 \le t \le 12$, where t is the time in months.

(a) What was the average score on the original exam $(t = 0)$?

(b) What was the average score after four months?

(c) What was the average score after ten months?

Solution:

(a) $f(0) = 80 - 17 \log_{10} 1 = 80.0$

(b) $f(4) = 80 - 17 \log_{10} 5 \approx 68.1$

(c) $f(10) = 80 - 17 \log_{10} 11 \approx 62.3$

61. Use the model $y = 80.4 - 11 \ln x$ which approximates the minimum required ventilation rate in terms of the air space per child in a public school classroom. In the model, x is the air space per child in cubic feet and y is the ventilation rate in cubic feet per minute. Use the model to approximate the required ventilation rate if there are 300 cubic feet of air space per child.

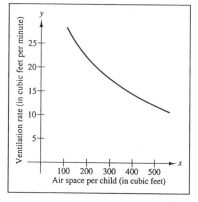

Solution:

$$y = 80.4 - 11 \ln 300 \approx 17.658 \text{ cubic feet per minute}$$

67. The work (in foot-pounds) done in compressing an initial volume of 9 cubic feet at a pressure of 15 pounds per square inch to a volume of 3 cubic feet is $W = 19{,}440(\ln 9 - \ln 3)$. Find W.

Solution:

$$W = 19{,}440(\ln 9 - \ln 3) \approx 21{,}357.023 \text{ foot-pounds}$$

69. (a) Use a calculator to complete the table (shown in the textbook) for the function

$$f(x) = \frac{\ln x}{x}.$$

(b) Use the table in part (a) to determine what $f(x)$ approaches as x increases without bound.

Solution:

(a)

x	1	5	10	10^2	10^4	10^6
$f(x)$	0	0.322	0.230	0.046	0.00092	0.0000138

(b) As $x \to \infty$, $f(x) \to 0$.

SECTION 6.3

Properties of Logarithms

- You should know the following properties of logarithms.

  (a) $\log_a(uv) = \log_a u + \log_a v$

  (b) $\log_a(u/v) = \log_a u - \log_a v$

  (c) $\log_a u^n = n \log_a u$

  (d) $\log_a x = \dfrac{\log_b x}{\log_b a}$

- You should be able to rewrite logarithmic expressions.

Solutions to Selected Exercises

1. Use the change of base formula to write $\log_3 5$ as a multiple of a common logarithm.

Solution:

$$\log_3 5 = \frac{\log_{10} 5}{\log_{10} 3}$$

5. Use the change of base formula to write $\log_3 5$ as a multiple of a natural logarithm.

Solution:

$$\log_3 5 = \frac{\ln 5}{\ln 3}$$

9. Evaluate $\log_3 7$ using the change of base formula. Do the problem twice; once with common logarithms and once with natural logarithms. Round to three decimal places.

Solution:

$$\log_3 7 = \frac{\log_{10} 7}{\log_{10} 3} \approx 1.771$$

$$\log_3 7 = \frac{\ln 7}{\ln 3} \approx 1.771$$

13. Evaluate $\log_9(0.4)$ using the change of base formula. Do the problem twice; once with common logarithms and once with natural logarithms. Round to three decimal places.

Solution:

$$\log_9(0.4) = \frac{\log_{10} 0.4}{\log_{10} 9} \approx -0.417$$

$$\log_9(0.4) = \frac{\ln 0.4}{\ln 9} \approx -0.417$$

17. Use the properties of logarithms to write $\log_{10} 5x$ as a sum, difference and/or multiple of logarithms.

Solution:

$$\log_{10} 5x = \log_{10} 5 + \log_{10} x$$

21. Use the properties of logarithms to write $\log_8 x^4$ as a sum, difference, and/or multiple of logarithms.

Solution:

$$\log_8 x^4 = 4 \log_8 x$$

25. Use the properties of logarithms to write $\ln xyz$ as a sum, difference, and/or multiple of logarithms.

Solution:

$$\ln xyz = \ln[x(yz)]$$
$$= \ln x + \ln yz$$
$$= \ln x + \ln y + \ln z$$

29. Use the properties of logarithms to write $\ln z(z-1)^2$ as a sum, difference and/or multiple of logarithms.

Solution:

$$\ln z(z-1)^2 = \ln z + \ln(z-1)^2$$
$$= \ln z + 2\ln(z-1)$$

33. Use the properties of logarithms to write the following expression as a sum, difference, and/or multiple of logarithms.

$$\ln \frac{x^4 \sqrt{y}}{z^5}$$

Solution:

$$\ln \frac{x^4 \sqrt{y}}{z^5} = \ln x^4 \sqrt{y} - \ln z^5$$
$$= \ln x^4 + \ln \sqrt{y} - \ln z^5$$
$$= 4\ln x + \frac{1}{2}\ln y - 5\ln z$$

35. Use the properties of logarithms to write the following expression as a sum, difference, and/or multiple of logarithms.

$$\log_b \frac{x^2}{y^2 z^3}$$

Solution:

$$\log_b \frac{x^2}{y^2 z^3} = \log_b x^2 - \log_b y^2 z^3$$
$$= \log_b x^2 - [\log_b y^2 + \log_b z^3]$$
$$= 2\log_b x - 2\log_b y - 3\log_b z$$

39. Write $\log_4 z - \log_4 y$ as the logarithm of a single quantity.

Solution:

$$\log_4 z - \log_4 y = \log_4 \frac{z}{y}$$

45. Write $\ln x - 3\ln(x+1)$ as the logarithm of a single quantity.

Solution:

$$\ln x - 3\ln(x+1) = \ln x - \ln(x+1)^3$$
$$= \ln \frac{x}{(x+1)^3}$$

49. Write $\ln x - 2[\ln(x+2) + \ln(x-2)]$ as the logarithm of a single quantity.

Solution:

$$\ln x - 2[\ln(x+2) + \ln(x-2)] = \ln x - 2\ln(x+2)(x-2)$$
$$= \ln x - 2\ln(x^2 - 4)$$
$$= \ln x - \ln(x^2-4)^2$$
$$= \ln \frac{x}{(x^2-4)^2}$$

53. Write $\frac{1}{3}[\ln y + 2\ln(y+4)] - \ln(y-1)$ as the logarithm of a single quantity.

Solution:

$$\frac{1}{3}[\ln y + 2\ln(y+4)] - \ln(y-1) = \frac{1}{3}[\ln y + \ln(y+4)^2] - \ln(y-1)$$

$$= \frac{1}{3}\ln[y(y+4)^2] - \ln(y-1)$$

$$= \ln\sqrt[3]{y(y+4)^2} - \ln(y-1)$$

$$= \ln\frac{\sqrt[3]{y(y+4)^2}}{y-1}$$

57. Approximate $\log_b 6$ using the properties of logarithms, given $\log_b 2 \approx 0.3562$ and $\log_b 3 \approx 0.5646$.

Solution:

$$\log_b 6 = \log_b(2 \cdot 3) = \log_b 2 + \log_b 3 \approx 0.3562 + 0.5646 = 0.9208$$

63. Approximate $\log_b \sqrt{2}$ using the properties of logarithms, given $\log_b 2 \approx 0.3562$.

Solution:

$$\log_b \sqrt{2} = \log_b(2^{1/2}) = \frac{1}{2}\log_b 2 \approx \frac{1}{2}(0.3562) = 0.1781$$

65. Approximate $\log_b \frac{1}{4}$ using the properties of logarithms, given $\log_b 2 \approx 0.3562$.

Solution:

$$\log_b \frac{1}{4} = \log_b 1 - \log_b 4 = 0 - \log_b 2^2 = -2\log_b 2 \approx -2(0.3562) = -0.7124$$

69. Approximate the following using the properties of logarithms, given $\log_b 2 \approx 0.3562$ and $\log_b 3 \approx 0.5646$.

$$\log_b\left[\frac{(4.5)^3}{\sqrt{3}}\right]$$

Solution:

$$\log_b\left[\frac{(4.5)^3}{\sqrt{3}}\right] = 3\log_b 4.5 - \frac{1}{2}\log_b 3$$

$$= 3\log_b \frac{9}{2} - \frac{1}{2}\log_b 3$$

$$= 3[\log_b 9 - \log_b 2] - \frac{1}{2}\log_b 3$$

$$= 3[2\log_b 3 - \log_b 2] - \frac{1}{2}\log_b 3$$

$$\approx 3[2(0.5646) - 0.3562] - \frac{1}{2}(0.5646) = 2.0367$$

73. Find the exact value of $\log_4 16^{1.2}$.

Solution:

$$\log_4 16^{1.2} = 1.2 \log_4 16 = 1.2 \log_4 4^2 = (1.2)(2) \log_4 4 = (2.4)(1) = 2.4$$

77. Use the properties of logarithms to simplify $\log_4 8$.

Solution:

$$\log_4 8 = \log_4 2^3 = 3 \log_4 2 = 3 \log_4 \sqrt{4} = 3 \log_4 4^{1/2} = 3 \left(\tfrac{1}{2}\right) \log_4 4 = \tfrac{3}{2}$$

81. Use the properties of logarithms to simplify $\log_5 \frac{1}{250}$.

Solution:

$$\log_5 \tfrac{1}{250} = \log_5 1 - \log_5 250 = 0 - \log_5(125 \cdot 2)$$
$$= -\log_5(5^3 \cdot 2) = -[\log_5 5^3 + \log_5 2]$$
$$= -[3 \log_5 5 + \log_5 2] = -3 - \log_5 2$$

85. The relationship between the number of decibels β and the intensity of a sound I in watts per meter squared is given by

$$\beta = 10 \log_{10}\left(\frac{I}{10^{-16}}\right).$$

Use properties of logarithms to write the formula in simpler form, and determine the number of decibels of a sound with an intensity of 10^{-10} watts per meter squared.

Solution:

$$\beta = 10 \log_{10}\left(\frac{I}{10^{-16}}\right)$$
$$= 10 \left[\log_{10} I - \log_{10} 10^{-16}\right]$$
$$= 10[\log_{10} I + 16]$$
$$= 160 + 10 \log_{10} I$$

When $I = 10^{-10}$, we have

$$\beta = 160 + 10 \log_{10} 10^{-10}$$
$$= 160 + 10(-10)$$
$$= 60 \text{ decibels.}$$

87. Prove that $\log_b \dfrac{u}{v} = \log_b u - \log_b v$.

Solution:

Let $x = \log_b u$ and $y = \log_b v$, then $b^x = u$ and $b^y = v$.

$$\frac{u}{v} = \frac{b^x}{b^y} = b^{x-y}$$
$$\log_b \left(\frac{u}{v}\right) = \log_b(b^{x-y})$$
$$= x - y$$
$$= \log_b u - \log_b v$$

SECTION 6.4

Solving Exponential and Logarithmic Equations

- You should be able to solve exponential and logarithmic equations.

- To solve an exponential equation, take the logarithm of both sides.

- To solve a logarithmic equation, rewrite it in exponential form.

Solutions to Selected Exercises

5. Solve $\left(\frac{3}{4}\right)^x = \frac{27}{64}$ for x without a calculator.

Solution:

$$\left(\frac{3}{4}\right)^x = \frac{27}{64}$$

$$\left(\frac{3}{4}\right)^x = \left(\frac{3}{4}\right)^3$$

$$x = 3$$

9. Solve $\log_{10} x = -1$ for x without a calculator.

Solution:

$$\log_{10} x = -1$$

$$x = 10^{-1} = \tfrac{1}{10}$$

13. Apply the inverse properties of $\ln x$ and e^x to simplify $e^{\ln(5x+2)}$.

Solution:

$$e^{\ln(5x+2)} = 5x + 2$$

17. Solve $e^x = 10$. Round to three decimal places.

Solution:

$$e^x = 10$$

$$x = \ln 10 \approx 2.303$$

21. Solve $e^x - 5 = 10$. Round to three decimal places.

Solution:

$$e^x - 5 = 10$$

$$e^x = 15$$

$$x = \ln 15 \approx 2.708$$

27. Solve $500e^{-x} = 300$. Round to three decimal places.

Solution:

$$500e^{-x} = 300$$

$$e^{-x} = \tfrac{3}{5}$$

$$-x = \ln \tfrac{3}{5}$$

$$x = -\ln \tfrac{3}{5} = \ln \tfrac{5}{3} \approx 0.511$$

31. Solve $e^{2x} - 4e^x - 5 = 0$. Round to three decimal places.

Solution:

$$e^{2x} - 4e^x - 5 = 0$$

$$(e^x + 1)(e^x - 5) = 0$$

$$e^x + 1 = 0 \quad \text{or} \quad e^x - 5 = 0$$

$$e^x = -1 \qquad\qquad e^x = 5$$

$$\text{No solution} \qquad x = \ln 5 \approx 1.609$$

33. Solve $3(1 + e^{2x}) = 4$. Round to three decimal places.

Solution:

$$3(1 + e^{2x}) = 4$$

$$1 + e^{2x} = \tfrac{4}{3}$$

$$e^{2x} = \tfrac{1}{3}$$

$$2x = \ln \tfrac{1}{3}$$

$$x = \tfrac{1}{2} \ln \tfrac{1}{3} \approx -0.549$$

37. Solve $10^x = 42$. Round to three decimal places.

Solution:

$$10^x = 42$$

$$x = \log_{10} 42 \approx 1.623$$

41. Solve $5^{-t/2} = 0.20$. Round to three decimal places.

Solution:

$$5^{-t/2} = 0.20$$

$$5^{-t/2} = \frac{1}{5}$$

$$5^{-t/2} = 5^{-1}$$

$$-\frac{t}{2} = -1$$

$$t = 2$$

45. Solve $3\left(5^{x-1}\right) = 21$. Round to three decimal places.

Solution:

$$3\left(5^{x-1}\right) = 21$$

$$5^{x-1} = 7$$

$$\ln 5^{x-1} = \ln 7$$

$$(x - 1)\ln 5 = \ln 7$$

$$x - 1 = \frac{\ln 7}{\ln 5}$$

$$x = 1 + \frac{\ln 7}{\ln 5} \approx 2.209$$

49. Solve $\left(1 + \frac{0.10}{12}\right)^{12t} = 2$. Round to three decimal places.

Solution:

$$\left(1 + \frac{0.10}{12}\right)^{12t} = 2$$

$$\ln\left(1 + \frac{0.10}{12}\right)^{12t} = \ln 2$$

$$12t \ln\left(1 + \frac{0.10}{12}\right) = \ln 2$$

$$t = \frac{\ln 2}{12 \ln\left(1 + \frac{0.10}{12}\right)}$$

$$\approx 6.960$$

53. Solve $\ln 2x = 2.4$. Round to three decimal places.

Solution:

$$\ln 2x = 2.4$$
$$2x = e^{2.4}$$
$$x = \frac{e^{2.4}}{2} \approx 5.512$$

57. Solve $\ln \sqrt{x+2} = 1$. Round to three decimal places.

Solution:

$$\ln \sqrt{x+2} = 1$$
$$\sqrt{x+2} = e^1$$
$$x + 2 = e^2$$
$$x = -2 + e^2 \approx 5.389$$

61. Solve $\log_{10}(z - 3) = 2$. Round to three decimal places.

Solution:

$$\log_{10}(z - 3) = 2$$
$$z - 3 = 10^2$$
$$z = 10^2 + 3 = 103$$

63. Solve $\log_{10}(x + 4) - \log_{10} x = \log_{10}(x + 2)$. Round to three decimal places.

Solution:

$$\log_{10}(x + 4) - \log_{10} x = \log_{10}(x + 2)$$
$$\log_{10}\left(\frac{x + 4}{x}\right) = \log_{10}(x + 2)$$
$$\frac{x + 4}{x} = x + 2$$
$$x + 4 = x^2 + 2x$$
$$0 = x^2 + x - 4$$
$$x = \frac{-1 \pm \sqrt{17}}{2} = -\frac{1}{2} \pm \frac{\sqrt{17}}{2} \qquad \text{Quadratic Formula}$$
$$x = -\frac{1}{2} + \frac{\sqrt{17}}{2} \qquad \left(\text{since } -\frac{1}{2} - \frac{\sqrt{17}}{2} \text{ is not in the domain}\right)$$

Choosing the positive value of x (the negative value is extraneous), we have $-\frac{1}{2} + \frac{\sqrt{17}}{2} \approx 1.562$.

67. Solve $\ln(x + 5) = \ln(x - 1) - \ln(x + 1)$.
Round to three decimal places.

Solution:

$$\ln(x + 5) = \ln(x - 1) - \ln(x + 1)$$

$$\ln(x + 5) = \ln\left(\frac{x - 1}{x + 1}\right)$$

$$x + 5 = \frac{x - 1}{x + 1}$$

$$(x + 5)(x + 1) = x - 1$$

$$x^2 + 6x + 5 = x - 1$$

$$x^2 + 5x + 6 = 0$$

$$(x + 2)(x + 3) = 0$$

$$x = -2 \text{ or } x = -3$$

Both of these solutions are extraneous, so
the equation has no solution.

71. Find the time required for a $1000
investment to double at an interest rate of
$r = 0.085$ compounded continuously.

Solution:

$$A = Pe^{rt}$$

$$2000 = 1000e^{0.085t}$$

$$2 = e^{0.085t}$$

$$\ln 2 = 0.085t$$

$$\frac{\ln 2}{0.085} = t$$

$$t \approx 8.2 \text{ years}$$

75. The demand equation for a certain product is given by $p = 500 - 0.5(e^{0.004x})$. Find the
demand x for a price of (a) $p = \$350$ and (b) $p = \$300$.

Solution:

(a) $\quad 350 = 500 - 0.5(e^{0.004x})$

$\quad\quad -150 = -0.5(e^{0.004x})$

$\quad\quad\quad 300 = e^{0.004x}$

$\quad\quad 0.004x = \ln 300$

$$x = \frac{\ln 300}{0.004} \approx 1426 \text{ units}$$

(b) $\quad 300 = 500 - 0.5(e^{0.004x})$

$\quad\quad -200 = -0.5(e^{0.004x})$

$\quad\quad\quad 400 = e^{0.004x}$

$\quad\quad 0.004x = \ln 400$

$$x = \frac{\ln 400}{0.004} \approx 1498 \text{ units}$$

SECTION 6.5

Exponential and Logarithmic Applications

■ You should be able to solve compound interest problems.

(a) Compound interest formulas:

1. $A = P\left(1 + \dfrac{r}{n}\right)^{nt}$

2. $A = Pe^{rt}$

(b) Doubling time:

1. $t = \dfrac{\ln 2}{n \ln[1 + (r/n)]}$, n compoundings per year

2. $t = \dfrac{\ln 2}{r}$, continuous compounding

(c) Effective yield:

1. Effective yield $= \left(1 + \dfrac{r}{n}\right)^{n} - 1$, n compoundings per year

2. Effective yield $= e^r - 1$, continuous compounding

■ You should be able to solve growth and decay problems.

$$Q(t) = Ce^{kt}$$

(a) If $k > 0$, the population grows.

(b) If $k < 0$, the population decays.

(c) Ratio of Carbon 14 to Carbon 12 is $R(t) = \dfrac{1}{10^{12}} e^{-t/8223}$

■ You should be able to solve logistics model problems.

$$y = \dfrac{a}{1 + be^{-(x-c)/d}}$$

■ You should be able to solve intensity model problems.

$$S = k \log_{10} \dfrac{I}{I_0}$$

Solutions to Selected Exercises

5. Five hundred dollars is deposited into an account with continuously compounded interest. If the balance is $1292.85 after 10 years, find the annual percentage rate, the effective yield, and the time to double.

Solution:

$P = 500$, $A = 1292.85$, $t = 10$

$A = Pe^{rt}$

$$1292.85 = 500e^{10r}$$

$$\frac{1292.85}{500} = e^{10r}$$

$$10r = \ln\left(\frac{1292.85}{500}\right)$$

$$r = \frac{1}{10}\ln\left(\frac{1292.85}{100}\right) \approx 0.095 = 9.5\%$$

Effective yield $= e^{0.095} - 1 \approx 0.09966 \approx 9.97\%$

Time to double: $1000 = 500e^{0.095t}$

$$2 = e^{0.095t}$$

$$0.095t = \ln 2$$

$$t = \frac{\ln 2}{0.095} \approx 7.30 \text{ years}$$

9. Five thousand dollars is deposited into an account with continuously compounded interest. If the effective yield is 8.33%, find the annual percentage rate, the time to double, and the amount after 10 years.

Solution:

$P = 5000$

Effective yield $= 8.33\%$

$0.0833 = e^r - 1$

$$r = \ln 1.0833 \approx 0.0800 = 8\%$$

Time to double: $10{,}000 = 5000e^{0.08t}$

$$t = \frac{\ln 2}{0.08} \approx 8.66 \text{ years}$$

After 10 years: $A = 5000e^{0.08(10)} = \$11{,}127.70$

13. Determine the time necessary for $1000 to double if it is invested at 11% compounded (a) annually, (b) monthly, (c) daily, and (d) continuously.

Solution:

$P = 1000, \ r = 11\%$

(a) $n = 1$

$$t = \frac{\ln 2}{\ln(1 + 0.11)} \approx 6.642 \text{ years}$$

(b) $n = 12$

$$t = \frac{\ln 2}{12 \ln\left(1 + \frac{0.11}{12}\right)} \approx 6.330 \text{ years}$$

(c) $n = 365$

$$t = \frac{\ln 2}{365 \ln\left(1 + \frac{0.11}{365}\right)} \approx 6.302 \text{ years}$$

(d) Continuously

$$t = \frac{\ln 2}{0.11} \approx 6.301 \text{ years}$$

17. The half-life of the isotope Ra^{226} is 1620 years. If the initial quantity is 10 grams, how much will remain after 1000 years, and after 10,000 years?

Solution:

$$Q(t) = Ce^{kt}$$

$$Q = 10 \quad \text{when } t = 0 \Rightarrow 10 = Ce^0 \Rightarrow 10 = C$$

$$Q(t) = 10e^{kt}$$

$$Q = 5 \quad \text{when } t = 1620$$

$$5 = 10e^{1620k}$$

$$k = \frac{1}{1620} \ln\left(\frac{1}{2}\right)$$

$$Q(t) = 10e^{[\ln(1/2)/1620]t}$$

When $t = 1000, \ Q(t) = 10e^{[\ln(1/2)/1620](1000)} \approx 6.52$ grams.

When $t = 10,000, \ Q(t) = 10e^{[\ln(1/2)/1620](10000)} \approx 0.14$ gram.

21. The half-life of the isotope Pu^{230} is 24,360 years. If 2.1 grams remain after 1000 years, what is the initial quantity and how much will remain after 10,000 years?

Solution:

$$y = Ce^{[\ln(1/2)/24360]t}$$

$$2.1 = Ce^{[\ln(1/2)/24360](1000)}$$

$$C \approx 2.16$$

The initial quantity is 2.16 grams.

When $t = 10,000, \ y = 2.16e^{[\ln(1/2)/24360](10000)} \approx 1.63$ grams.

23. Find the constant k such that the exponential function $y = Ce^{kt}$ passes through the points (0, 1) and (4, 10).

Solution:

$$y = Ce^{kt}$$

Since the graph passes through the point (0, 1), we have

$$1 = Ce^{k(0)},$$

$$1 = C.$$

$$y = e^{kt}$$

Since the graph passes through the point (4, 10), we have

$$10 = e^{4k},$$

$$4k = \ln 10$$

$$k = \frac{\ln 10}{4} \approx 0.5756.$$

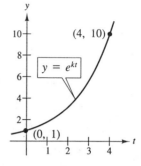

27. The population P of a city is given by $P = 105{,}300e^{0.015t}$ where t is the time in years with $t = 0$ corresponding to 1990. According to this model, in what year will the city have a population of 150,000?

Solution:

$$150{,}000 = 105{,}300e^{0.015t}$$

$$0.015t = \ln\left(\frac{150{,}000}{105{,}300}\right)$$

$$t = \frac{1}{0.015} \ln\left(\frac{150{,}000}{105{,}300}\right) \approx 23.588 \text{ years}$$

$$1990 + 23 = 2013$$

The city will have a population of 150,000 in the year 2013.

31. The population of Dhaka, Bangladesh was 4.22 million in 1990, and its projected population for the year 2000 is 6.49 million. (*Source:* U.S. Bureau of Census) Find the exponential growth model $y = Ce^{kt}$ for the population growth of Dhaka by letting $t = 0$ correspond to 1990. Use the model to predict the population of the city in 2010.

–CONTINUED ON NEXT PAGE–

31. –CONTINUED–

Solution:

$$P = Ce^{kt}$$

$$4.22 = Ce^{k(0)} \Rightarrow C = 4.22$$

$$6.49 = 4.22e^{10k}$$

$$\frac{6.49}{4.22} = e^{10k}$$

$$k = \frac{1}{10}\ln\left(\frac{6.49}{4.22}\right) \approx 0.0430$$

$$P = 4.22e^{0.0430t}$$

When $t = 20$: $P \approx 9.97$ million.

35. The half-life of radioactive radium (Ra^{226}) is 1620 years. What percentage of a present amount of radioactive radium will remain after 100 years?

Solution:

$$Q(t) = Ce^{kt}$$

$$\tfrac{1}{2}C = Ce^{k(1620)}$$

$$\tfrac{1}{2} = e^{1620k}$$

$$k = \tfrac{1}{1620}\ln(\tfrac{1}{2}) \approx -0.0004$$

$$Q(t) = Ce^{-0.0004t}$$

When $t = 100$: $Q(100) \approx 0.961C = 96.1\%$ of C.

39. The sales S (in thousands of units) of a new product after it has been on the market t years are given by $S(t) = 100(1 - e^{kt})$.

(a) Find S as a function of t if 15,000 units have been sold after one year.

(b) How many units will be sold after five years?

Solution:

(a) $S(t) = 100(1 - e^{kt})$

$\qquad S = 15$ when $t = 1$

$\qquad 15 = 100(1 - e^k)$

$\qquad 0.15 = 1 - e^k$

$\qquad e^k = 0.85$

$\qquad k = \ln 0.85 \approx -0.1625$

$\qquad S(t) = 100[1 - e^{-0.1625t}]$

(b) $S(5) = 100[1 - e^{-0.1625t}]$

$\qquad \approx 55.625$ thousands of units

$\qquad = 55{,}625$ units

41. A certain lake was stocked with 500 fish and the fish population increased according to the logistics curve

$$p(t) = \frac{10{,}000}{1 + 19e^{-t/5}}$$

where t is measured in months (see figure).

(a) Estimate the fish population after 5 months.

(b) After how many months will the fish population be 2000?

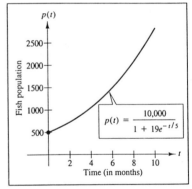

Solution:

$$p(t) = \frac{10{,}000}{1 + 19e^{-t/5}}$$

(a) $p(5) = \dfrac{10{,}000}{1 + 19e^{-1}} \approx 1252$ fish

(b) $\qquad 2000 = \dfrac{10{,}000}{1 + 19e^{-t/5}}$

$\qquad\qquad 1 + 19e^{-t/5} = 5$

$\qquad\qquad e^{-t/5} = \dfrac{4}{19}$

$\qquad\qquad -\dfrac{t}{5} = \ln\left(\dfrac{4}{19}\right)$

$\qquad\qquad t = -5\ln\left(\dfrac{4}{19}\right) \approx 7.8$ months

45. Find the magnitude R of an earthquake of intensity I (let $I_0 = 1$).

(a) $I = 80{,}500{,}000$ (b) $I = 48{,}275{,}000$

Solution:

$$R = \log_{10} \frac{I}{I_0} = \log_{10} I \text{ since } I_0 = 1$$

(a) $R = \log_{10} 80{,}500{,}000 \approx 7.9$ (b) $R = \log_{10} 48{,}275{,}000 \approx 7.7$

47. The intensity level β, in decibels, of a sound wave is defined by

$$\beta(I) = 10 \log_{10} \frac{I}{I_0}$$

where I_0 is an intensity of 10^{-16} watts per square centimeter, corresponding roughly to the faintest sound that can be heard. Determine $\beta(I)$ for the following conditions.

(a) $I = 10^{-14}$ watts per square centimeter (whisper)

(b) $I = 10^{-9}$ watts per square centimeter (busy street corner)

(c) $I = 10^{-6.5}$ watts per square centimeter (air hammer)

(d) $I = 10^{-4}$ watts per square centimeter (threshold of pain)

Solution:

$$\beta(I) = 10 \log_{10} \frac{I}{I_0} \text{ where } I_0 = 10^{-16} \text{ watt/cm}^2$$

(a) $\beta(10^{-14}) = 10 \log_{10} \dfrac{10^{-14}}{10^{-16}} = 10 \log_{10} 10^2 = 20$ decibels

(b) $\beta(10^{-9}) = 10 \log_{10} \dfrac{10^{-9}}{10^{-16}} = 10 \log_{10} 10^7 = 70$ decibels

(c) $\beta(10^{-6.5}) = 10 \log_{10} \dfrac{10^{-6.5}}{10^{-16}} = 10 \log_{10} 10^{9.5} = 95$ decibels

(d) $\beta(10^{-4}) = 10 \log_{10} \dfrac{10^{-4}}{10^{-16}} = 10 \log_{10} 10^{12} = 120$ decibels

51. Use the acidity model $\text{pH} = -\log_{10}[\text{H}^+]$, where acidity (pH) is a measure of the hydrogen ion concentration $[\text{H}^+]$ (measured in moles of hydrogen per liter) of a solution. Find the pH if $[\text{H}^+] = 2.3 \times 10^{-5}$.

Solution:

$$\text{pH} = -\log_{10}[\text{H}^+] = -\log_{10}[2.3 \times 10^{-5}] \approx 4.64$$

57. At 8:30 A.M. a coroner was called to the home of a person who had died during the night. In order to estimate the time of death, the coroner took the person's temperature twice. At 9:00 A.M. the temperature was 85.7° and at 9:30 A.M. the temperature was 82.8°. From these two temperatures the coroner was able to determine that the time elapsed since death and the body temperature were related by the formula

$$t = -2.5 \ln \frac{T - 70}{98.6 - 70}$$

where t is the time in hours that has elapsed since the person died and T is the temperature (in degrees Fahrenheit) of the person's body at 9:00 A.M. Assume that the person had a normal body temperature of 98.6° at death, and that the room temperature was a constant 70°. (This formula is derived from a general cooling principle called Newton's Law of Cooling.) Use this formula to estimate the time of death of the person.

Solution:

$$t = -2.5 \ln \left(\frac{T - 70}{98.6 - 70} \right)$$

At 9:00 A.M. we have: $t = -2.5 \ln \left(\dfrac{85.7 - 70}{98.6 - 70} \right) \approx 1.5$ hours. From this we can conclude that the person died at 7:30 A.M.

REVIEW EXERCISES FOR CHAPTER 6

Solutions to Selected Exercises

5. Match $f(x) = \log_2 x$ with the sketch of its graph.

Solution:

$f(x) = \log_2 x$
Vertical asymptote: $x = 0$
Intercept: $(1,\ 0)$
Matches (c)

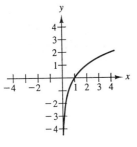

9. Sketch the graph of $g(x) = 6^{-x}$.

Solution:

$$g(x) = 6^{-x} = \left(\frac{1}{6}\right)^x$$

x	0	1	-1
$g(x)$	1	$\frac{1}{6}$	6

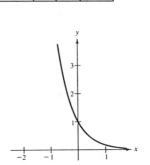

---

15. Use the table in the textbook to determine the balance A for \$3500 invested at 10.5% for 10 years and compounded n times per year.

Solution:

$n = 1:\quad A = 3500(1 + 0.105)^{10} \quad \approx \$9{,}499.28$

$n = 2:\quad A = 3500\left(1 + \dfrac{0.105}{2}\right)^{20} \quad \approx \$9{,}738.91$

$n = 4:\quad A = 3500\left(1 + \dfrac{0.105}{4}\right)^{40} \quad \approx \$9{,}867.22$

$n = 12:\quad A = 3500\left(1 + \dfrac{0.105}{12}\right)^{120} \quad \approx \$9{,}956.20$

$n = 365:\ A = 3500\left(1 + \dfrac{0.105}{365}\right)^{3650} \quad \approx \$10{,}000.27$

Continuous: $A = 3500e^{(0.105)(10)} \approx \$10{,}001.78$

n	1	2	4	12	365	Continuous compounding
A	\$9,499.28	\$9,738.91	\$9,867.22	\$9,956.20	\$10,000.27	\$10,001.78

17. Use the table in the textbook to determine the amount of money P that should be invested at 8% compounded continuously to produce a final balance of $200,000 in t years.

Solution:

$$A = Pe^{rt}$$
$$P = Ae^{-rt} = 200{,}000e^{-0.08t}$$

t	1	10	20	30	40	50
P	$184,623.27	$89,865.79	$40,379.30	$18,143.59	$8,152.44	$3,663.13

21. A solution of a certain drug contained 500 units per milliliter when prepared. It was analyzed after 40 days and found to contain 300 units per milliliter. Assuming that the rate of decomposition is proportional to the amount present, the equation giving the amount A after t days is $A = 500e^{-0.013t}$. Use this model to find A when $t = 60$.

Solution:

$$A = 500e^{-0.013(60)} \approx 229.2 \text{ units per milliliter}$$

23. A certain automobile gets 28 miles per gallon of gasoline for speeds up to 50 miles per hour. Over 50 miles per hour, the number of miles per gallon drops at the rate of 12% for each 10 miles per hour. If s is the speed and y is the number of miles per gallon, then

$$y = 28e^{0.6-0.012s}, \quad s \geq 50.$$

Use this function to complete the table shown in the textbook.

Solution:

When $s = 50$, $y = 28e^{0.6-0.012(50)} = 28$ miles per gallon

When $s = 55$, $y = 28e^{0.6-0.012(55)} \approx 26.4$ miles per gallon

When $s = 60$, $y = 28e^{0.6-0.012(60)} \approx 24.8$ miles per gallon

When $s = 65$, $y = 28e^{0.6-0.012(65)} \approx 23.4$ miles per gallon

When $s = 70$, $y = 28e^{0.6-0.012(70)} \approx 22.0$ miles per gallon

Speed	50	55	60	65	70
Miles per gallon	28	26.4	24.8	23.4	22.0

27. Sketch the graph of $f(x) = \ln x + 3$.

Solution:

$f(x) = \ln x + 3$
Domain: $(0, \infty)$

x	1	2	3	$\frac{1}{2}$	$\frac{1}{4}$
$f(x)$	3	3.69	4.10	2.31	1.61

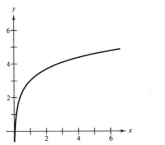

29. Sketch the graph of $h(x) = \ln(e^{x-1})$.

Solution:

$$h(x) = \ln(e^{x-1})$$
$$= (x-1)\ln e$$
$$= x - 1$$

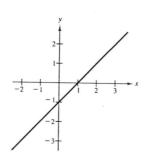

33. Evaluate $\log_{10} 1000$ without using a calculator.

Solution:

$$\log_{10} 1000 = \log_{10} 10^3 = 3$$

37. Evaluate $\ln e^7$ without using a calculator.

Solution:

$$\ln e^7 = 7 \ln e = 7(1) = 7$$

41. Evaluate $\log_4 9$ using the change of base formula. Do the problem twice; once with common logarithms and once with natural logarithms. Round to three decimal places.

Solution:

$$\log_4 9 = \frac{\log_{10} 9}{\log_{10} 4} \approx 1.585$$

$$\log_4 9 = \frac{\ln 9}{\ln 4} \approx 1.585$$

47. Use the properties of logarithms to write the following expression as a sum, difference, and/or multiple of logarithms.

$$\log_{10} \frac{5\sqrt{y}}{x^2}$$

Solution:

$$\log_{10} \frac{5\sqrt{y}}{x^2} = \log_{10} 5\sqrt{y} - \log_{10} x^2$$

$$= \log_{10} 5 + \log_{10} \sqrt{y} - \log_{10} x^2$$

$$= \log_{10} 5 + \frac{1}{2} \log_{10} y - 2 \log_{10} x$$

49. Use the properties of logarithms to write the following expression as a sum, difference, and/or multiple of logarithms.

$$\ln[(x^2 + 1)(x - 1)]$$

Solution:

$$\ln[(x^2 + 1)(x - 1)] = \ln(x^2 + 1) + \ln(x - 1)$$

53. Write $\frac{1}{2}\ln|2x - 1| - 2\ln|x + 1|$ as the logarithm of a single quantity.

Solution:

$$\frac{1}{2}\ln|2x - 1| - 2\ln|x + 1| = \ln\sqrt{|2x - 1|} - \ln(x + 1)^2 = \ln\frac{\sqrt{|2x - 1|}}{(x + 1)^2}$$

55. Write $\ln 3 + \frac{1}{3}\ln(4 - x^2) - \ln x$ as the logarithm of a single quantity.

Solution:

$$\ln 3 + \frac{1}{3}\ln(4 - x^2) - \ln x = \ln 3 + \ln \sqrt[3]{4 - x^2} - \ln x = \ln\left(3\sqrt[3]{4 - x^2}\right) - \ln x = \ln\frac{3\sqrt[3]{4 - x^2}}{x}$$

59. Determine whether the equation $\ln(x + y) = \ln x + \ln y$ is true or false.

Solution:

False, since $\ln x + \ln y = \ln(xy)$

63. Approximate $\log_b \sqrt{3}$ using the properties of logarithms given $\log_b 3 \approx 0.5646$.

Solution:

$$\log_b \sqrt{3} = \frac{1}{2}\log_b 3 \approx \frac{1}{2}(0.5646) = 0.2823$$

67. Solve $e^x = 12$. Round to three decimal places.

Solution:

$$e^x = 12$$

$$x = \ln 12 \approx 2.485$$

71. Solve $e^{2x} - 7e^x + 10 = 0$. Round to three decimal places.

Solution:

$$e^{2x} - 7e^x + 10 = 0$$

$$(e^x - 2)(e^x - 5) = 0$$

$$e^x = 2 \qquad \text{or} \quad e^x = 5$$

$$x = \ln 2 \qquad\qquad x = \ln 5$$

$$x \approx 0.693 \qquad\qquad x \approx 1.609$$

75. Solve $\ln x - \ln 3 = 2$. Round to three decimal places.

Solution:

$$\ln x - \ln 3 = 2$$

$$\ln\left(\frac{x}{3}\right) = 2$$

$$\frac{x}{3} = e^2$$

$$x = 3e^2 \approx 22.167$$

79. Find the exponential function $y = Ce^{kt}$ that passes through the points $(0, 4)$ and $\left(5, \frac{1}{2}\right)$.

Solution:

Since the graph passes through the point $(0, \ 4)$, we have

$$4 = Ce^{k(0)}$$

$$4 = C(1) \quad \text{so} \quad y = 4e^{kt}.$$

Since the graph passes through the point $\left(5, \frac{1}{2}\right)$, we have

$$\tfrac{1}{2} = 4e^{5k}$$

$$\tfrac{1}{8} = e^{5k}$$

$$5k = \ln \tfrac{1}{8}$$

$$k \approx -0.4159.$$

Thus, $y = 4e^{-0.4159t}$.

81. The demand equation for a certain product is given by $p = 500 - 0.5e^{0.004x}$. Find the demand x for a price of (a) $p = \$450$ and (b) $p = \$400$.

Solution:

(a) $p = 450$

$$450 = 500 - 0.5e^{0.004x}$$

$$0.5e^{0.004x} = 50$$

$$e^{0.004x} = 100$$

$$0.004x = \ln 100$$

$$x \approx 1151 \text{ units}$$

(b) $p = 400$

$$400 = 500 - 0.5e^{0.004x}$$

$$0.5e^{0.004x} = 100$$

$$e^{0.004x} = 200$$

$$0.004x = \ln 200$$

$$x \approx 1325 \text{ units}$$

Practice Test for Chapter 6

1. Solve for x: $x^{3/5} = 8$.

2. Solve for x: $3^{x-1} = \frac{1}{81}$.

3. Graph $f(x) = 2^{-x}$.

4. Graph $g(x) = e^x + 1$.

5. If \$5000 is invested at 9% interest, find the amount after three years if the interest is compounded (a) monthly, (b) quarterly, and (c) continuously.

6. Write the equation in logarithmic form: $7^{-2} = \frac{1}{49}$.

7. Solve for x: $x - 4 = \log_2 \frac{1}{64}$.

8. Given $\log_b 2 = 0.3562$ and $\log_b 5 = 0.8271$, evaluate $\log_b \sqrt[4]{8/25}$.

9. Write $5 \ln x - \frac{1}{2} \ln y + 6 \ln z$ as a single logarithm.

10. Using your calculator and the change of base formula, evaluate $\log_9 28$.

11. Use your calculator to solve for N: $\log_{10} N = 0.6646$.

12. Graph $y = \log_4 x$.

13. Determine the domain of
$f(x) = \log_3(x^2 - 9)$.

14. Graph $y = \ln(x - 2)$.

15. True or false: $\dfrac{\ln x}{\ln y} = \ln(x - y)$

16. Solve for x: $5^x = 41$.

17. Solve for x: $x - x^2 = \log_5 \frac{1}{25}$.

18. Solve for x: $\log_2 x + \log_2(x - 3) = 2$.

19. Solve for x: $\dfrac{e^x + e^{-x}}{3} = 4$.

20. Six thousand dollars is deposited into a fund at an annual percentage rate of 13%. Find the time required for the investment to double if the interest is compounded continuously.

CHAPTER 7

Some Topics in Analytic Geometry

SECTION 7.1

Lines

- The **inclination** of a non-horizontal line is the positive angle θ ($\theta < 180°$) measured counterclockwise from the x-axis to the line. A horizontal line has an inclination of zero.

- If a nonvertical line has inclination θ and slope m, then $m = \tan\theta$.

- If two non-perpendicular lines have slopes m_1 and m_2, then the angle between the lines is given by
$$\tan\theta = \left|\frac{m_2 - m_1}{1 + m_1 m_2}\right|.$$

- The distance between a point (x_1, y_1) and a line $Ax + By + C = 0$ is given by
$$d = \frac{|Ax_1 + By_1 + C|}{\sqrt{A^2 + B^2}}.$$

Solutions to Selected Exercises

5. Find the slope of the line with inclination $\theta = 38.2°$.

Solution:

$$m = \tan 38.2° \approx 0.7869$$

11. Find the inclination, θ, of the line with slope $m = \frac{3}{4}$.

Solution:

$$\frac{3}{4} = \tan\theta$$

$$\theta = \tan^{-1}\frac{3}{4} \approx 36.9°$$

15. Find the inclination, θ, of the line passing through the points $(-2, 20)$ and $(10, 0)$.

Solution:

$$m = \frac{0 - 20}{10 - (-2)} = \frac{-20}{12} = -\frac{5}{3}$$

$$-\frac{5}{3} = \tan\theta$$

$$\theta = 180° + \tan^{-1}\left(-\frac{5}{3}\right) \approx 121.0°$$

19. Find the inclination, θ, of the line $5x + 3y = 0$.

Solution:

$$5x + 3y = 0$$

$$3y = -5x$$

$$y = -\tfrac{5}{3}x \Rightarrow m = -\tfrac{5}{3}$$

$$-\tfrac{5}{3} = \tan\theta$$

$$\theta = 180° + \tan^{-1}\left(-\tfrac{5}{3}\right) \approx 121.0°$$

23. Find the angle, θ, between the lines $x - y = 0$ and $3x - 2y + 1 = 0$.

Solution:

$$x - y = 0 \Rightarrow y = x \Rightarrow m_1 = 1$$

$$3x - 2y + 1 = 0 \Rightarrow y = \frac{3}{2}x + \frac{1}{2} \Rightarrow m_2 = \frac{3}{2}$$

$$\tan\theta = \left|\frac{(3/2) - 1}{1 + (1)(3/2)}\right| = \left|\frac{1/2}{5/2}\right| = \frac{1}{5}$$

$$\theta = \tan^{-1}\left(\frac{1}{5}\right) \approx 11.3°$$

29. Find the angle, θ, between the lines $0.05x - 0.03y - 0.21 = 0$ and $0.07x + 0.02y - 0.16 = 0$.

Solution:

$$0.05x - 0.03y - 0.21 = 0 \Rightarrow 5x - 3y - 21 = 0 \Rightarrow y = \frac{5}{3}x - 7 \Rightarrow m_1 = \frac{5}{3}$$

$$0.07x + 0.02y - 0.16 = 0 \Rightarrow 7x + 2y - 16 = 0 \Rightarrow y = -\frac{7}{2}x + 8 \Rightarrow m_2 = -\frac{7}{2}$$

$$\tan\theta = \left|\frac{-(7/2) - (5/3)}{1 + (5/3)(-7/2)}\right| = \left|\frac{-31/6}{-29/6}\right| = \frac{31}{29}$$

$$\theta = \tan^{-1}\left(\frac{31}{29}\right) \approx 46.9°$$

33. Find the distance between the point $(2, 3)$ and the line $4x + 3y - 10 = 0$.

Solution:

$(2, 3) \Rightarrow x_1 = 2$ and $y_1 = 3$

$4x + 3y - 10 = 0 \Rightarrow A = 4,\ B = 3,$ and $C = -10$

$$d = \frac{|4(2) + 3(3) + (-10)|}{\sqrt{4^2 + 3^2}} = \frac{7}{5} = 1.4$$

37. Find the distance between the point $(0, 8)$ and the line $6x - y = 0$.

Solution:

$(0, 8) \Rightarrow x_1 = 0$ and $y_1 = 8$

$6x - y = 0 \Rightarrow A = 6,\ B = -1,$ and $C = 0$

$$d = \frac{|6(0) + (-1)(8) + 0|}{\sqrt{6^2 + (-1)^2}} = \frac{8}{\sqrt{37}} = \frac{8\sqrt{37}}{37} \approx 1.3152$$

41. A straight road rises with an inclination of 6.5° from the horizontal. Find the slope of the road and the change in elevation after driving two miles.

Solution:

Slope: $m = \tan 6.5° \approx 0.1139$

Change in elevation: $\sin 6.5° = \dfrac{x}{2}$

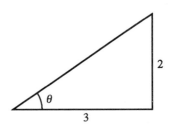

$$2 \sin 6.5° = x$$

$$x \approx 0.2264 \text{ mile}$$

$$\approx 0.2264(5280)$$

$$\approx 1195 \text{ feet}$$

45. There is a rise of two feet for every horizontal change of three feet on a roof. Find the inclination of the roof.

Solution:

$\tan \theta = \frac{2}{3}$

$\theta = \tan^{-1}\left(\frac{2}{3}\right)$

$\approx 33.7°$

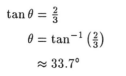

49. (a) Find the altitude from vertex B of a triangle to the side AC, and (b) find the area of the triangle given $A = \left(-\frac{1}{2}, \frac{1}{2}\right)$, $B = (2, 3)$, and $C = \left(\frac{5}{2}, 0\right)$.

Solution:

(a) The slope of the line through AC is

$$m = \frac{0 - (1/2)}{(5/2) - (-1/2)} = -\frac{1}{6}.$$

The equation of the line is

$$y - 0 = -\frac{1}{6}\left(x - \frac{5}{2}\right)$$

$$y = -\frac{1}{6}x + \frac{5}{12}$$

$$12y = -2x + 5$$

$$2x + 12y - 5 = 0.$$

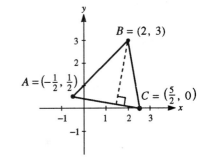

The distance between $B = (2, 3)$ and this line is

$$d = \frac{|2(2) + 12(3) + (-5)|}{\sqrt{2^2 + 12^2}} = \frac{35}{2\sqrt{37}} = \frac{35\sqrt{37}}{74}.$$

(b) The distance between A and C is

$$d = \sqrt{\left(\frac{5}{2} - \left(-\frac{1}{2}\right)\right)^2 + \left(0 - \frac{1}{2}\right)^2} = \sqrt{9 + \frac{1}{4}} = \sqrt{\frac{37}{4}} = \frac{\sqrt{37}}{2}.$$

The area of the triangle is

$$A = \frac{1}{2}bh = \frac{1}{2}\left(\frac{\sqrt{37}}{2}\right)\left(\frac{35\sqrt{37}}{74}\right) = \frac{35}{8} \text{ square units.}$$

53. Find the slope of each side of the triangle and use the slopes to find the magnitude of the interior angles.

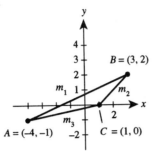

Solution:

Let $A = (-4, -1)$, $B = (3, 2)$, and $C = (1, 0)$. The slopes are as follows.

$$AB: \quad m_1 = \frac{2 - (-1)}{3 - (-4)} = \frac{3}{7}$$

$$BC: \quad m_2 = \frac{0 - 2}{1 - 3} = 1$$

$$AC: \quad m_3 = \frac{0 - (-1)}{1 - (-4)} = \frac{1}{5}$$

The angle at A is found by

$$\tan A = \left| \frac{m_3 - m_1}{1 + m_1 m_3} \right| = \left| \frac{(1/5) - (3/7)}{1 + (3/7)(1/5)} \right| = \frac{4}{19}$$

$$A = \tan^{-1} \frac{4}{19} \approx 11.9°.$$

The angle at B is found by

$$\tan B = \left| \frac{m_2 - m_1}{1 + m_1 m_2} \right| = \left| \frac{1 - (3/7)}{1 + (3/7)(1)} \right| = \frac{2}{5}$$

$$B = \tan^{-1} \left(\frac{2}{5} \right) \approx 21.8°.$$

The angle at C is found by

$$C = 180° - A - B = 180° - 11.9° - 21.8° = 146.3°.$$

SECTION 7.2

Introduction to Conics: Parabolas

- A *parabola* is the set of all points (x, y) that are equidistant from a fixed line (*directrix*) and a fixed point (*focus*) not on the line.

- The standard equation of a parabola with vertex (h, k) and:

  (a) Vertical axis $x = h$ and directrix $y = k - p$ is:
  $$(x - h)^2 = 4p(y - k), \quad p \neq 0$$

  (b) Horizontal axis $y = k$ and directrix $x = h - p$ is:
  $$(y - k)^2 = 4p(x - h), \quad p \neq 0$$

Solutions to Selected Exercises

5. Match $(y - 1)^2 = 4(x - 2)$ with the correct graph.

Solution:

The vertex is at $(2, 1)$ and the axis is horizontal. Therefore, it matches graph (d).

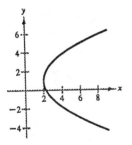

11. Find the vertex, focus, and directrix of the parabola $(x - 1)^2 + 8(y + 2) = 0$ and sketch its graph.

Solution:

$$(x - 1)^2 + 8(y + 2) = 0$$
$$(x - 1)^2 = -8(y + 2)$$
$$(x - 1)^2 = 4(-2)(y + 2)$$

$h = 1, \ k = -2, \ p = -2$
Vertex: $(1, -2)$
Focus: $(1, \ -2 + (-2))$ or $(1, \ -4)$
Directrix: $y = -2 - (-2)$ or $y = 0$

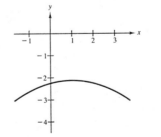

13. Find the vertex, focus, and directrix of the parabola $y = \frac{1}{4}(x^2 - 2x + 5)$ and sketch its graph.

Solution:

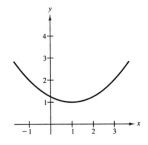

$$y = \frac{1}{4}(x^2 - 2x + 5)$$
$$4y = x^2 - 2x + 1 - 1 + 5$$
$$4y = (x-1)^2 + 4$$
$$4y - 4 = (x-1)^2$$
$$(x-1)^2 = 4(y-1)$$
$$(x-1)^2 = 4(1)(y-1)$$

$h = 1$, $k = 1$, $p = 1$
Vertex: $(1, 1)$
Focus: $(1, 1+1)$ or $(1, 2)$
Directrix: $y = 1 - 1$ or $y = 0$

15. Find the vertex, focus, and directrix of the parabola $y^2 + 6y + 8x + 25 = 0$ and sketch its graph.

Solution:

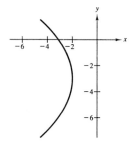

$$y^2 + 6y + 8x + 25 = 0$$
$$y^2 + 6y = -8x - 25$$
$$y^2 + 6y + 9 = -8x - 25 + 9$$
$$(y+3)^2 = -8x - 16$$
$$(y+3)^2 = -8(x+2)$$
$$(y+3)^2 = 4(-2)(x+2)$$

$h = -2$, $k = -3$, $p = -2$
Vertex: $(-2, -3)$
Focus: $(-2 + (-2), -3)$ or $(-4, -3)$
Directrix: $x = -2 - (-2)$ or $x = 0$

17. Find the vertex, focus, and directrix of the parabola $y^2 - 4x - 4 = 0$ and sketch its graph.

Solution:

$$y^2 - 4x - 4 = 0$$
$$y^2 = 4x + 4$$
$$(y - 0)^2 = 4(x + 1)$$
$$(y - 0)^2 = 4(1)(x + 1)$$

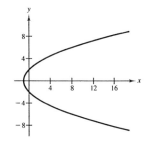

$h = -1$, $k = 0$, $p = 1$
Vertex: $(-1, \ 0)$
Focus: $(-1 + 1, \ 0)$ or $(0, \ 0)$
Directrix: $x = -1 - 1$ or $x = -2$

21. Find an equation of the specified parabola.

Vertex: $(0, \ 0)$
Directrix: $x = 3$

Solution:

The vertex is $(0, \ 0)$ and the axis is horizontal with $p = -3$.

$$(y - 0)^2 = 4(-3)(x - 0)$$
$$y^2 = -12x$$

25. Find an equation of the specified parabola.

Axis: parallel to the y-axis
Passes through the points $(0, 3)$, $(3, 4)$, and $(4, 11)$

Solution:

Since the axis is vertical, we have $(x - h)^2 = 4p(y - k)$. Now, substituting the x- and y-values of the given points into this equation yields:

$(0, \ 3)$: $\quad (0 - h)^2 = 4p(3 - k) \Rightarrow h^2 = 12p - 4pk$
$(3, \ 4)$: $\quad (3 - h)^2 = 4p(4 - k) \Rightarrow (3 - h)^2 = 16p - 4pk$
$(4, \ 11)$: $\quad (4 - h)^2 = 4p(11 - k) \Rightarrow (4 - h)^2 = 44p - 4pk$

By subtraction we have: $h^2 - (3 - h)^2 = (12p - 4pk) - (16p - 4pk)$

$$6h - 9 = -4p$$

$$h^2 - (4 - h)^2 = (12p - 4pk) - (44p - 4pk)$$

$$8h - 16 = -32p$$

–CONTINUED ON NEXT PAGE–

25. –CONTINUED–

Using the method of elimination yields:

$$8h - 16 = -32p \Rightarrow \quad 2h - \quad 4 = -8p$$
$$6h - \quad 9 = \quad -4p \Rightarrow \underline{-12h + \quad 18 = \quad 8p}$$
$$-10h + \quad 14 = \quad 0$$
$$h = \tfrac{-14}{-10} = \tfrac{7}{5}$$
$$2\left(\tfrac{7}{5}\right) - 4 = -8p$$
$$p = \tfrac{3}{20}$$
$$\left(\tfrac{7}{5}\right)^2 = 12\left(\tfrac{3}{20}\right) - 4\left(\tfrac{3}{20}\right)k$$
$$k = -\tfrac{4}{15}$$

Thus,

$$\left(x - \frac{7}{5}\right)^2 = 4\left(\frac{3}{20}\right)\left(y + \frac{4}{15}\right)$$
$$x^2 - \frac{14}{5}x + \frac{49}{25} = \frac{3}{5}y + \frac{4}{25}$$
$$25x^2 - 70x + 49 = 15y + 4$$
$$25x^2 - 70x - 15y + 45 = 0$$
$$5x^2 - 14x - 3y + 9 = 0$$

27. Find an equation of the specified parabola.

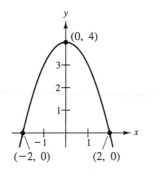

Solution:

The x-intercepts occur at $(\pm 2, \ 0)$ and the parabola opens downward.

$$y = -(x + 2)(x - 2)$$
$$y = -(x^2 - 4)$$
$$y = 4 - x^2$$
$$x^2 + y - 4 = 0$$

29. The receiver in a parabolic television dish antenna is three feet from the vertex and is located at the focus, as shown in the figure. Find an equation of a cross section of the reflector. (Assume the dish is directed upward and the vertex is at the origin.)

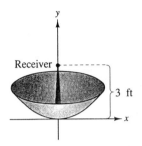

Solution:

The vertex is at $(0, 0)$ and the focus is at $(0, 3)$. Therefore, $p = 3$.

$$(x - 0)^2 = 4(3)(y - 0)$$
$$x^2 = 12y$$

33. A satellite in a 100-mile-high circular orbit around the earth has a velocity of approximately 17,500 miles per hour. If this velocity is multiplied by $\sqrt{2}$, then the satellite will have the minimum velocity necessary to escape the earth's gravity and it will follow a parabolic path with the center of the earth as the focus (see figure).

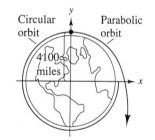

(a) Find the escape velocity of the satellite.

(b) Find the equation of its path (assume that the radius of the earth is 4000 miles.)

Solution:

(a) $17,500\sqrt{2} \approx 24,748.737 \approx 24,749$ mph

(b) Since the vertex is at $(0, 4100)$ and the focus is at $(0, 0)$, we have

$$(x - 0)^2 = 4(-4100)(y - 4100)$$
$$x^2 = -16,400(y - 4100).$$

35. A ball is thrown horizontally from the top of a 75-foot tower with a velocity of 32 feet per second.

(a) Find the equation of the parabolic path.

(b) How far does the ball travel horizontally before striking the ground?

Solution:

(a)
$$y = -\frac{16}{v^2}x^2 + s$$

$$= -\frac{16}{(32)^2}x^2 + 75$$

$$= -\frac{x^2}{64} + 75 \text{ or}$$

$$x^2 + 64y = 4800$$

(b) When $y = 0$, we have

$$x^2 = 4800$$

$$x = \sqrt{4800}$$

$$= 40\sqrt{3} \approx 69.3 \text{ feet.}$$

41. Find the equation of the tangent line to the parabola $y = -2x^2$ at the point $(-1, -2)$ and find the x-intercept of the line.

Solution:

$$y = -2x^2$$

$$x^2 = -\frac{1}{2}y$$

$$x^2 = 4\left(-\frac{1}{8}\right)y \Rightarrow p = -\frac{1}{8}$$

The focus is at $\left(0, -\frac{1}{8}\right)$.

$$d_1 = \frac{1}{8} + b$$

$$d_2 = \sqrt{(-1 - 0)^2 + \left(-2 - \left(-\frac{1}{8}\right)\right)^2} = \sqrt{1 + \frac{225}{64}} = \frac{17}{8}$$

$$d_1 = d_2$$

$$\frac{1}{8} + b = \frac{17}{8}$$

$$b = 2$$

$$m = \frac{-2 - 2}{-1 - 0} = 4$$

$$y = 4x + 2$$

x-intercept: $\left(-\frac{1}{2}, 0\right)$

SECTION 7.3

Ellipses

- An *ellipse* is the set of all points (x, y) the sum of whose distances from two distinct fixed points (*foci*) is constant.

- The standard equation of an ellipse with center (h, k) and major and minor axes of lengths $2a$ and $2b$ is:

  (a) $\dfrac{(x - h)^2}{a^2} + \dfrac{(y - k)^2}{b^2} = 1$ if the major axis is horizontal.

  (b) $\dfrac{(x - h)^2}{b^2} + \dfrac{(y - k)^2}{a^2} = 1$ if the major axis is vertical.

- $c^2 = a^2 - b^2$ where c is the distance from the center to a focus.

- The eccentricity of an ellipse is $e = \dfrac{c}{a}$.

Solutions to Selected Exercises

3. Match the following equation with the correct graph.

$$\frac{x^2}{9} + \frac{y^2}{4} = 1$$

Solution:

$a = 3$, $b = 2$
Center: $(0, 0)$
Major axis is horizontal.
Therefore, it matches graph (c).

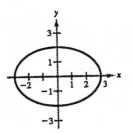

7. Find the center, foci, vertices, and eccentricity of the following ellipse and sketch its graph.

$$\frac{x^2}{25} + \frac{y^2}{16} = 1$$

Solution:

$a^2 = 25, \ b^2 = 16, \ c^2 = 9$

Center: $(0, 0)$

Foci: $(\pm 3, \ 0)$

Vertices: $(\pm 5, \ 0), \quad e = \frac{3}{5}$

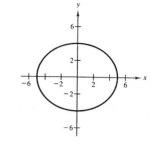

9. Find the center, foci, vertices, and eccentricity of the following ellipse and sketch its graph.

$$\frac{x^2}{144} + \frac{y^2}{169} = 1$$

Solution:

$a^2 = 169, \ b^2 = 144, \ c^2 = 25$

Center: $(0, 0)$

Foci: $(0, \ \pm 5)$

Vertices: $(0, \ \pm 13), \quad e = \frac{5}{13}$

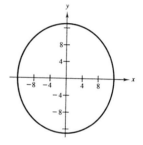

11. Find the center, foci, vertices, and eccentricity of the ellipse $3x^2 + 2y^2 = 6$ and sketch its graph.

Solution:

$$3x^2 + 2y^2 = 6$$

$$\frac{x^2}{2} + \frac{y^2}{3} = 1$$

$a^2 = 3, \ b^2 = 2, \ c^2 = 1$

Center: $(0, 0)$

Foci: $(0, \ \pm 1)$

Vertices: $(0, \ \pm\sqrt{3}), \quad e = \frac{1}{\sqrt{3}} = \frac{\sqrt{3}}{3}$

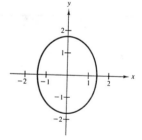

13. Find the center, foci, vertices, and eccentricity of the following ellipse and sketch its graph.

$$\frac{(x-1)^2}{9} + \frac{(y-5)^2}{25} = 1$$

Solution:

$a^2 = 25,\ b^2 = 9,\ c^2 = 16$

Center: $(1,\ 5)$

Foci: $(1,\ 5 \pm 4)$ or $(1,\ 9),\ (1,\ 1)$

Vertices: $(1,\ 5 \pm 5)$ or $(1,\ 10),\ (1,\ 0),\ \ e = \frac{4}{5}$

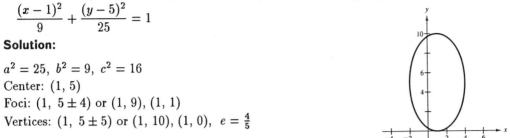

17. Find the center, foci, vertices, and eccentricity of the ellipse $16x^2 + 25y^2 - 32x + 50y + 16 = 0$ and sketch its graph.

Solution:

$$16x^2 + 25y^2 - 32x + 50y + 16 = 0$$

$$16(x^2 - 2x + 1) + 25(y^2 + 2y + 1) = -16 + 16 + 25$$

$$16(x-1)^2 + 25(y+1)^2 = 25$$

$$\frac{(x-1)^2}{25/16} + \frac{(y+1)^2}{1} = 1$$

$a^2 = \frac{25}{16},\ b^2 = 1,\ c^2 = \frac{9}{16}$

Center: $(1,\ -1)$

Foci: $\left(1 \pm \frac{3}{4},\ -1\right)$ or $\left(\frac{1}{4},\ -1\right),\ \left(\frac{7}{4},\ -1\right)$

Vertices: $\left(1 \pm \frac{5}{4},\ -1\right)$ or $\left(-\frac{1}{4},\ -1\right),\ \left(\frac{9}{4},\ -1\right),\ \ e = \frac{3}{5}$

21. Find an equation of the specified ellipse.

Vertices: $(\pm 6,\ 0)$

Foci: $(\pm 5,\ 0)$

Solution:

The major axis is horizontal with the center at $(0,\ 0)$.

$a = 6,\ c = 5$ implies $b = \sqrt{11}$.

$$\frac{(x-0)^2}{(6)^2} + \frac{(y-0)^2}{(\sqrt{11})^2} = 1$$

$$\frac{x^2}{36} + \frac{y^2}{11} = 1$$

25. Find an equation of the specified ellipse.

Foci: $(0,\ 0),\ (0,\ 8)$

Major axis of length 16

Solution:

The major axis is vertical with center at $(0,\ 4)$.

$2a = 16 \Rightarrow a = 8$

$c = 4 \Rightarrow b = \sqrt{48} = 4\sqrt{3}$

$$\frac{(x-0)^2}{(\sqrt{48})^2} + \frac{(y-4)^2}{(8)^2} = 1$$

$$\frac{x^2}{48} + \frac{(y-4)^2}{64} = 1$$

29. A fireplace arch is to be constructed in the shape of a semi-ellipse. The opening is to have a height of 2 feet at the center and a width of 5 feet along the base, as shown in the figure. The contractor will first draw the form of the ellipse by the method shown in Figure 11.16. Where should the tacks be placed and what should be the length of the piece of string?

Solution:

$a = \frac{5}{2}$, $b = 2$, $c = \sqrt{\left(\frac{5}{2}\right)^2 - (2)^2} = \frac{3}{2}$

The tacks should be placed 1.5 feet from the center.

$d_1 + d_2 = 2a = 2\left(\frac{5}{2}\right) = 5$

The string should be $2a = 5$ feet.

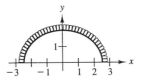

33. A line segment through a focus with endpoints on the ellipse and perpendicular to the major axis is called a **latus rectum** of the ellipse. Therefore, an ellipse has two latus recta. Knowing the length of the latus recta is helpful in sketching an ellipse because it yields other points on the curve (see figure). The length of each latus rectum is $2b^2/a$. Graph $(x^2/4) + (y^2/1) = 1$ making use of the latus recta.

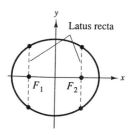

Solution:

Since $a = 2$, $b = 1$, $c = \sqrt{3}$, and $(2b^2)/a = 1$, we have the following graph.

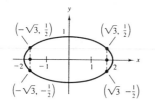

37. The earth moves in an elliptical orbit with the sun at one of the foci. The length of half of the major axis is 92.957×10^6 miles and the eccentricity is 0.017. Find the least and greatest distances of the earth from the sun.

Solution:

$e = \dfrac{c}{a}$, $a = 92.957 \times 10^6$, $e = 0.017$, $0.017 = \dfrac{c}{92.957 \times 10^6}$, $c \approx 1{,}580{,}269$

Least distance: $a - c \approx 91{,}376{,}731$ miles ≈ 91.377 million miles

Greatest distance: $a + c \approx 94{,}537{,}269$ miles ≈ 94.537 million miles

43. Show that the equation of an ellipse can be written as

$$\frac{(x-h)^2}{a^2} + \frac{(y-k)^2}{a^2(1-e^2)} = 1.$$

Note that as e approaches zero, with a remaining fixed, the ellipse approaches a circle of radius a.

Solution:

$$\frac{(x-h)^2}{a^2} + \frac{(y-k)^2}{b^2} = 1$$

$$\frac{(x-h)^2}{a^2} + \frac{(y-k)^2}{a^2(b^2/a^2)} = 1$$

$$\frac{(x-h)^2}{a^2} + \frac{(y-k)^2}{a^2(a^2-c^2)/a^2} = 1$$

$$\frac{(x-h)^2}{a^2} + \frac{(y-k)^2}{a^2(1-e^2)} = 1$$

As $e \Rightarrow 0$, $1 - e^2 \Rightarrow 1$ and we have $\dfrac{(x-h)^2}{a^2} + \dfrac{(y-k)^2}{a^2} = 1$ or the circle $(x-h)^2 + (y-k)^2 = a^2$.

SECTION 7.4

Hyperbolas

- A *hyperbola* is the set of all points (x, y) the difference of whose distances from two distinct fixed points (*foci*) is constant.

- The standard equation of a hyperbola with center (h, k) and transverse and conjugate axes of lengths $2a$ and $2b$ is:

  (a) $\dfrac{(x-h)^2}{a^2} - \dfrac{(y-k)^2}{b^2} = 1$ if the transverse axis is horizontal.

  (b) $\dfrac{(y-k)^2}{a^2} - \dfrac{(x-h)^2}{b^2} = 1$ if the transverse axis is vertical.

- $c^2 = a^2 + b^2$ where c is the distance from the center to a focus.

- The asymptotes of a hyperbola are:

  (a) $y = k \pm \dfrac{b}{a}(x - h)$ if the transverse axis is horizontal.

  (b) $y = k \pm \dfrac{a}{b}(x - h)$ if the transverse axis is vertical.

- The eccentricity of a hyperbola is $e = \dfrac{c}{a}$.

- To classify a nondegenerate conic from its general equation $Ax^2 + Cy^2 + Dx + Ey + F = 0$:

  (a) If $A = C$ $(A \neq 0, C \neq 0)$, then it is a circle.
  (b) If $AC = 0$ $(A = 0$ or $C = 0$, but not both), then it is a parabola.
  (c) If $AC > 0$, then it is an ellipse.
  (d) If $AC < 0$, then it is a hyperbola.

Solutions to Selected Exercises

5. Match the following equation with its graph.

$$\frac{(x-2)^2}{9} - \frac{y^2}{4} = 1$$

Solution:

$a = 3,\ b = 2$

Center: $(2, 0)$

Horizontal transverse axis

Matches graph (d)

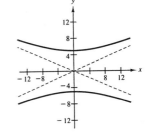

9. Find the center, foci, and vertices of the following hyperbola and sketch its graph, using asymptotes as an aid.

$$\frac{y^2}{25} - \frac{x^2}{144} = 1$$

Solution:

$a = 5,\ b = 12,\ c = \sqrt{25 + 144} = 13$

Vertical transverse axis

Center: $(0, 0)$

Vertices: $(0, \pm 5)$

Foci: $(0, \pm 13)$

Asymptotes: $y = \pm \frac{5}{12}x$

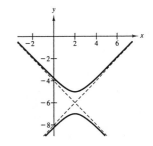

15. Find the center, foci, and vertices of the hyperbola $(y + 6)^2 - (x - 2)^2 = 1$ and sketch its graph, using asymptotes as an aid.

Solution:

$$\frac{(y+6)^2}{1} - \frac{(x-2)^2}{1} = 1$$

$a = 1,\ b = 1,\ c = \sqrt{2}$

Center: $(2, -6)$

Foci: $(2, -6 \pm \sqrt{2})$

Vertices: $(2, -6 \pm 1)$ or $(2, -5),\ (2, -7)$

Asymptotes: $y = -6 \pm (x - 2)$

17. Find the center, foci, and vertices of the hyperbola $9y^2 - x^2 + 2x + 54y + 62 = 0$ and sketch its graph, using asymptotes as an aid.

Solution:

$$9y^2 - x^2 + 2x + 54y + 62 = 0$$

$$9(y^2 + 6y + 9) - (x^2 - 2x + 1) = -62 - 1 + 81$$

$$\frac{(y+3)^2}{2} - \frac{(x-1)^2}{18} = 1$$

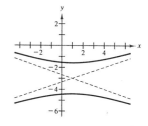

$a = \sqrt{2}$, $b = 3\sqrt{2}$, $c = 2\sqrt{5}$

Center: $(1, -3)$

Foci: $(1, -3 \pm 2\sqrt{5})$

Vertices: $(1, -3 \pm \sqrt{2})$

Asymptotes: $y = -3 \pm \frac{1}{3}(x - 1)$

21. Find an equation of the specified hyperbola.

Vertices: $(0, \pm 2)$

Foci: $(0, \pm 4)$

Solution:

The transverse axis is vertical.

Center: $(0, 0)$

$a = 2$, $c = 4 \Rightarrow b = \sqrt{16 - 4} = 2\sqrt{3}$

$$\frac{(y - 0)^2}{2^2} - \frac{(x - 0)^2}{(2\sqrt{3})^2} = 1$$

$$\frac{y^2}{4} - \frac{x^2}{12} = 1$$

25. Find an equation of the specified hyperbola.

Vertices: $(2, 0)$, $(6, 0)$

Foci: $(0, 0)$, $(8, 0)$

Solution:

The transverse axis is horizontal.

Center: $(4, 0)$

$a = 2$, $c = 4$, $b = \sqrt{16 - 4} = 2\sqrt{3}$

$$\frac{(x - 4)^2}{2^2} - \frac{(y - 0)^2}{(2\sqrt{3})^2} = 1$$

$$\frac{(x - 4)^2}{4} - \frac{y^2}{12} = 1$$

29. Find an equation of the specified hyperbola.

Vertices: $(0, 2)$, $(6, 2)$

Asymptotes: $y = \frac{2}{3}x$ and $y = 4 - \frac{2}{3}x$

Solution:

The transverse axis is horizontal.

Center: $(3, 2)$

$a = 3$, $\pm\dfrac{b}{a} = \pm\dfrac{2}{3} \Rightarrow b = 2$

$$\frac{(x - 3)^2}{9} - \frac{(y - 2)^2}{4} = 1$$

33. A hyperbolic mirror (used in some telescopes) has the property that a light ray directed at the focus will be reflected to the other focus (see figure). The focus of a hyperbolic mirror has coordinates $(12, 0)$. Find the vertex of the mirror if its mount has coordinates $(12, 12)$.

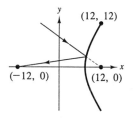

Solution:

The transverse axis is horizontal.

Center: $(0, 0)$

$c = 12 \Rightarrow b = \sqrt{144 - a^2}$

$$\frac{x^2}{a^2} - \frac{y^2}{144 - a^2} = 1$$

Since the hyperbola passes through $(12, 12)$, we have:

$$\frac{144}{a^2} - \frac{144}{144 - a^2} = 1$$

$$144(144 - a^2) - 144a^2 = a^2(144 - a^2)$$

$$20{,}736 - 288a^2 = 144a^2 - a^4$$

$$a^4 - 432a^2 + 20{,}736 = 0$$

$$a^2 = \frac{432 \pm \sqrt{432^2 - 4(20{,}736)}}{2} = \frac{432 \pm 144\sqrt{5}}{2} = 216 \pm 72\sqrt{5}$$

$$a = \sqrt{216 \pm 72\sqrt{5}}$$

$$a \approx 19.416 \text{ or } a \approx 7.416$$

Since $a < c$ for a hyperbola, we use the smaller value.

Vertex: $\left(\sqrt{216 - 72\sqrt{5}},\ 0\right) \approx (7.42,\ 0)$

37. Classify the graph of the equation $4x^2 - y^2 - 4x - 3 = 0$ as a circle, a parabola, an ellipse, or a hyperbola.

Solution:

$4x^2 - y^2 - 4x - 3 = 0$

$A = 4,\ C = -1$

$AC = (4)(-1) = -4 < 0$

Therefore, the graph is a hyperbola.

41. Classify the graph of the equation $25x^2 - 10x - 200y - 119 = 0$ as a circle, a parabola, an ellipse, or a hyperbola.

Solution:

$25x^2 - 10x - 200y - 119 = 0$

$A = 25,\ C = 0$

$AC = (25)(0) = 0$

Therefore, the graph is a parabola.

SECTION 7.5

Rotation and the General Second-Degree Equation

■ The general second-degree equation $Ax^2+Bxy+Cy^2+Dx+Ey+F=0$ can be rewritten as $A'(x')^2 + C'(y')^2 + D'x' + E'y' + F' = 0$ by rotating the coordinate axes through the angle θ, where $\cot 2\theta = (A-C)/B$.

■ $x = x' \cos\theta - y' \sin\theta$
  $y = x' \sin\theta + y' \cos\theta$

■ The graph of the nondegenerate equation $Ax^2 + Bxy + Cy^2 + Dx + Ey + F = 0$ is:

(a) An ellipse or circle if $B^2 - 4AC < 0$.
(b) A parabola if $B^2 - 4AC = 0$.
(c) A hyperbola if $B^2 - 4AC > 0$.

Solutions to Selected Exercises

5. Rotate the axes to eliminate the xy-term in the equation $xy - 2y - 4x = 0$. Sketch the graph of the resulting equation, showing both sets of axes.

Solution:

$xy - 2y - 4x = 0$

$A = 0, \ B = 1, \ C = 0$

$$\cos 2\theta = \frac{A-C}{B} = 0 \Rightarrow 2\theta = \frac{\pi}{2} \Rightarrow \theta = \frac{\pi}{4}$$

$x = x' \cos\dfrac{\pi}{4} - y' \sin\dfrac{\pi}{4}$ $\qquad\qquad$ $y = x' \sin\dfrac{\pi}{4} + y' \cos\dfrac{\pi}{4}$

$\quad = x'\left(\dfrac{\sqrt{2}}{2}\right) - y'\left(\dfrac{\sqrt{2}}{2}\right)$ $\qquad\qquad$ $= x'\left(\dfrac{\sqrt{2}}{2}\right) + y'\left(\dfrac{\sqrt{2}}{2}\right)$

$\quad = \dfrac{x' - y'}{\sqrt{2}}$ $\qquad\qquad\qquad\quad$ $= \dfrac{x' + y'}{\sqrt{2}}$

–CONTINUED ON NEXT PAGE–

5. –CONTINUED–

$$xy - 2y - 4x = 0$$

$$\left(\frac{x' - y'}{\sqrt{2}}\right)\left(\frac{x' + y'}{\sqrt{2}}\right) - 2\left(\frac{x' + y'}{\sqrt{2}}\right) - 4\left(\frac{x' - y'}{\sqrt{2}}\right) = 0$$

$$\frac{(x')^2}{2} - \frac{(y')^2}{2} - \sqrt{2}x' - \sqrt{2}y' - 2\sqrt{2}x' + 2\sqrt{2}y' = 0$$

$$\left[(x')^2 - 6\sqrt{2}x' + (3\sqrt{2})^2\right] - \left[(y')^2 - 2\sqrt{2}y' + (\sqrt{2})^2\right] = 0 + (3\sqrt{2})^2 - (\sqrt{2})^2$$

$$(x' - 3\sqrt{2})^2 - (y' - \sqrt{2})^2 = 16$$

$$\frac{(x' - 3\sqrt{2})^2}{16} - \frac{(y' - \sqrt{2})^2}{16} = 1$$

The graph is a hyperbola.

9. Rotate the axes to eliminate the xy-term in the equation $3x^2 - 2\sqrt{3}xy + y^2 + 2x + 2\sqrt{3}y = 0$. Sketch the graph of the resulting equation, showing both sets of axes.

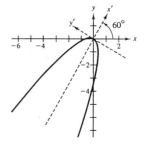

Solution:

$$3x^2 - 2\sqrt{3}xy + y^2 + 2x + 2\sqrt{3}y = 0$$

$$A = 3, \ B = -2\sqrt{3}, \ C = 1, \ \cot 2\theta = \frac{A - C}{B} = -\frac{1}{\sqrt{3}} \Rightarrow \theta = 60°$$

$$x = x'\cos 60° - y'\sin 60° \qquad\qquad y = x'\sin 60° + y'\cos 60°$$

$$= x'\left(\frac{1}{2}\right) - y'\left(\frac{\sqrt{3}}{2}\right) = \frac{x' - \sqrt{3}y'}{2} \qquad = x'\left(\frac{\sqrt{3}}{2}\right) + y'\left(\frac{1}{2}\right) = \frac{\sqrt{3}x' + y'}{2}$$

$$3x^2 - 2\sqrt{3}xy + y^2 + 2x + 2\sqrt{3}y = 0$$

$$3\left(\frac{x' - \sqrt{3}y'}{2}\right)^2 - 2\sqrt{3}\left(\frac{x' - \sqrt{3}y'}{2}\right)\left(\frac{\sqrt{3}x' + y'}{2}\right) + \left(\frac{\sqrt{3}x' + y'}{2}\right)^2$$

$$+ 2\left(\frac{x' - \sqrt{3}y'}{2}\right) + 2\sqrt{3}\left(\frac{\sqrt{3}x' + y'}{2}\right) = 0$$

$$\frac{3(x')^2}{4} - \frac{6\sqrt{3}x'y'}{4} + \frac{9(y')^2}{4} - \frac{6(x')^2}{4} + \frac{4\sqrt{3}x'y'}{4} + \frac{6(y')^2}{4} + \frac{3(x')^2}{4} + \frac{2\sqrt{3}x'y'}{4} + \frac{(y')^2}{4}$$

$$+ x' - \sqrt{3}y' + 3x' + \sqrt{3}y' = 0$$

$$4(y')^2 + 4x' = 0$$

$$x' = -(y')^2$$

The graph is a parabola.

11. Rotate the axes to eliminate the xy-term in the equation $9x^2 + 24xy + 16y^2 + 90x - 130y = 0$. Sketch the graph of the resulting equation, showing both sets of axes.

Solution:

$9x^2 + 24xy + 16y^2 + 90x - 130y = 0$

$A = 9, \ B = 24, \ C = 16$

$\cot 2\theta = \dfrac{A - C}{B} = -\dfrac{7}{24} \Rightarrow \theta \approx 53.13°$

$\cos 2\theta = -\dfrac{7}{25}$

$\sin \theta = \sqrt{\dfrac{1 - \cos 2\theta}{2}} = \sqrt{\dfrac{1 - (-7/25)}{2}} = \dfrac{4}{5}$

$\cos \theta = \sqrt{\dfrac{1 + \cos 2\theta}{2}} = \sqrt{\dfrac{1 + (-7/25)}{2}} = \dfrac{3}{5}$

$x = x' \cos \theta - y' \sin \theta \qquad\qquad y = x' \sin \theta + y' \cos \theta$

$\quad = x'\left(\dfrac{3}{5}\right) - y'\left(\dfrac{4}{5}\right) \qquad\qquad = x'\left(\dfrac{4}{5}\right) + y'\left(\dfrac{3}{5}\right)$

$\quad = \dfrac{3x' - 4y'}{5} \qquad\qquad\qquad = \dfrac{4x' + 3y'}{5}$

$$9x^2 + 24xy + 16y^2 + 90x - 130y = 0$$

$$9\left(\dfrac{3x' - 4y'}{5}\right)^2 + 24\left(\dfrac{3x' - 4y'}{5}\right)\left(\dfrac{4x' + 3y'}{5}\right) + 16\left(\dfrac{4x' + 3y'}{5}\right)^2$$

$$+ 90\left(\dfrac{3x' - 4y'}{5}\right) - 130\left(\dfrac{4x' + 3y'}{5}\right) = 0$$

$$\dfrac{81(x')^2}{25} - \dfrac{216x'y'}{25} + \dfrac{144(y')^2}{25} + \dfrac{288(x')^2}{25} - \dfrac{168x'y'}{25} - \dfrac{288(y')^2}{25} + \dfrac{256(x')^2}{25}$$

$$+ \dfrac{384x'y'}{25} + \dfrac{144(y')^2}{25} + 54x' - 72y' - 104x' - 78y' = 0$$

$$25(x')^2 - 50x' - 150y' = 0$$

$$(x')^2 - 2x' + 1 = 6y' + 1$$

$$(x' - 1)^2 = 4\left(\dfrac{3}{2}\right)\left(y' + \dfrac{1}{6}\right)$$

The graph is a parabola.

15. Rotate the axes to eliminate the xy-term in the equation $32x^2 + 50xy + 7y^2 = 52$. Sketch the gaph of the resulting equation, showing both sets of axes.

Solution:

$32x^2 + 50xy + 7y^2 = 52$

$A = 32, \ B = 50, \ C = 7$

$$\cot 2\theta = \frac{A - C}{B} = \frac{1}{2} \Rightarrow \theta \approx 31.72°$$

$$\cos 2\theta = \frac{1}{\sqrt{5}}$$

$$\sin \theta = \sqrt{\frac{1 - \cos 2\theta}{2}} = \sqrt{\frac{1 - (1/\sqrt{5})}{2}} = \sqrt{\frac{\sqrt{5} - 1}{2\sqrt{5}}}$$

$$\cos \theta = \sqrt{\frac{1 + \cos 2\theta}{2}} = \sqrt{\frac{1 + (1/\sqrt{5})}{2}} = \sqrt{\frac{\sqrt{5} + 1}{2\sqrt{5}}}$$

$x = x' \cos \theta - y' \sin \theta \qquad\qquad y = x' \sin \theta + y' \cos \theta$

$$= x'\sqrt{\frac{\sqrt{5} + 1}{2\sqrt{5}}} - y'\sqrt{\frac{\sqrt{5} - 1}{2\sqrt{5}}} \qquad = x'\sqrt{\frac{\sqrt{5} - 1}{2\sqrt{5}}} + y'\sqrt{\frac{\sqrt{5} + 1}{2\sqrt{5}}}$$

$$32x^2 + 50xy + 7y^2 = 52$$

$$32\left(x'\sqrt{\frac{\sqrt{5} + 1}{2\sqrt{5}}} - y'\sqrt{\frac{\sqrt{5} - 1}{2\sqrt{5}}} \right)^2$$

$$+ 50\left(x'\sqrt{\frac{\sqrt{5} + 1}{2\sqrt{5}}} - y'\sqrt{\frac{\sqrt{5} - 1}{2\sqrt{5}}} \right)\left(x'\sqrt{\frac{\sqrt{5} - 1}{2\sqrt{5}}} + y'\sqrt{\frac{\sqrt{5} + 1}{2\sqrt{5}}} \right)$$

$$+ 7\left(x'\sqrt{\frac{\sqrt{5} - 1}{2\sqrt{5}}} + y'\sqrt{\frac{\sqrt{5} + 1}{2\sqrt{5}}} \right)^2 = 52$$

$$47.451(x')^2 - 8.451(y')^2 = 52$$

$$\frac{(x')^2}{1.096} - \frac{(y')^2}{6.153} = 1$$

The graph is a hyperbola.

19. Use the discriminant to determine whether the graph of $13x^2 - 8xy + 7y^2 - 45 = 0$ is a parabola, an ellipse, or a hyperbola.

Solution:

$A = 13$, $B = -8$, $C = 7$

$B^2 - 4AC = (-8)^2 - 4(13)(7) = -300 < 0$

Therefore, the graph is an ellipse or a circle.

23. Use the discriminant to determine whether the graph of $x^2 + 4xy + 4y^2 - 5x - y - 3 = 0$ is a parabola, an ellipse, or a hyperbola.

Solution:

$A = 1$, $B = 4$, $C = 4$

$B^2 - 4AC = (4)^2 - 4(1)(4) = 0$

Therefore, the graph is a parabola.

25. Show that the equation $x^2 + y^2 = r^2$ is invariant under rotation of axes.

Solution:

$$(x')^2 + (y')^2 = [x \cos \theta + y \sin \theta]^2 + [y \cos \theta - x \sin \theta]^2$$
$$= x^2 \cos^2 \theta + 2xy \cos \theta \sin \theta + y^2 \sin^2 \theta + y^2 \cos^2 \theta - 2xy \cos \theta \sin \theta + x^2 \sin^2 \theta$$
$$= x^2(\cos^2 \theta + \sin^2 \theta) + y^2(\sin^2 \theta + \cos^2 \theta)$$
$$= x^2 + y^2 = r^2$$

SECTION 7.6

Polar Coordinates

- In polar coordinates you do not have unique representation of points. The point (r, θ) can be represented by $(r, \theta \pm 2n\pi)$ or by $(-r, \theta \pm (2n+1)\pi)$ where n is any integer. The pole is represented by $(0, \theta)$ where θ is any angle.

- To convert from polar coordinates to rectangular coordinates, use the following relationships.

    $$x = r\cos\theta$$
    $$y = r\sin\theta$$

- To convert from rectangular coordinates to polar coordinates, use the following relationships.

    $$r = \pm\sqrt{x^2 + y^2}$$
    $$\tan\theta = y/x$$

    If θ is in the same quadrant as the point (x, y), then r is positive. If θ is in the opposite quadrant as the point (x, y), then r is negative.

- You should be able to convert rectangular equations to polar form and vice versa.

Solutions to Selected Exercises

3. Plot the polar point $(-1, 5\pi/4)$ and find the corresponding rectangular coordinates for the point.

Solution:

$$r = -1, \ \theta = \frac{5\pi}{4}$$

$$x = (-1)\cos\frac{5\pi}{4} = (-1)\left(-\frac{\sqrt{2}}{2}\right) = \frac{\sqrt{2}}{2}$$

$$y = (-1)\sin\frac{5\pi}{4} = (-1)\left(-\frac{\sqrt{2}}{2}\right) = \frac{\sqrt{2}}{2}$$

$\left(-1, \dfrac{5\pi}{4}\right)$ corresponds to $\left(\dfrac{\sqrt{2}}{2}, \dfrac{\sqrt{2}}{2}\right)$.

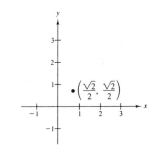

9. Plot the polar point $(\sqrt{2},\ 2.36)$ and find the corresponding rectangular coordinates for the point.

Solution:

$r = \sqrt{2},\ \theta = 2.36$ (in radians)

$\quad x = \sqrt{2}\cos 2.36 \approx -1.004$

$\quad y = \sqrt{2}\sin 2.36 \approx 0.996$

$(\sqrt{2},\ 2.36)$ corresponds to $(-1.004,\ 0.996)$.

15. Plot the rectangular point $(-3,\ 4)$ and find two sets of polar coordinates for $0 \le \theta < 2\pi$.

Solution:

$x = -3,\ y = 4$

$r = \pm\sqrt{(-3)^2 + (4)^2} = \pm 5$

$\tan\theta = -\frac{4}{3},\ \theta \approx 2.214$

The point $(-3,\ 4)$ is in Quadrant II as is the angle $\theta = 2.214$.
Thus, one polar representation is $(5,\ 2.214)$. Another
representation is $(-5,\ 2.214 + \pi) \approx (-5,\ 5.356)$.

19. Plot the the rectangular point $(4,\ 6)$ and find two sets of polar coordinates for $0 \le \theta < 2\pi$.

Solution:

$x = 4,\ y = 6$

$r = \pm\sqrt{(4)^2 + (6)^2} = \pm 2\sqrt{13}$

$\tan\theta = \frac{6}{4},\ \theta \approx 0.983$

Since $(4,\ 6)$ is in Quadrant I and $\theta = 0.983$ is in Quadrant I, one
representation in polar coordinates is $(2\sqrt{13},\ 0.983)$. Another
representation is $(-2\sqrt{13},\ 0.983 + \pi) \approx (-2\sqrt{13},\ 4.124)$.

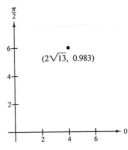

23. Convert the rectangular equation $x^2 + y^2 - 2ax = 0$ to polar form.

Solution:

$$x^2 + y^2 - 2ax = 0$$
$$r^2 - 2ar\cos\theta = 0$$
$$r(r - 2a\cos\theta) = 0$$
$$r = 0 \quad\text{or}\quad r = 2a\cos\theta$$

Since $r = 0$ is the pole and is also on the graph of $r = 2a\cos\theta$, we only have $r = 2a\cos\theta$.

27. Convert the rectangular equation $x = 10$ to polar form.

Solution:

$$x = 10$$
$$r\cos\theta = 10$$
$$r = \frac{10}{\cos\theta}$$
$$r = 10\sec\theta$$

31. Convert the rectangular equation $xy = 4$ to polar form.

Solution:

$$xy = 4$$
$$(r\cos\theta)(r\sin\theta) = 4$$
$$r^2 = \frac{4}{\cos\theta\sin\theta}$$
$$r^2 = 4\sec\theta\csc\theta$$
$$r^2 = 8\csc 2\theta$$

35. Convert the polar equation $r = 4\sin\theta$ to rectangular form.

Solution:

$$r = 4\sin\theta$$
$$r^2 = 4r\sin\theta$$
$$x^2 + y^2 = 4y$$
$$x^2 + y^2 - 4y = 0$$

39. Convert the polar equation $r = 2\csc\theta$ to rectangular form.

Solution:

$$r = 2\csc\theta$$
$$r = \frac{2}{\sin\theta}$$
$$r\sin\theta = 2$$
$$y = 2$$

43. Convert the polar equation $r = \dfrac{6}{2 - 3\sin\theta}$ to rectangular form.

Solution:

$$r = \frac{6}{2 - 3\sin\theta}$$
$$r(2 - 3\sin\theta) = 6$$
$$2r - 3r\sin\theta = 6$$
$$2r = 6 + 3r\sin\theta$$
$$2(\pm\sqrt{x^2 + y^2}) = 6 + 3y$$
$$4(x^2 + y^2) = (6 + 3y)^2$$
$$4x^2 + 4y^2 = 36 + 36y + 9y^2$$
$$4x^2 - 5y^2 - 36y - 36 = 0$$

47. Convert the polar equation $\theta = \pi/4$ to rectangular form and sketch its graph.

Solution:

$$\theta = \frac{\pi}{4}$$

$$\tan \theta = \tan \frac{\pi}{4}$$

$$\frac{y}{x} = 1$$

$$y = x$$

$$x - y = 0$$

51. Show that the distance between $(r_1,\ \theta_1)$ and $(r_2,\ \theta_2)$ is $\sqrt{r_1{}^2 + r_2{}^2 - 2r_1r_2 \cos(\theta_1 - \theta_2)}$.

Solution:

$(r_1,\ \theta_1)$ corresponds to the point $(r_1 \cos \theta_1,\ r_1 \sin \theta_1)$ in rectangular coordinates. Likewise, $(r_2,\ \theta_2)$ corresponds to the point $(r_2 \cos \theta_2,\ r_2 \sin \theta_2)$. In rectangular coordinates we use the distance formula, $d = \sqrt{(x_2 - x_1)^2 + (y_2 - y_1)^2}$, to find the distance between two points.

$$d = \sqrt{(r_2 \cos \theta_2 - r_1 \cos \theta_1)^2 + (r_2 \sin \theta_2 - r_1 \sin \theta_1)^2}$$

$$= \sqrt{r_2{}^2 \cos^2 \theta_2 - 2r_1r_2 \cos \theta_1 \cos \theta_2 + r_1{}^2 \cos^2 \theta_1 + r_2{}^2 \sin^2 \theta_2 - 2r_1r_2 \sin \theta_1 \sin \theta_2 + r_1{}^2 \sin^2 \theta_1}$$

$$= \sqrt{r_1{}^2(\cos^2 \theta_1 + \sin^2 \theta_1) + r_2{}^2(\cos^2 \theta_2 + \sin^2 \theta_2) - 2r_1r_2(\cos \theta_1 \cos \theta_2 + \sin \theta_1 \sin \theta_2)}$$

$$= \sqrt{r_1{}^2(1) + r_2{}^2(1) - 2r_1r_2 \cos(\theta_1 - \theta_2)}$$

$$= \sqrt{r_1{}^2 + r_2{}^2 - 2r_1r_2 \cos(\theta_1 - \theta_2)}$$

SECTION 7.7

Graphs of Polar Equations

- When graphing polar equations:
  1. Test for symmetry
     - (a) $\theta = \pi/2$: Replace (r, θ) by $(r, \pi - \theta)$ or $(-r, -\theta)$.
     - (b) Polar axis: Replace (r, θ) by $(r, -\theta)$ or $(-r, \pi - \theta)$.
     - (c) Pole: Replace (r, θ) by $(r, \pi + \theta)$ or $(-r, \theta)$.
     - (d) $r = f(\sin \theta)$ is symmetric with respect to the line $\theta = \pi/2$.
     - (e) $r = f(\cos \theta)$ is symmetric with respect to the polar axis.

  2. Find the θ values for which $|r|$ is maximum.

  3. Find the θ values for which $r = 0$.

  4. Know the different types of polar graphs.

     (a) Limaçons
     $$r = a \pm b \cos \theta$$
     $$r = a \pm b \sin \theta$$

     (b) Rose Curves, $n \geq 2$
     $$r = a \cos n\theta$$
     $$r = a \sin n\theta$$

     (c) Circles
     $$r = a \cos \theta$$
     $$r = a \sin \theta$$
     $$r = a$$

     (d) Lemniscates
     $$r^2 = a^2 \cos 2\theta$$
     $$r^2 = a^2 \sin 2\theta$$

  5. Plot additional points.

Solutions to Selected Exercises

3. Test $r = 2/(1 + \sin \theta)$ for symmetry with respect to $\theta = \pi/2$, the polar axis, and the pole.

Solution:

$$\theta = \frac{\pi}{2}: \quad r = \frac{2}{1 + \sin(\pi - \theta)} = \frac{2}{1 + \sin \pi \cos \theta - \cos \pi \sin \theta} = \frac{2}{1 + \sin \theta}$$

The graph **is** symmetric with respect to the line $\theta = \pi/2$. None of the other substitutions will yield an equivalent equation. The graph is **not** symmetric with respect to the polar axis or the pole.

7. Find the maximum values of $|r|$ and any zeros of r for $r = 5 \cos 3\theta$.

Solution:

$$|r| = |5 \cos 3\theta| = 5|\cos 3\theta| \le 5$$

The maximum value of $|r|$ is 5. This occurs when $\cos 3\theta = \pm 1$ or when $\theta = 0,\ \pi/3,\ 2\pi/3$. $r = 0$ when $\cos 3\theta = 0$. This occurs when $\theta = \pi/6,\ \pi/2,\ 5\pi/6$ (for $0 \le \theta < 2\pi$).

13. Sketch the graph of $\theta = \pi/6$.

Solution:

$$\theta = \frac{\pi}{6}$$

$$\tan \theta = \tan \frac{\pi}{6}$$

$$\frac{y}{x} = \frac{1}{\sqrt{3}}$$

$$\sqrt{3}\, y = x$$

$$y = \frac{x}{\sqrt{3}} \quad \text{Straight line}$$

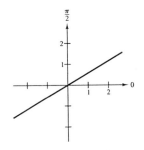

17. Sketch the graph of $r = 4(1 + \sin \theta)$.

Solution:

$$r = 4 + 4 \sin \theta$$

$a/b = 4/4 = 1$, so the graph is a cardioid. Since r is a function of $\sin \theta$, the graph is symmetric with respect to $\theta = \pi/2$. The maximum value of $|r|$ is 8 and occurs when $\theta = \pi/2$. The zero of r occurs when $\theta = 3\pi/2$.

θ	0	$\dfrac{\pi}{6}$	$\dfrac{\pi}{2}$	$\dfrac{5\pi}{6}$	π	$\dfrac{7\pi}{6}$	$\dfrac{3\pi}{2}$	$\dfrac{11\pi}{6}$	2π
r	4	6	8	6	4	2	0	2	4

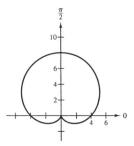

21. Sketch the graph of $r = 3 - 4\cos\theta$.

Solution:

$r = 3 - 4\cos\theta$

Since $a/b = 3/4 < 1$, the graph is a limaçon with an inner loop. Also, since r is a function of $\cos\theta$, the graph is symmetric with respect to the polar axis. The maximum value of $|r|$ is 7 and occurs when $\theta = \pi$. The zeros of r occur when $\cos\theta = 3/4$ or when $\theta \approx 0.723,\ 5.560$.

θ	0	$\dfrac{\pi}{3}$	$\dfrac{\pi}{2}$	$\dfrac{2\pi}{3}$	π	$\dfrac{4\pi}{3}$	$\dfrac{3\pi}{2}$	$\dfrac{5\pi}{3}$	2π
r	-1	1	3	5	7	5	3	1	-1

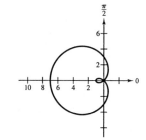

25. Sketch the graph of $r = \dfrac{3}{\sin\theta - 2\cos\theta}$.

Solution:

$$r = \frac{3}{\sin\theta - 2\cos\theta}$$

$$r(\sin\theta - 2\cos\theta) = 3$$

$$r\sin\theta - 2r\cos\theta = 3$$

$$y - 2x = 3$$

$$y = 2x + 3$$

The graph is a line.

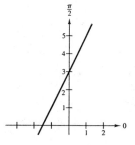

27. Sketch the graph of $r^2 = 4\cos 2\theta$.

Solution:

The graph is a lemniscate. Symmetric to the polar axis, the line $\theta = \pi/2$, and the pole. Maximum value of $|r|$ is 2 and occurs when $\theta = 0$ and $\theta = \pi$. The zeros of r occur when $\theta = \pi/4$, $3\pi/4$, $5\pi/4$, and $7\pi/4$.

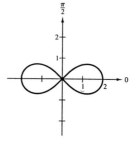

θ	0	$\dfrac{\pi}{6}$	$\dfrac{\pi}{4}$
r	± 2	$\pm\sqrt{2}$	0

31. Convert $r = 2 - \sec\theta$ to rectangular form and show that $x = -1$ is an asymptote to the graph.

Solution:

$$r = 2 - \sec\theta = 2 - \frac{1}{\cos\theta}$$

$$r\cos\theta = 2\cos\theta - 1$$

$$r(r\cos\theta) = 2r\cos\theta - r$$

$$(\pm\sqrt{x^2+y^2}\,)x = 2x - (\pm\sqrt{x^2+y^2}\,)$$

$$(\pm\sqrt{x^2+y^2}\,)(x+1) = 2x$$

$$(\pm\sqrt{x^2+y^2}\,) = \frac{2x}{x+1}$$

$$x^2 + y^2 = \frac{4x^2}{(x+1)^2}$$

$$y^2 = \frac{4x^2}{(x+1)^2} - x^2$$

$$= \frac{4x^2 - x^2(x+1)^2}{(x+1)^2} = \frac{4x^2 - x^2(x^2+2x+1)}{(x+1)^2}$$

$$= \frac{-x^4 - 2x^3 + 3x^2}{(x+1)^2} = \frac{-x^2(x^2+2x-3)}{(x+1)^2}$$

$$y = \pm\sqrt{\frac{x^2(3 - 2x - x^2)}{(x+1)^2}} = \pm\left|\frac{x}{x+1}\right|\sqrt{3 - 2x - x^2}$$

The graph has an asymptote at $x = -1$.

35. Write the equation for the limaçon $r = 2 - \sin \theta$ after it has been rotated by the given amount.

(a) $\dfrac{\pi}{4}$ (b) $\dfrac{\pi}{2}$ (c) π (d) $\dfrac{3\pi}{2}$

Solution:

Refer to Exercises 33 and 34.

(a) $r = 2 - \sin\left(\theta - \dfrac{\pi}{4}\right)$

     $= 2 - \dfrac{\sqrt{2}}{2}(\sin\theta - \cos\theta)$

(b) $r = 2 - (-\cos\theta) = 2 + \cos\theta$

(c) $r = 2 - (-\sin\theta) = 2 + \sin\theta$

(d) $r = 2 - \cos\theta$

37. Sketch the graphs of the equations.

(a) $r = 1 - \sin\theta$

(b) $r = 1 - \sin\left(\theta - \dfrac{\pi}{4}\right)$

Solution:

(a) Cardioid

θ	0	$\dfrac{\pi}{2}$	π	$\dfrac{3\pi}{2}$
r	1	0	1	2

(b) Rotate the graph of $r = 1 - \sin\theta$ through the angle $\pi/4$.

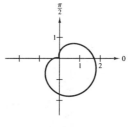

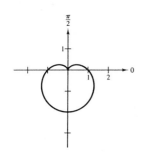

SECTION 7.8

Polar Equations of Conics

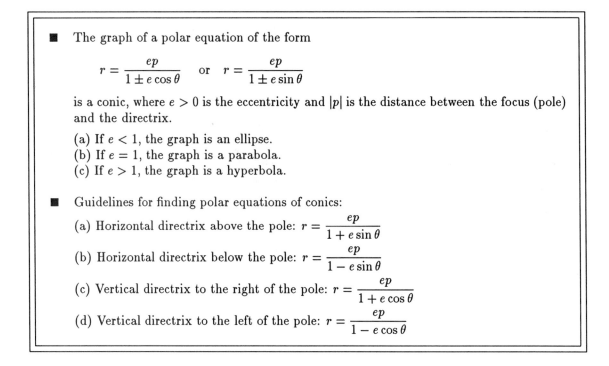

- The graph of a polar equation of the form

$$r = \frac{ep}{1 \pm e \cos \theta} \quad \text{or} \quad r = \frac{ep}{1 \pm e \sin \theta}$$

  is a conic, where $e > 0$ is the eccentricity and $|p|$ is the distance between the focus (pole) and the directrix.

  (a) If $e < 1$, the graph is an ellipse.
  (b) If $e = 1$, the graph is a parabola.
  (c) If $e > 1$, the graph is a hyperbola.

- Guidelines for finding polar equations of conics:

  (a) Horizontal directrix above the pole: $r = \dfrac{ep}{1 + e \sin \theta}$

  (b) Horizontal directrix below the pole: $r = \dfrac{ep}{1 - e \sin \theta}$

  (c) Vertical directrix to the right of the pole: $r = \dfrac{ep}{1 + e \cos \theta}$

  (d) Vertical directrix to the left of the pole: $r = \dfrac{ep}{1 - e \cos \theta}$

Solutions to Selected Exercises

5. Match the polar equation $r = 6/(2 - \sin \theta)$ with the correct graph.

Solution:

$$r = \frac{6}{2 - \sin \theta} = \frac{3}{1 - \frac{1}{2}\sin \theta}$$

$e = \frac{1}{2} < 1 \Rightarrow$ the graph is an ellipse with a horizontal directrix below the pole.

θ	0	$\dfrac{\pi}{2}$	π	$\dfrac{3\pi}{2}$
r	3	6	3	2

Matches graph (b).

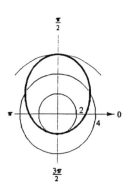

7. Identify and sketch the graph of
$r = 2/(1 - \cos\theta)$.

Solution:

$e = 1 \Rightarrow$ the graph is a parabola.

Vertex: $(1, \pi)$

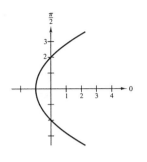

θ	$\dfrac{\pi}{2}$	π	$\dfrac{3\pi}{2}$
r	2	1	2

11. Identify and sketch the graph of
$r = 2/(2 - \cos\theta)$.

Solution:

$$r = \frac{2}{2 - \cos\theta} = \frac{1}{1 - \frac{1}{2}\cos\theta}$$

$e = \frac{1}{2} < 1 \Rightarrow$ the graph is an ellipse.

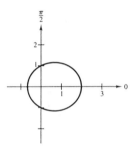

θ	0	$\dfrac{\pi}{2}$	π	$\dfrac{3\pi}{2}$
r	2	1	$\dfrac{2}{3}$	1

17. Identify and sketch the graph of
$r = 3/(2 - 6\cos\theta)$.

Solution:

$$r = \frac{3}{2 - 6\cos\theta}$$

$$r = \frac{3/2}{1 - 3\cos\theta}$$

$e = 3 > 1 \Rightarrow$ the graph is a hyperbola.

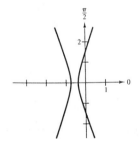

θ	0	$\dfrac{\pi}{2}$	π	$\dfrac{3\pi}{2}$
r	$-\dfrac{3}{4}$	$\dfrac{3}{2}$	$\dfrac{3}{8}$	$\dfrac{3}{2}$

21. Find a polar equation of the ellipse with focus at $(0, 0)$, $e = \frac{1}{2}$, and directrix $y = 1$.

Solution:

$e = \dfrac{1}{2}$, $y = 1$, $p = 1$

Horizontal directrix above the pole

$$r = \frac{ep}{1 + e\sin\theta}$$

$$r = \frac{\frac{1}{2}}{1 + \frac{1}{2}\sin\theta}$$

$$r = \frac{1}{2 + \sin\theta}$$

25. Find a polar equation of the parabola with focus at $(0, 0)$ and vertex at $(1, -\pi/2)$.

Solution:

$e = 1$, $p = 2$

Horizontal directrix below the pole

$$r = \frac{ep}{1 - e\sin\theta}$$

$$r = \frac{2}{1 - \sin\theta}$$

27. Find a polar equation of the parabola with focus at $(0, 0)$ and vertex at $(5, \pi)$.

Solution:

Directrix: $x = -10$, $e = 1$, $p = 10$

Vertical directrix to the left of the pole

$$r = \frac{ep}{1 - e\cos\theta}$$

$$r = \frac{10}{1 - \cos\theta}$$

33. Find a polar equation of the hyperbola with focus at $(0, 0)$ and vertices at $(1, 3\pi/2)$, $(9, 3\pi/2)$.

Solution:

Center: $(5, 3\pi/2)$

$c = 5$, $a = 4$, $e = c/a = 5/4$

Horizontal directrix below the pole

$$r = \frac{ep}{1 - e\sin\theta} = \frac{\frac{5}{4}p}{1 - \frac{5}{4}\sin\theta} = \frac{5p}{4 - 5\sin\theta}$$

$$1 = \frac{5p}{4 - 5\sin\frac{3\pi}{2}} = \frac{5p}{9}$$

$$p = \frac{9}{5}$$

$$r = \frac{5\left(\frac{9}{5}\right)}{4 - 5\sin\theta} = \frac{9}{4 - 5\sin\theta}$$

37. Use the results of Exercises 35 and 36 to write the polar form of

$$\frac{x^2}{169} + \frac{y^2}{144} = 1.$$

Solution:

$a = 13$, $b = 12$, $c = 5$, $e = \frac{5}{13}$

$$r^2 = \frac{b^2}{1 - e^2\cos^2\theta} = \frac{144}{1 - \left(\frac{25}{169}\right)\cos^2\theta} = \frac{24{,}336}{169 - 25\cos^2\theta}$$

41. Use the results of Exercises 35 and 36 to write the polar form of the hyperbola with one focus at $(5, 0)$ and vertices at $(4, 0)$, $(4, \pi)$.

Solution:

Center: $(0, 0)$, $a = 4$, $c = 5$, $b = 3$, $e = \frac{5}{4}$

$$\frac{x^2}{16} - \frac{y^2}{9} = 1$$

$$r^2 = \frac{-b^2}{1 - e^2 \cos^2 \theta} = \frac{-9}{1 - \left(\frac{25}{16}\right) \cos^2 \theta} = \frac{-144}{16 - 25 \cos^2 \theta} = \frac{144}{25 \cos^2 \theta - 16}$$

45. The planets travel in elliptical orbits with the sun as a focus. Assume that the focus is at the pole, the major axis lies on the polar axis, and the length of the major axis is $2a$ (see figure). Show that the polar equation of the orbit is given by

$$r = \frac{(1 - e^2)a}{1 - e \cos \theta}$$

where e is the eccentricity.

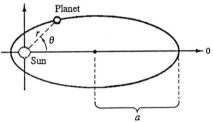

Solution:

When $\theta = 0$, $r = c + a = ea + a = a(1 + e)$. Therefore,

$$a(1 + e) = \frac{ep}{1 - e}$$

$$a(1 + e)(1 - e) = ep$$

$$a(1 - e^2) = ep.$$

Thus, $r = \dfrac{ep}{1 - e \cos \theta} = \dfrac{(1 - e^2)a}{1 - e \cos \theta}.$

49. A satellite in a 100-mile-high circular orbit around the earth has a velocity of approximately 17,500 miles per hour. If this velocity is multiplied by $\sqrt{2}$, then the satellite will have the minimum velocity necessary to escape the earth's gravity and it will follow a parabolic path with the center of the earth as the focus. Find a polar equation of the parabolic path of the satellite (assume the radius of the earth is 4000 miles).

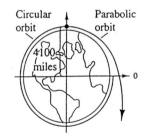

Solution:

Directrix: $y = 8200$, $e = 1$, $p = 8200$

$$r = \frac{ep}{1 + e \sin \theta} = \frac{8200}{1 + \sin \theta}$$

SECTION 7.9

Plane Curves and Parametric Equations

- If f and g are continuous functions of t on an interval I, then the set of ordered pairs $(f(t),\ g(t))$ is a *plane curve C*. The equations $x = f(t)$ and $y = g(t)$ are *parametric equations* for C and t is the *parameter*.

- To eliminate the parameter:

    (a) Solve for t in one equation and substitute into the second equation.
    (b) Use trigonometric identities.

- You should be able to find the parametric equations for a graph.

Solutions to Selected Exercises

5. Sketch the curve represented by the parametric equations (indicate the direction of the curve), and write the corresponding rectangular equation by eliminating the parameter.

$$x = \tfrac{1}{4}t$$
$$y = t^2$$

Solution:

$$x = \tfrac{1}{4}t \Rightarrow 4x = t$$
$$y = t^2 \Rightarrow y = (4x)^2 = 16x^2$$

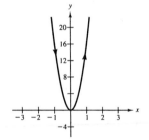

t	-2	-1	0	1	2
x	$-\frac{1}{2}$	$-\frac{1}{4}$	0	$\frac{1}{4}$	$\frac{1}{2}$
y	4	1	0	1	4

9. Sketch the curve represented by the parametric equations (indicate the direction of the curve), and write the corresponding rectangular equation by eliminating the parameter.

$$x = t^3, \; y = \frac{t}{2}$$

Solution:

$$y = \frac{t}{2} \Rightarrow 2y = t$$

$$x = t^3 \Rightarrow x = (2y)^3 \Rightarrow x = 8y^3 \Rightarrow y = \frac{\sqrt[3]{x}}{2}$$

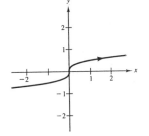

t	-2	-1	0	1	2
x	-8	-1	0	1	8
y	-1	$-\frac{1}{2}$	0	$\frac{1}{2}$	1

13. Sketch the curve represented by the parametric equations (indicate the direction of the curve), and write the corresponding rectangular equation by eliminating the parameter.

$$x = \cos\theta, \; y = 2\sin^2\theta$$

Solution:

$$x = \cos\theta \Rightarrow x^2 = \cos^2\theta$$

$$y = 2\sin^2\theta \Rightarrow \frac{y}{2} = \sin^2\theta$$

Using the identity $\sin^2\theta + \cos^2\theta = 1$ yields

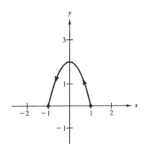

$$\frac{y}{2} + x^2 = 1$$

$$\frac{y}{2} = 1 - x^2$$

$$y = 2(1 - x^2) = 2 - 2x^2.$$

Also, since $x = \cos\theta$ and $y = 2\sin^2\theta$, we know that $-1 \le x \le 1$ and $0 \le y \le 2$.

θ	0	$\frac{\pi}{2}$	π	$\frac{3\pi}{2}$	2π
x	1	0	-1	0	1
y	0	2	0	2	0

The graph oscillates.

15. Sketch the curve represented by the parametric equations (indicate the direction of the curve), and write the corresponding rectangular equation by eliminating the parameter.

$$x = 4 + 2\cos\theta$$

$$y = -1 + 4\sin\theta$$

Solution:

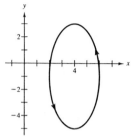

$$x = 4 + 2\cos\theta \Rightarrow \frac{x-4}{2} = \cos\theta$$

$$y = -1 + 4\sin\theta \Rightarrow \frac{y+1}{4} = \sin\theta$$

$$\left(\frac{x-4}{2}\right)^2 + \left(\frac{y+1}{4}\right)^2 = 1$$

$$\frac{(x-4)^2}{4} + \frac{(y+1)^2}{16} = 1$$

θ	0	$\dfrac{\pi}{2}$	π	$\dfrac{3\pi}{2}$
x	6	4	2	4
y	-1	3	-1	-5

17. Sketch the curve represented by the parametric equations (indicate the direction of the curve), and write the corresponding rectangular equation by eliminating the parameter.

$$x = e^{-t}$$

$$y = e^{3t}$$

Solution:

Since $x = e^{-t}$ and $y = e^{3t}$, we have $x > 0$ and $y > 0$.

$$x = e^{-t} \Rightarrow \frac{1}{x} = e^t$$

$$y = e^{3t} = (e^t)^3 = \left(\frac{1}{x}\right)^3 = \frac{1}{x^3}$$

where $x > 0$ and $y > 0$.

t	-1	0	1
x	2.718	1	0.368
y	0.050	1	20.086

21. Determine how the plane curves differ from each other.

(a) $x = t$

$y = 2t + 1$

(b) $x = \cos\theta$

$y = 2\cos\theta + 1$

(c) $x = e^{-t}$

$y = 2e^{-t} + 1$

(d) $x = e^t$

$y = 2e^t + 1$

Solution:

By eliminating the parameter, each curve becomes $y = 2x + 1$.

(a) $x = t$

$y = 2t + 1$

There are no restrictions on x and y.

(b) $\quad x = \cos\theta \Rightarrow -1 \le x \le 1$

$y = 2\cos\theta + 1 \Rightarrow -1 \le y \le 3$

The graph oscillates.

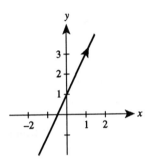

(c) $\quad x = e^{-t} \Rightarrow x > 0$

$y = 2e^{-t} + 1 \Rightarrow y > 1$

This graph is oriented downward.

(d) $\quad x = e^t \Rightarrow x > 0$

$y = 2e^t + 1 \Rightarrow y > 1$

This graph is oriented upward.

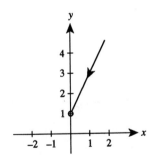

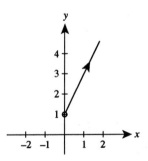

25. Eliminate the parameter and obtain the standard form of the rectangular equation.

Ellipse: $x = h + a\cos\theta$, $y = k + b\sin\theta$

Solution:

$$x = h + a\cos\theta \Rightarrow \frac{x-h}{a} = \cos\theta$$

$$y = k + b\sin\theta \Rightarrow \frac{y-k}{b} = \sin\theta$$

$$\left(\frac{x-h}{a}\right)^2 + \left(\frac{y-k}{b}\right)^2 = 1$$

$$\frac{(x-h)^2}{a^2} + \frac{(y-k)^2}{b^2} = 1$$

29. Find a set of parametric equations for the circle with center at $(2, 1)$ and radius 4.

Solution:

From Exercise 24 we have $x = h + r\cos\theta$, $y = k + r\sin\theta$. Using $h = 2$, $k = 1$ and $r = 4$, we have $x = 2 + 4\cos\theta$, $y = 1 + 4\sin\theta$. This solution is not unique.

33. Find a set of parametric equations for the hyperbola with vertices at $(\pm 4, 0)$ and foci at $(\pm 5, 0)$.

Solution:

From Exercise 26 we have $x = h + a\sec\theta$, $y = k + b\tan\theta$. Using $(h, k) = (0, 0)$, $a = 4$, $c = 5$, and $b = 3$, we have $x = 4\sec\theta$, $y = 3\tan\theta$. This solution is not unique.

35. Find two different sets of parametric equations for the rectangular equation $y = x^3$.

Solution:

Examples

$x = t,$	$y = t^3$
$x = \sqrt[3]{t},$	$y = t$
$x = \tan t,$	$y = \tan^3 t$
$x = t - 4,$	$y = (t-4)^3$

and so on.

41. Sketch the curve represented by the parametric equations.

Witch of Agnesi: $x = 2\cot\theta$, $y = 2\sin^2\theta$

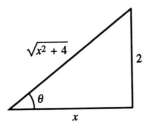

Solution:

$$x = 2\cot\theta \Rightarrow \theta = \operatorname{arccot}\frac{x}{2}$$

$$y = 2\sin^2\theta \Rightarrow y = 2\sin^2\left(\operatorname{arccot}\frac{x}{2}\right)$$

$$y = 2\left(\frac{2}{\sqrt{x^2+4}}\right)^2$$

$$y = \frac{8}{x^2+4}$$

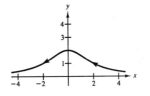

45. Match the equations with the correct graph.

Involute of a Circle: $x = \cos\theta + \theta\sin\theta$

$$y = \sin\theta - \theta\cos\theta$$

Solution:

$$x = \cos\theta + \theta\sin\theta$$

$$y = \sin\theta - \theta\cos\theta$$

θ	0	$\dfrac{\pi}{2}$	π	$\dfrac{3\pi}{2}$	2π
x	1	$\dfrac{\pi}{2}$	-1	$-\dfrac{3\pi}{2}$	1
y	0	1	π	-1	-2π

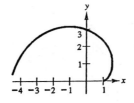

Matches graph (d).

47. A wheel of radius a rolls along a straight line without slipping (see figure). Find the parametric equations for the curve generated by a point P that is b units from the center of the wheel. This curve is called a *curtate cycloid* when $b < a$.

Solution:

When the circle has rolled θ radians, we know that the center is at $(a\theta, a)$.

$$\sin\theta = \sin(180° - \theta) = \frac{|AC|}{b} = \frac{|BD|}{b} \quad \text{or}$$

$$|BD| = b\sin\theta$$

$$\cos\theta = -\cos(180° - \theta) = \frac{|AP|}{-b} \quad \text{or}$$

$$|AP| = -b\cos\theta$$

Therefore, $x = a\theta - b\sin\theta$ and $y = a - b\cos\theta$.

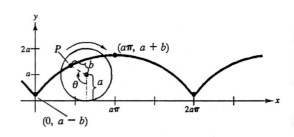

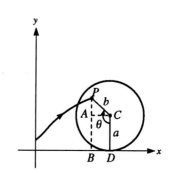

REVIEW EXERCISES FOR CHAPTER 7

Solutions to Selected Exercises

5. Find the distance between the point $(1, 2)$ and the line $x - y - 3 = 0$.

Solution:

$(1,\ 2) \Rightarrow x_1 = 1$ and $y_1 = 2$

$x - y - 3 = 0 \Rightarrow A = 1,\ B = -1,$ and $C = -3$

$$d = \frac{|1(1) + (-1)(2) + (-3)|}{\sqrt{(1)^2 + (-1)^2}} = \frac{4}{\sqrt{2}} = 2\sqrt{2}$$

11. Identify and sketch the graph of the rectangular equation $3x^2 + 2y^2 - 12x + 12y + 29 = 0$.

Solution:

Since $AC = 3(2) = 6 > 0$, the graph is an ellipse.

$$3x^2 + 2y^2 - 12x + 12y + 29 = 0$$

$$3(x^2 - 4x + 4) + 2(y^2 + 6y + 9) = -29 + 12 + 18$$

$$3(x - 2)^2 + 2(y + 3)^2 = 1$$

$$\frac{(x - 2)^2}{1/3} + \frac{(y + 3)^2}{1/2} = 1$$

Center: $(2,\ -3)$; Vertices: $\left(2,\ -3 \pm \frac{\sqrt{2}}{2}\right)$

15. Identify and sketch the graph of the rectangular equation
$x^2 + y^2 + 2xy + 2\sqrt{2}\,x - 2\sqrt{2}\,y + 2 = 0$.

Solution:

Since $B^2 - 4AC = 2^2 - 4(1)(1) = 0$, the graph is a parabola.

$$\cot 2\theta = \frac{A - C}{B} = 0 \Rightarrow 2\theta = \frac{\pi}{2} \Rightarrow \theta = \frac{\pi}{4}$$

$$x = x' \cos \frac{\pi}{4} - y' \sin \frac{\pi}{4} = \frac{x' - y'}{\sqrt{2}}$$

$$y = x' \sin \frac{\pi}{4} + y' \cos \frac{\pi}{4} = \frac{x' + y'}{\sqrt{2}}$$

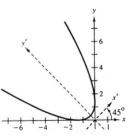

–CONTINUED ON NEXT PAGE–

15. –CONTINUED–

$$\left(\frac{x'-y'}{\sqrt{2}}\right)^2 + \left(\frac{x'+y'}{\sqrt{2}}\right)^2 + 2\left(\frac{x'-y'}{\sqrt{2}}\right)\left(\frac{x'+y'}{\sqrt{2}}\right) + 2\sqrt{2}\left(\frac{x'-y'}{\sqrt{2}}\right)$$

$$- 2\sqrt{2}\left(\frac{x'+y'}{\sqrt{2}}\right) + 2 = 0$$

$$2(x')^2 - 4y' + 2 = 0$$

$$(x')^2 = 2y' - 1$$

Vertex: $(x', y') = \left(0, \frac{1}{2}\right)$, $\theta = 45°$

19. Find a rectangular equation for the parabola with vertex at $(0, 2)$ and directrix $x = -3$.

Solution:

$p = 3$, $(h, k) = (0, 2)$
Horizontal axis

$$(y - k)^2 = 4p(x - h)$$
$$(y - 2)^2 = 4(3)(x - 0)$$
$$(y - 2)^2 = 12x$$

23. Find a rectangular equation for the ellipse with vertices at $(0, \pm 6)$ and passes through the point $(2, 2)$.

Solution:

$(h, k) = (0, 0)$
Vertical major axis with $a = 6$

$$\frac{x^2}{b^2} + \frac{y^2}{36} = 1$$

Since the graph passes through the point $(2, 2)$, we have:

$$\frac{4}{b^2} + \frac{4}{36} = 1$$
$$36 + b^2 = 9b^2$$
$$36 = 8b^2$$
$$\frac{36}{8} = b^2$$
$$\frac{9}{2} = b^2$$
$$\frac{x^2}{9/2} + \frac{y^2}{36} = 1$$

27. Find a rectangular equation of the hyperbola with foci at $(0, 0)$, $(8, 0)$ and asymptotes $y = \pm 2(x - 4)$.

Solution:

$(h, k) = (4, 0)$
The transverse axis is horizontal with $c = 4$. Also from the slopes of the asymptotes $\pm b/a = \pm 2$ or $\pm b = \pm 2a$. Now $c^2 = a^2 + b^2 = a^2 + (2a)^2 = 16$. Therefore,

$$a^2 = \frac{16}{5}, \quad b^2 = \frac{64}{5} \quad \text{and} \quad \frac{(x-4)^2}{16/5} - \frac{y^2}{64/5} = 1.$$

31. Find an equation of the tangent line to

$$\frac{x^2}{100} + \frac{y^2}{25} = 1$$ at the point $(-8, \ 3)$. The tangent line to the conic

$$\frac{x^2}{a^2} \pm \frac{y^2}{b^2} = 1$$ at the point $(x_0, \ y_0)$ is given by

$$\frac{x_0 x}{a^2} \pm \frac{y_0 y}{b^2} = 1.$$

Solution:

$(x_0, \ y_0) = (-8, \ 3)$
$a^2 = 100, \ b^2 = 25$

$$\frac{-8x}{100} + \frac{3y}{25} = 1$$

$$-8x + 12y = 100$$

$$-2x + 3y = 25$$

39. Identify and sketch the graph of the polar equation $r = -2(1 + \cos \theta)$.

Solution:

$r = -2(1 + \cos \theta)$ is a cardioid; symmetric to the polar axis.

θ	0	$\dfrac{\pi}{3}$	$\dfrac{\pi}{2}$	$\dfrac{2\pi}{3}$	π
r	-4	-3	-2	-1	0

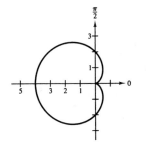

35. Identify and sketch the graph of the polar equation $r = 4$.

Solution:

$r = 4$ is a circle of radius 4 centered at the pole.

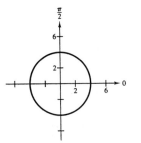

43. Identify and sketch the graph of the polar equation $r = -3 \cos 3\theta$.

Solution:

$r = -3 \cos 3\theta$ is a rose curve with three petals; symmetric to the polar axis. Maximum value of $|r|$ is 3.

$$(-3, \ 0), \ \left(3, \ \frac{\pi}{3}\right), \ \left(-3, \ \frac{2\pi}{3}\right)$$

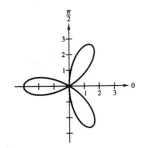

47. Identify and sketch the graph of the polar equation

$$r = \frac{3}{\cos(\theta - (\pi/4))}.$$

Solution:

$$r = \frac{3}{\cos(\theta - (\pi/4))}$$

$$r \cos\left(\theta - \frac{\pi}{4}\right) = 3$$

$$r\left[\cos\theta \cos\frac{\pi}{4} + \sin\theta \sin\frac{\pi}{4}\right] = 3$$

$$r\left[\frac{\sqrt{2}}{2}\cos\theta + \frac{\sqrt{2}}{2}\sin\theta\right] = 3$$

$$\frac{\sqrt{2}}{2}r\cos\theta + \frac{\sqrt{2}}{2}r\sin\theta = 3$$

$$r\cos\theta + r\sin\theta = 3\sqrt{2}$$

$$x + y = 3\sqrt{2}$$

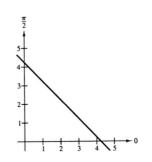

The graph is a line.

51. Convert $r = 3\cos\theta$ to rectangular form.

Solution:

$$r = 3\cos\theta$$

$$r^2 = 3r\cos\theta$$

$$x^2 + y^2 = 3x$$

$$x^2 + y^2 - 3x = 0$$

55. Convert $r^2 = \cos 2\theta$ to rectangular form.

Solution:

$$r^2 = \cos 2\theta$$

$$r^2 = 2\cos^2\theta - 1$$

$$x^2 + y^2 = 2\left(\frac{x^2}{x^2 + y^2}\right) - 1$$

$$(x^2 + y^2)^2 = 2x^2 - (x^2 + y^2)$$

$$(x^2 + y^2)^2 - x^2 + y^2 = 0$$

59. Find a polar equation for a circle with center at $(5, \pi/2)$ and passes through $(0, 0)$.

Solution:

The radius is 5.

$$x^2 + (y - 5)^2 = 25$$
$$x^2 + y^2 - 10y = 0$$
$$r^2 - 10r \sin \theta = 0$$
$$r(r - 10 \sin \theta) = 0$$
$$r = 10 \sin \theta$$

61. Find a polar equation for a parabola with vertex at $(2, \pi)$ and focus at $(0, 0)$.

Solution:

$e = 1$, $p = 4$

Vertical directrix to the left of the pole

$$r = \frac{ep}{1 - e \cos \theta}$$

$$r = \frac{4}{1 - \cos \theta}$$

67. Sketch the curve represented by the parametric equations, $x = 1 + 4t$, $y = 2 - 3t$, and where possible, write the corresponding rectangular equation by eliminating the parameter.

Solution:

$$x = 1 + 4t \Rightarrow t = \frac{x - 1}{4}$$

$$y = 2 - 3t \Rightarrow y = 2 - 3\left(\frac{x - 1}{4}\right)$$

$$y = -\frac{3}{4}x + \frac{11}{4}$$

$$3x + 4y = 11$$

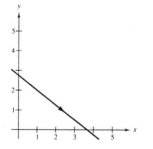

71. Sketch the curve represented by the parametric equations, $x = 6 \cos \theta$, $y = 6 \sin \theta$, and where possible, write the corresponding rectangular equation by eliminating the parameter.

Solution:

$$x = 6 \cos \theta \Rightarrow \cos \theta = \frac{x}{6}$$

$$y = 6 \sin \theta \Rightarrow \sin \theta = \frac{y}{6}$$

$$\left(\frac{x}{6}\right)^2 + \left(\frac{y}{6}\right)^2 = 1$$

$$x^2 + y^2 = 36$$

$$\frac{x^2}{36} + \frac{y^2}{36} = 1$$

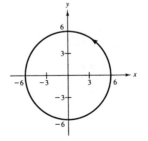

73. Sketch the curve represented by the parametric equations, $x = \cos^3\theta$, $y = 4\sin^3\theta$, and where possible, write the corresponding rectangular equation by eliminating the parameter.

Solution:

$$x = \cos^3\theta \Rightarrow \cos\theta = x^{1/3}$$

$$y = 4\sin^3\theta \Rightarrow \sin\theta = \left(\frac{y}{4}\right)^{1/3}$$

$$\left(x^{1/3}\right)^2 + \left[\left(\frac{y}{4}\right)^{1/3}\right]^2 = 1$$

$$x^{2/3} + \left(\frac{y}{4}\right)^{2/3} = 1$$

79. Show that the Cartesian equation of a cycloid is

$$x = a\arccos\left(\frac{a-y}{a}\right) \pm \sqrt{2ay - y^2}.$$

Solution:

The parametric equations of a cycloid are $x = a(\theta - \sin\theta)$ and $y = a(1 - \cos\theta)$. See Example 5 in Section 7.9.

$$\cos\theta = \frac{a-y}{a}$$

$$\theta = \arccos\left(\frac{a-y}{a}\right)$$

Thus,

$$x = a(\theta - \sin\theta)$$

$$= a\left\{\arccos\left(\frac{a-y}{a}\right) - \sin\left[\arccos\left(\frac{a-y}{a}\right)\right]\right\}$$

$$= a\arccos\left(\frac{a-y}{a}\right) \pm a\left[\frac{\sqrt{2ay - y^2}}{a}\right]$$

$$= a\arccos\left(\frac{a-y}{a}\right) \pm \sqrt{2ay - y^2}$$

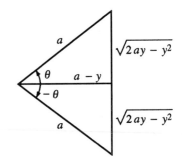

Practice Test for Chapter 7

1. Find the angle, θ, between the lines $3x + 4y = 12$ and $4x - 3y = 12$.

2. Find the distance between the point $(5, -9)$ and the line $3x - 7y = 21$.

3. Find the vertex, focus, and directrix of the parabola $x^2 - 6x - 4y + 1 = 0$.

4. Find an equation of the parabola with its vertex at $(2, -5)$ and focus at $(2, -6)$.

5. Find the center, foci, vertices, and eccentricity of the ellipse $x^2 + 4y^2 - 2x + 32y + 61 = 0$.

6. Find an equation of the ellipse with vertices $(0, \pm 6)$ and eccentricity $e = \frac{1}{2}$.

7. Find the center, vertices, foci, and asymptotes of the hyperbola $16y^2 - x^2 - 6x - 128y + 231 = 0$.

8. Find an equation of the hyperbola with vertices at $(\pm 3, 2)$ and foci at $(\pm 5, 2)$.

9. Rotate the axes to eliminate the xy-term. Sketch the graph of the resulting equation, showing both sets of axes.
   $$5x^2 + 2xy + 5y^2 - 10 = 0$$

10. Use the discriminant to determine whether the graph of the equation is a parabola, ellipse, or hyperbola.
    (a) $6x^2 - 2xy + y^2 = 0$ (b) $x^2 + 4xy + 4y^2 - x - y + 17 = 0$

11. Convert the polar point $(\sqrt{2}, (3\pi)/4)$ to rectangular coordinates.

12. Convert the rectangular point $(\sqrt{3}, -1)$ to polar coordinates.

13. Convert the rectangular equation $4x - 3y = 12$ to polar form.

14. Convert the polar equation $r = 5\cos\theta$ to rectangular form.

15. Sketch the graph of $r = 1 - \cos\theta$.

16. Sketch the graph of $r = 5\sin 2\theta$.

17. Sketch the graph of $r = \dfrac{3}{6 - \cos\theta}$.

18. Find a polar equation of the parabola with its vertex at $(6, \pi/2)$ and focus at $(0, 0)$.

For Exercises 19 and 20, eliminate the parameter and write the corresponding rectangular equation.

19. $x = 3 - 2\sin\theta, \quad y = 1 + 5\cos\theta$ **20.** $x = e^{2t}, \quad y = e^{4t}$

CHAPTER 1

Practice Test Solutions

1. $-|-17| - 17 = -17 - 17$

$\qquad = -34$

2. $d = \left| \frac{12}{5} - \left(-\frac{7}{15} \right) \right|$

$\qquad = \left| \frac{36}{15} + \frac{7}{15} \right|$

$\qquad = \frac{43}{15}$

3. $|z - (-5)| \leq 12$

$\qquad |z + 5| \leq 12$

4. The midpoint of the interval is -2 and the distance between -2 and either endpoint is 6. Therefore, we have

$$|x - (-2)| \leq 6$$

$$|x + 2| \leq 6$$

5. $\dfrac{6x + 5}{2x - 9} = \dfrac{3}{5}$

$5(6x + 5) = 3(2x - 9)$

$30x + 25 = 6x - 27$

$24x = -52$

$$x = -\frac{52}{24} = -\frac{13}{6}$$

6. $4x^2 + 3x - 5 = 0$

$a = 4, \ b = 3, \ c = -5$

$$x = \frac{-3 \pm \sqrt{(3)^2 - 4(4)(-5)}}{2(4)} = \frac{-3 \pm \sqrt{89}}{8}$$

7. $21.4x^2 + 6.9x - 1.4 = 0$

$a = 21.4, \ b = 6.9, \ c = -1.4$

$$x = \frac{-6.9 \pm \sqrt{(6.9)^2 - 4(21.4)(-1.4)}}{2(21.4)}$$

$$= \frac{-6.9 \pm \sqrt{167.45}}{42.8}$$

$$x = \frac{-6.9 + \sqrt{167.45}}{42.8} \approx 0.141$$

$$x = \frac{-6.9 - \sqrt{167.48}}{42.8} \approx -0.464$$

8. $x^6 - 7x^3 - 8 = 0$

$(x^3 - 8)(x^3 + 1) = 0$

$x^3 = 8$ or $x^3 = -1$

$x = 2 \qquad x = -1$

9. $d = \sqrt{(-2 - 4)^2 + (5 - 7)^2}$

$\qquad = \sqrt{36 + 4}$

$\qquad = \sqrt{40}$

$\qquad = 2\sqrt{10}$

10. $\left(\dfrac{-1 + 3}{2}, \ \dfrac{16 + (-5)}{2} \right) = \left(1, \ \dfrac{11}{2} \right)$

11. $\sqrt{(-6-2)^2 + (x-0)^2} = 9$

$$\sqrt{64 + x^2} = 9$$

$$64 + x^2 = 81$$

$$x^2 = 17$$

$$x = \pm\sqrt{17}$$

12. $y = x\sqrt{3-x}$

x-intercepts:

$$0 = x\sqrt{3-x} \Rightarrow x = 0 \text{ or } x = 3$$

$$(0,\ 0) \text{ and } (3,\ 0)$$

y-intercept: $y = 0\sqrt{3-0} = 0$

$$(0,\ 0)$$

13. $y = \dfrac{(-x)^2}{(-x)^3 - 1} = \dfrac{x^2}{-x^3 - 1} \neq \dfrac{x^2}{x^3 - 1};$ *Not* symmetric with respect to the y-axis

$-y = \dfrac{x^2}{x^3 - 1} \Rightarrow y = -\dfrac{x^2}{x^3 - 1} \neq \dfrac{x^2}{x^3 - 1};$ *Not* symmetric with respect to the x-axis

$-y = \dfrac{(-x)^2}{(-x)^3 - 1} \Rightarrow -y = \dfrac{x^2}{-x^3 - 1} \Rightarrow y = \dfrac{x^2}{x^3 + 1} \neq \dfrac{x^2}{x^3 - 1};$ *Not* symmetric with respect to the origin

14. $y = \sqrt{x+2}$

x	-2	-1	2	7
y	0	1	2	3

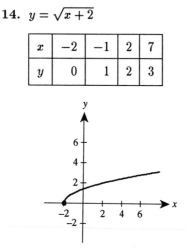

15. $y = |x - 3|$

x	0	1	2	3	4	5
y	3	2	1	0	1	2

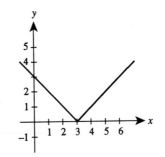

16. $x^2 + y^2 - 14x + 6y + 42 = 0$

$$x^2 - 14x + 49 + y^2 + 6y + 9 = -42 + 49 + 9$$

$$(x - 7)^2 + (y + 3)^2 = 16$$

17. $f(x) = 5x + 11$

$$f(2) = 10 + 11 = 21$$

$$\frac{f(x) - f(2)}{x - 2} = \frac{(5x + 11) - 21}{x - 2} = \frac{5x - 10}{x - 2} = \frac{5(x - 2)}{x - 2} = 5$$

18. $f(x) = \sqrt{\dfrac{x-1}{x+3}}$

Domain: $\dfrac{x-1}{x+3} \geq 0$

Critical numbers: $x = 1,\ x = -3$

$$\dfrac{(-)}{(-)} > 0 \ \Big|\ \dfrac{(-)}{(+)} < 0 \ \Big|\ \dfrac{(+)}{(+)} > 0$$

YES   NO   YES

$x < -3$ OR $x \geq 1$

19. $V = l \cdot w \cdot h$

$V = (16 - 2x)(11 - 2x)(x)$

$V = 4x^3 - 54x^2 + 176x$

20. $f(x) = x^2 - 9$
Intercepts:
$(-3,\ 0),\ (3,\ 0),\ (0,\ -9)$
y-axis symmetry

21. $f(x) = -1 + |x|$
Intercepts:
$(-1,\ 0),\ (1,\ 0),\ (0,\ -1)$
y-axis symmetry

22. $f(x) = \dfrac{3x^2}{x^2 - 4}$
Vertical asymptotes:
$x = \pm 2$
Horizontal asymptote:
$y = 3$
y-axis symmetry

23. $f(x) = x^2 + 2$

$g(x) = 3x - 8$

$(f \circ g)(x) = f(g(x)) = f(3x - 8) = (3x - 8)^2 + 2 = 9x^2 - 48x + 66$

24. $f(x) = \dfrac{x+3}{x}$

$y = \dfrac{x+3}{x}$

$x = \dfrac{y+3}{y}$

$xy = y + 3$

$xy - y = 3$

$y(x - 1) = 3$

$y = \dfrac{3}{x-1}$

$f^{-1}(x) = \dfrac{3}{x-1}$

25. $f(x) = \dfrac{x^3}{4}$

$f^{-1}(x) = \sqrt[3]{4x}$

$g(x) = 3x$

$g^{-1}(x) = \dfrac{x}{3}$

$g^{-1} \circ f^{-1} = g^{-1}(f^{-1}(x))$

$= g^{-1}(\sqrt[3]{4x})$

$= \dfrac{\sqrt[3]{4x}}{3}$

CHAPTER 2

Practice Test Solutions

1. (a) $350° = 350\left(\dfrac{\pi}{180}\right) = \dfrac{35\pi}{18}$

(b) $\dfrac{5\pi}{9} = \dfrac{5\pi}{9} \cdot \dfrac{180}{\pi} = 100°$

2. (a) $135°14'12'' = \left(135 + \frac{14}{60} + \frac{12}{3600}\right)°$

$\approx 135.2367°$

(b) $-22.569° = -(22° + 0.569(60)')$

$= -22°34.14'$

$= -(22°34' + 0.14(60)'')$

$\approx -22°34'8''$

3. (a) $\dfrac{5\pi}{6}$ corresponds to the point $\left(-\dfrac{\sqrt{3}}{2}, \dfrac{1}{2}\right)$.

$\sin\dfrac{5\pi}{6} = y = \dfrac{1}{2}$

(b) $\dfrac{5\pi}{4}$ corresponds to the point $\left(-\dfrac{\sqrt{2}}{2}, -\dfrac{\sqrt{2}}{2}\right)$.

$\tan\dfrac{5\pi}{4} = \dfrac{y}{x} = 1$

4. (a) $\sin 7\pi = \sin(6\pi + \pi) = \sin\pi = 0$

(b) $\cos\left(-\dfrac{13\pi}{3}\right) = \cos\left(-4\pi - \dfrac{\pi}{3}\right)$

$= \cos\left(-\dfrac{\pi}{3}\right)$

$= \cos\dfrac{\pi}{3} = \dfrac{1}{2}$

5. $\cos\theta = \dfrac{2}{3}$

$x = 2, \ r = 3, \ y = \sqrt{9 - 4} = \sqrt{5}$

$\tan\theta = \dfrac{y}{x} = \dfrac{\sqrt{5}}{2}$

6. $\sin\theta = 0.9063$

$\theta = \arcsin(0.9063)$

$\theta \approx 65° \ \text{or} \ \dfrac{13\pi}{36}$

7. $\tan 20° = \dfrac{35}{x}$

$x = \dfrac{35}{\tan 20°} \approx 96.1617$

8. $\theta = \dfrac{6\pi}{5}$, θ is in Quadrant III.

Reference angle: $\dfrac{6\pi}{5} - \pi = \dfrac{\pi}{5}$ or $36°$

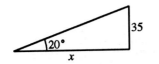

9. $\csc 3.92 = \dfrac{1}{\sin 3.92} \approx -1.4242$

10. $\tan \theta = 6 = \dfrac{6}{1}$, θ lies in Quadrant III.

$y = -6$, $x = -1$, $r = \sqrt{36 + 1} = \sqrt{37}$,

so $\sec \theta = \dfrac{\sqrt{37}}{-1} \approx -6.0828$.

11. Period: 4π
Amplitude: 3

12. Period: 2π
Amplitude: 2

13. Period: $\dfrac{\pi}{2}$

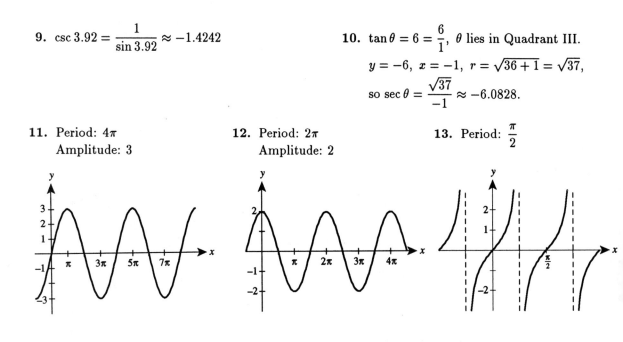

14. Period: 2π

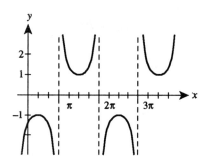

15.

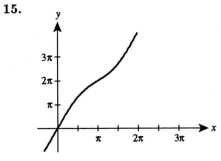

16.

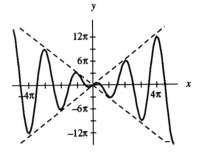

17. Let $\theta = \arcsin 1$.

$\sin \theta = 1$

$\theta = \dfrac{\pi}{2}$

18. $\arctan(-3) = -\arctan 3$

$\tan \theta = -3$

$\theta \approx -1.249 \approx -71.565°$

19. $\sin\left(\arccos \dfrac{4}{\sqrt{35}}\right)$

$\sin \theta = \dfrac{\sqrt{19}}{\sqrt{35}} \approx 0.7368$

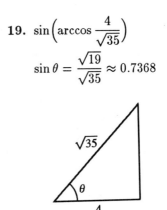

20. $\cos\left(\arcsin \dfrac{x}{4}\right)$

$\cos \theta = \dfrac{\sqrt{16 - x^2}}{4}$

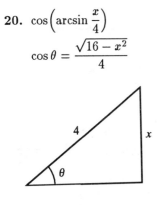

21. Given $A = 40°$, $c = 12$

$B = 90° - 40° = 50°$

$\sin 40° = \dfrac{a}{12}$

$a = 12 \sin 40° \approx 7.713$

$\cos 40° = \dfrac{b}{12}$

$b = 12 \cos 40° \approx 9.192$

22. Given $B = 6.84°$, $a = 21.3$

$A = 90° - 6.84° = 83.16°$

$\sin 83.16° = \dfrac{21.3}{c}$

$c = \dfrac{21.3}{\sin 83.16°} \approx 21.453$

$\tan 83.16° = \dfrac{21.3}{b}$

$b = \dfrac{21.3}{\tan 83.16°} \approx 2.555$

23. Given $a = 5$, $b = 9$

$c = \sqrt{25 + 81} = \sqrt{106} \approx 10.296$

$\tan A = \frac{5}{9}$

$A = \arctan \frac{5}{9} \approx 29.055°$

$B = 90° - 29.055° = 60.945°$

24. $\sin 67° = \dfrac{x}{20}$

$x = 20 \sin 67° \approx 18.41$ feet

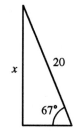

25. $\tan 5° = \dfrac{250}{x}$

$x = \dfrac{250}{\tan 5°}$

≈ 2857.513 ft

≈ 0.541 mi

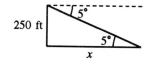

CHAPTER 3

Practice Test Solutions

1. $\tan x = \dfrac{4}{11}$, $\sec x < 0 \Rightarrow x$ is in Quadrant III.

$y = -4$, $x = -11$, $r = \sqrt{16 + 121} = \sqrt{137}$

$$\sin x = -\frac{4}{\sqrt{137}} = -\frac{4\sqrt{137}}{137} \qquad \csc x = -\frac{\sqrt{137}}{4}$$

$$\cos x = -\frac{11}{\sqrt{137}} = -\frac{11\sqrt{137}}{137} \qquad \sec x = -\frac{\sqrt{137}}{11}$$

$$\tan x = \frac{4}{11} \qquad\qquad\qquad \cot x = \frac{11}{4}$$

2.
$$\frac{\sec^2 x + \csc^2 x}{\csc^2 x(1 + \tan^2 x)} = \frac{\sec^2 x + \csc^2 x}{\csc^2 x + (\csc^2 x)\tan^2 x} = \frac{\sec^2 x + \csc^2 x}{\csc^2 x + \dfrac{1}{\sin^2 x} \cdot \dfrac{\sin^2 x}{\cos^2 x}}$$

$$= \frac{\sec^2 x + \csc^2 x}{\csc^2 x + \dfrac{1}{\cos^2 x}} = \frac{\sec^2 x + \csc^2 x}{\csc^2 x + \sec^2 x} = 1$$

3. $\ln|\tan\theta| - \ln|\cot\theta| = \ln\dfrac{|\tan\theta|}{|\cot\theta|} = \ln\left|\dfrac{\sin\theta/\cos\theta}{\cos\theta/\sin\theta}\right| = \ln\left|\dfrac{\sin^2\theta}{\cos^2\theta}\right| = \ln|\tan^2\theta| = 2\ln|\tan\theta|$

4. $\cos\left(\dfrac{\pi}{2} - x\right) = \dfrac{1}{\csc x}$ is true since $\cos\left(\dfrac{\pi}{2} - x\right) = \sin x = \dfrac{1}{\csc x}$.

5. $\sin^4 x + (\sin^2 x)\cos^2 x = \sin^2 x(\sin^2 x + \cos^2 x) = \sin^2 x(1) = \sin^2 x$

6. $(\csc x + 1)(\csc x - 1) = \csc^2 x - 1 = \cot^2 x$

7. $\dfrac{\cos^2 x}{1 - \sin x} \cdot \dfrac{1 + \sin x}{1 + \sin x} = \dfrac{\cos^2 x(1 + \sin x)}{1 - \sin^2 x} = \dfrac{\cos^2 x(1 + \sin x)}{\cos^2 x} = 1 + \sin x$

8. $\dfrac{1 + \cos\theta}{\sin\theta} + \dfrac{\sin\theta}{1 + \cos\theta} = \dfrac{(1 + \cos\theta)^2 + \sin^2\theta}{\sin\theta(1 + \cos\theta)}$

$$= \frac{1 + 2\cos\theta + \cos^2\theta + \sin^2\theta}{\sin\theta(1 + \cos\theta)} = \frac{2 + 2\cos\theta}{\sin\theta(1 + \cos\theta)} = \frac{2}{\sin\theta} = 2\csc\theta$$

9. $\tan^4 x + 2\tan^2 x + 1 = (\tan^2 x + 1)^2 = (\sec^2 x)^2 = \sec^4 x$

10. (a) $\sin 105° = \sin(60° + 45°) = \sin 60° \cos 45° + \cos 60° \sin 45°$

$$= \frac{\sqrt{3}}{2} \cdot \frac{\sqrt{2}}{2} + \frac{1}{2} \cdot \frac{\sqrt{2}}{2} = \frac{\sqrt{2}}{4}(\sqrt{3} + 1)$$

(b) $\tan 15° = \tan(60° - 45°) = \dfrac{\tan 60° - \tan 45°}{1 + \tan 60° \tan 45°}$

$$= \frac{\sqrt{3} - 1}{1 + \sqrt{3}} \cdot \frac{1 - \sqrt{3}}{1 - \sqrt{3}} = \frac{2\sqrt{3} - 1 - 3}{1 - 3} = \frac{2\sqrt{3} - 4}{-2} = 2 - \sqrt{3}$$

11. $(\sin 42°) \cos 38° - (\cos 42°) \sin 38° = \sin(42° - 38°) = \sin 4°$

12. $\tan\left(\theta + \dfrac{\pi}{4}\right) = \dfrac{\tan\theta + \tan(\pi/4)}{1 - (\tan\theta)\tan(\pi/4)} = \dfrac{\tan\theta + 1}{1 - \tan\theta(1)} = \dfrac{1 + \tan\theta}{1 - \tan\theta}$

13. $\sin(\arcsin x - \arccos x) = \sin(\arcsin x)\cos(\arccos x) - \cos(\arcsin x)\sin(\arccos x)$

$$= (x)(x) - (\sqrt{1 - x^2})(\sqrt{1 - x^2}) = x^2 - (1 - x^2) = 2x^2 - 1$$

14. (a) $\cos(120°) = \cos[2(60°)] = 2\cos^2 60° - 1 = 2\left(\dfrac{1}{2}\right)^2 - 1 = -\dfrac{1}{2}$

(b) $\tan(300°) = \tan[2(150°)] = \dfrac{2\tan 150°}{1 - \tan^2 150°} = \dfrac{-2\sqrt{3}/3}{1 - (1/3)} = -\sqrt{3}$

15. (a) $\sin 22.5° = \sin\dfrac{45°}{2} = \sqrt{\dfrac{1 - \cos 45°}{2}} = \sqrt{\dfrac{1 - \sqrt{2}/2}{2}} = \dfrac{\sqrt{2 - \sqrt{2}}}{2}$

(b) $\tan\dfrac{\pi}{12} = \tan\dfrac{\pi/6}{2} = \dfrac{\sin(\pi/6)}{1 + \cos(\pi/6)} = \dfrac{1/2}{1 + \sqrt{3}/2} = \dfrac{1}{2 + \sqrt{3}} = 2 - \sqrt{3}$

16. $\sin\theta = \dfrac{4}{5}$, θ lies in Quadrant II $\Rightarrow \cos\theta = -\dfrac{3}{5}$.

$$\cos\frac{\theta}{2} = \sqrt{\frac{1 + \cos\theta}{2}} = \sqrt{\frac{1 - 3/5}{2}} = \sqrt{\frac{2}{10}} = \frac{1}{\sqrt{5}} = \frac{\sqrt{5}}{5}$$

17. $(\sin^2 x)\cos^2 x = \dfrac{1 - \cos 2x}{2} \cdot \dfrac{1 + \cos 2x}{2} = \dfrac{1}{4}[1 - \cos^2 2x] = \dfrac{1}{4}\left[1 - \dfrac{1 + \cos 4x}{2}\right]$

$$= \frac{1}{8}[2 - (1 + \cos 4x)] = \frac{1}{8}[1 - \cos 4x]$$

18. $6(\sin 5\theta)\cos 2\theta = 6\left\{\dfrac{1}{2}[\sin(5\theta + 2\theta) + \sin(5\theta - 2\theta)]\right\} = 3[\sin 7\theta + \sin 3\theta]$

19. $\sin(x + \pi) + \sin(x - \pi) = 2\left(\sin\dfrac{[(x + \pi) + (x - \pi)]}{2}\right)\cos\dfrac{[(x + \pi) - (x - \pi)]}{2}$

$$= 2(\sin x)\cos\pi = -2\sin x$$

20. $\dfrac{\sin 9x + \sin 5x}{\cos 9x - \cos 5x} = \dfrac{2 \sin 7x \cos 2x}{-2 \sin 7x \sin 2x} = -\dfrac{\cos 2x}{\sin 2x} = -\cot 2x$

21. $\frac{1}{2}[\sin(u+v) - \sin(u-v)] = \frac{1}{2}\{(\sin u)\cos v + (\cos u)\sin v - [(\sin u)\cos v - (\cos u)\sin v]\}$

$$= \tfrac{1}{2}[2(\cos u)\sin v] = (\cos u)\sin v$$

22. $4\sin^2 x = 1$

$\sin^2 x = \dfrac{1}{4}$

$\sin x = \pm\dfrac{1}{2}$

$\sin x = \dfrac{1}{2}$ \qquad or $\sin x = -\dfrac{1}{2}$

$x = \dfrac{\pi}{6}$ or $\dfrac{5\pi}{6}$ \qquad $x = \dfrac{7\pi}{6}$ or $\dfrac{11\pi}{6}$

23. $\tan^2 \theta + (\sqrt{3} - 1)\tan\theta - \sqrt{3} = 0$

$(\tan\theta - 1)(\tan\theta + \sqrt{3}) = 0$

$\tan\theta = 1$ \qquad or $\tan\theta = -\sqrt{3}$

$\theta = \dfrac{\pi}{4}$ or $\dfrac{5\pi}{4}$ \qquad $\theta = \dfrac{2\pi}{3}$ or $\dfrac{5\pi}{3}$

24. $\qquad\qquad \sin 2x = \cos x$

$2(\sin x)\cos x - \cos x = 0$

$\cos x(2\sin x - 1) = 0$

$\cos x = 0$ \qquad or $\sin x = \dfrac{1}{2}$

$x = \dfrac{\pi}{2}$ or $\dfrac{3\pi}{2}$ \qquad $x = \dfrac{\pi}{6}$ or $\dfrac{5\pi}{6}$

25. $\tan^2 x - 6\tan x + 4 = 0$

$$\tan x = \dfrac{-(-6) \pm \sqrt{(-6)^2 - 4(1)(4)}}{2(1)}$$

$$\tan x = \dfrac{6 \pm \sqrt{20}}{2} = 3 \pm \sqrt{5}$$

$\tan x = 3 + \sqrt{5}$ \qquad or $\tan x = 3 - \sqrt{5}$

$x \approx 1.3821$ or 4.5237 \qquad $x \approx 0.6524$ or 3.7940

CHAPTER 4

Practice Test Solutions

1. $C = 180° - (40° + 12°) = 128°$

$a = \sin 40° \left(\dfrac{100}{\sin 12°} \right) \approx 309.164$

$c = \sin 128° \left(\dfrac{100}{\sin 12°} \right) \approx 379.012$

2. $\sin A = 5 \left(\dfrac{\sin 150°}{20} \right) = 0.1250$

$A \approx 7.181°$

$B \approx 180° - (150° + 7.181°) = 22.819°$

$b = \sin 22.819° \left(\dfrac{20}{\sin 150°} \right) \approx 15.513$

3. Area $= \frac{1}{2} ab \sin C$

$= \frac{1}{2}(3)(5) \sin 130°$

≈ 5.745 square units

4. $h = b \sin A, \ a = 10$

$= 35 \sin 22.5$

≈ 13.394

Since $a < h$ and A is acute, the triangle has solution.

5. $\cos A = \dfrac{(53)^2 + (38)^2 - (49)^2}{2(53)(38)} \approx 0.4598$

$A \approx 62.627°$

$\cos B = \dfrac{(49)^2 + (38)^2 - (53)^2}{2(49)(38)} \approx 0.2782$

$B \approx 73.847°$

$C = 180° - (62.627° + 73.847°) = 43.526°$

6. $c^2 = (100)^2 + (300)^2 - 2(100)(300) \cos 29°$

≈ 47522.8176

$c \approx 218$

$\cos A = \dfrac{(300)^2 + (218)^2 - (100)^2}{2(300)(218)} \approx 0.9750$

$A \approx 12.85°$

$B = 180° - (12.85° + 29°) = 138.15°$

7. $s = \dfrac{a+b+c}{2} = \dfrac{4.1 + 6.8 + 5.5}{2} = 8.2$

Area $= \sqrt{s(s-a)(s-b)(s-c)}$

$= \sqrt{8.2(8.2 - 4.1)(8.2 - 6.8)(8.2 - 5.5)}$

≈ 11.273 square units

8. $x^2 = (40)^2 + (70)^2 - 2(40)(70) \cos 168°$

≈ 11977.6266

$x \approx 109.442$ miles

9. $\mathbf{w} = 4(3\mathbf{i} + \mathbf{j}) - 7(-\mathbf{i} + 2\mathbf{j})$
$= 19\mathbf{i} - 10\mathbf{j}$

10. $\dfrac{\mathbf{v}}{||\mathbf{v}||} = \dfrac{5\mathbf{i} - 3\mathbf{j}}{\sqrt{25 + 9}} = \dfrac{5}{\sqrt{34}}\mathbf{i} - \dfrac{3}{\sqrt{34}}\mathbf{j}$
$= \dfrac{5\sqrt{34}}{34}\mathbf{i} - \dfrac{3\sqrt{34}}{34}\mathbf{j}$

11. $\mathbf{u} = 6\mathbf{i} + 5\mathbf{j}$
$||\mathbf{u}|| = \sqrt{61}$
$\mathbf{v} = 2\mathbf{i} - 3\mathbf{j}$
$||\mathbf{v}|| = \sqrt{13}$
$\mathbf{w} = -4\mathbf{i} - 8\mathbf{j}$
$||\mathbf{w}|| = \sqrt{80}$
$\cos\theta = \dfrac{61 + 13 - 80}{2\sqrt{61}\sqrt{13}}$
$\theta \approx 96.116°$

12. $\tan 30° = \dfrac{y}{x} = \dfrac{1}{\sqrt{3}}$

$\mathbf{u} = \sqrt{3}\mathbf{i} + \mathbf{j}$ but $||\mathbf{u}|| = 2$
$\mathbf{v} = 2\mathbf{u} = 2\sqrt{3}\mathbf{i} + 2\mathbf{j}$

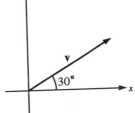

13. $\mathbf{u} \cdot \mathbf{v} = 3(-2) + (-5)(1) = -11$

14. $||\mathbf{u}|| = \sqrt{(3)^2 + (-5)^2} = \sqrt{34}$

15. $\cos\theta = \dfrac{-11}{\sqrt{34}\sqrt{5}}$
$\theta = \arccos\left(\dfrac{-11}{\sqrt{170}}\right) \approx 147.5288°$

16. $(\mathbf{v} \cdot \mathbf{u})\mathbf{u} = (\mathbf{u} \cdot \mathbf{v})\mathbf{u} = -11\mathbf{u} = \langle -33,\ 55 \rangle$

17. $\mathbf{u} \cdot \mathbf{v} = -11 \neq 0 \Rightarrow$ *not* orthogonal
$\mathbf{u} \neq k\mathbf{v}$ for any real number $k \Rightarrow$ *not* parallel
Neither

18. $\text{proj}_{\mathbf{v}}(\mathbf{u}) = \left(\dfrac{-11}{5}\right)\mathbf{v} = \left\langle \dfrac{22}{5},\ -\dfrac{11}{5} \right\rangle$

19. $\mathbf{u} - \text{proj}_{\mathbf{v}}(\mathbf{u}) = \langle 3,\ -5 \rangle - \left\langle \dfrac{22}{5},\ -\dfrac{11}{5} \right\rangle$
$= \left\langle -\dfrac{7}{5},\ -\dfrac{14}{5} \right\rangle$

20. $W = (\cos 40°)(70)(20) = 1072.4622$ ft-lb

CHAPTER 5

Practice Test Solutions

1. $i^{38} = i^{36}i^2 = (i^4)^9 i^2 = (1)^9(-1) = -1$

2. $(8 + \sqrt{-64}) + (6 + \sqrt{-25}) = (8 + 8i) + (6 + 5i) = 14 + 13i$

3. $-(4 + 4i) - (-3i) = -4 - 4i + 3i = -4 - i$

4. $(-8 + 2i)(-8 - 2i) = 64 + 16i - 16i - 4i^2 = 64 + 4 = 68 + 0i$

5.
$$\frac{12 + 16i}{4 - 2i} = \frac{6 + 8i}{2 - i} \cdot \frac{2 + i}{2 + i}$$
$$= \frac{12 + 6i + 16i + 8i^2}{4 + 1} = \frac{4 + 22i}{5}$$
$$= \frac{4}{5} + \frac{22}{5}i$$

6. $3x^2 + 2x + 2 = 0$
$$x = \frac{-2 \pm \sqrt{(2)^2 - 4(3)(2)}}{2(3)} = \frac{-2 \pm \sqrt{-20}}{6}$$
$$= \frac{-2 \pm 2i\sqrt{5}}{6} = -\frac{1}{3} \pm \frac{\sqrt{5}}{3}i$$

7. $3x^2 + 1 = -47$
$$3x^2 = -48$$
$$x^2 = -16$$
$$x = \pm\sqrt{-16}$$
$$x = \pm 4i = 0 \pm 4i$$

8. $x^4 - 1296 = 0$
$$(x^2 + 36)(x^2 - 36) = 0$$

$x^2 = -36$ OR $x^2 = 36$

$x = \pm\sqrt{-36}$ $x = \pm\sqrt{36}$

$x = \pm 6i$ $x = \pm 6$

$x = 0 \pm 6i$

9. $x^4 - 7x^2 - 60 = 0$
$$(x^2 - 12)(x^2 + 5) = 0$$

$x^2 = 12$ OR $x^2 = -5$

$x = \pm\sqrt{12}$ $x = \pm\sqrt{-5}$

$x = \pm 2\sqrt{3}$ $x = \pm\sqrt{5}\,i = 0 \pm \sqrt{5}\,i$

10. $x^3 + 2x^2 + 9x + 18 = 0$
$$x^2(x + 2) + 9(x + 2) = 0$$
$$(x + 2)(x^2 + 9) = 0$$

$x = -2$ OR $x^2 = -9$

$x = \pm 3i = 0 \pm 3i$

11. Since $-2i$ is a zero, so is $2i$.
$$P(x) = (x - 0)(x + 2i)(x - 2i)(x - 3)$$
$$= x(x^2 + 4)(x - 3)$$
$$= x(x^3 - 3x^2 + 4x - 12)$$
$$= x^4 - 3x^3 + 4x^2 - 12x$$

12. Since $1 + 2i$ is a zero, so is $1 - 2i$. Thus,

$$[x - (1 + 2i)][x - (1 - 2i)] = [(x - 1) - 2i][(x - 1) + 2i]$$
$$= (x - 1)^2 - 4i^2$$
$$= x^2 - 2x + 5.$$

is a factor of $f(x)$.

$$\begin{array}{r}
x + 6 \\
x^2 - 2x + 5 \overline{) x^3 + 4x^2 - 7x + 30} \\
\underline{x^3 - 2x^2 + 5x} \\
6x^2 - 12x + 30 \\
\underline{6x^2 - 12x + 30} \\
0
\end{array}$$

Therefore, $f(x) = (x^2 - 2x + 5)(x + 6)$ and the corresponding zeros are -6, $1 + 2i$, and $1 - 2i$.

13. $r = \sqrt{25 + 25} = \sqrt{50} = 5\sqrt{2}$

$\tan \theta = \dfrac{-5}{5} = -1$

Since z is in Quadrant IV,

$\theta = 315°$

$z = 5\sqrt{2}(\cos 315° + i \sin 315°).$

14. $\cos 225° = -\dfrac{\sqrt{2}}{2} \quad \sin 225° = -\dfrac{\sqrt{2}}{2}$

$$z = 6\left(-\dfrac{\sqrt{2}}{2} - i\dfrac{\sqrt{2}}{2}\right)$$
$$= -3\sqrt{2} - 3\sqrt{2}\,i$$

15. $[7(\cos 23° + i \sin 23°)][4(\cos 7° + i \sin 7°)] = 7(4)[\cos(23° + 7°) + i \sin(23° + 7°)]$
$$= 28(\cos 30° + i \sin 30°)$$

16. $\dfrac{9\left(\cos \dfrac{5\pi}{4} + i \sin \dfrac{5\pi}{4}\right)}{3(\cos \pi + i \sin \pi)} = \dfrac{9}{3}\left[\cos\left(\dfrac{5\pi}{4} - \pi\right) + i \sin\left(\dfrac{5\pi}{4} - \pi\right)\right] = 3\left(\cos \dfrac{\pi}{4} + i \sin \dfrac{\pi}{4}\right)$

17. $(2 + 2i)^8 = [2\sqrt{2}(\cos 45° + i \sin 45°)]^8 = (2\sqrt{2})^8[\cos(8)(45°) + i \sin(8)(45°)]$
$$= 4096[\cos 360° + i \sin 360°] = 4096$$

18. $z = 8 \left(\cos \dfrac{\pi}{3} + i \sin \dfrac{\pi}{3} \right), \quad n = 3$; The cube roots of z are:

For $k = 0,$ $\sqrt[3]{8} \left[\cos \dfrac{\pi/3}{3} + i \sin \dfrac{\pi/3}{3} \right] = 2 \left(\cos \dfrac{\pi}{9} + i \sin \dfrac{\pi}{9} \right)$

For $k = 1,$ $\sqrt[3]{8} \left[\cos \dfrac{\pi/3 + 2\pi}{3} + i \sin \dfrac{\pi/3 + 2\pi}{3} \right] = 2 \left(\cos \dfrac{7\pi}{9} + i \sin \dfrac{7\pi}{9} \right)$

For $k = 2,$ $\sqrt[3]{8} \left[\cos \dfrac{\pi/3 + 4\pi}{3} + i \sin \dfrac{\pi/3 + 4\pi}{3} \right] = 2 \left(\cos \dfrac{13\pi}{9} + i \sin \dfrac{13\pi}{9} \right)$

19. $x^3 = -125 = 125(\cos \pi + i \sin \pi)$

For $k = 0,$ $\sqrt[3]{125} \left(\cos \dfrac{\pi}{3} + i \sin \dfrac{\pi}{3} \right) = 5 \left(\cos \dfrac{\pi}{3} + i \sin \dfrac{\pi}{3} \right)$

For $k = 1,$ $\sqrt[3]{125} \left(\cos \dfrac{\pi + 2\pi}{3} + i \sin \dfrac{\pi + 2\pi}{3} \right) = -5$

For $k = 2,$ $\sqrt[3]{125} \left(\cos \dfrac{\pi + 4\pi}{3} + i \sin \dfrac{\pi + 4\pi}{3} \right) = 5 \left(\cos \dfrac{5\pi}{3} + i \sin \dfrac{5\pi}{3} \right)$

20. $x^4 = -i = 1 \left(\cos \dfrac{3\pi}{2} + i \sin \dfrac{3\pi}{2} \right)$

For $k = 0,$ $\cos \dfrac{3\pi/2}{4} + i \sin \dfrac{3\pi/2}{4} = \cos \dfrac{3\pi}{8} + i \sin \dfrac{3\pi}{8}$

For $k = 1,$ $\cos \dfrac{3\pi/2 + 2\pi}{4} + i \sin \dfrac{3\pi/2 + 2\pi}{4} = \cos \dfrac{7\pi}{8} + i \sin \dfrac{7\pi}{8}$

For $k = 2,$ $\cos \dfrac{3\pi/2 + 4\pi}{4} + i \sin \dfrac{3\pi/2 + 4\pi}{4} = \cos \dfrac{11\pi}{8} + i \sin \dfrac{11\pi}{8}$

For $k = 3,$ $\cos \dfrac{3\pi/2 + 6\pi}{4} + i \sin \dfrac{3\pi/2 + 6\pi}{4} = \cos \dfrac{15\pi}{8} + i \sin \dfrac{15\pi}{8}$

CHAPTER 6

Practice Test Solutions

1. $x^{3/5} = 8$

$$x = 8^{5/3} = (\sqrt[3]{8})^5 = 2^5 = 32$$

2. $3^{x-1} = \frac{1}{81}$

$$3^{x-1} = 3^{-4}$$
$$x - 1 = -4$$
$$x = -3$$

3. $f(x) = 2^{-x} = \left(\frac{1}{2}\right)^x$

x	-2	-1	0	1	2
$f(x)$	4	2	1	$\frac{1}{2}$	$\frac{1}{4}$

4. $g(x) = e^x + 1$

x	-2	-1	0	1	2
$g(x)$	1.14	1.37	2	3.72	8.39

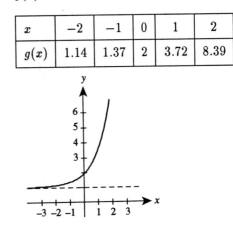

5. $A = P\left(1 + \dfrac{r}{n}\right)^{nt}$

(a) $A = 5000\left(1 + \dfrac{0.09}{12}\right)^{12(3)} \approx \$6543.23$

(b) $A = 5000\left(1 + \dfrac{0.09}{4}\right)^{4(3)} \approx \$6530.25$

(c) $A = 5000e^{(0.09)(3)} \approx \$6549.82$

6. $7^{-2} = \dfrac{1}{49}$

$$\log_7 \tfrac{1}{49} = -2$$

7. $x - 4 = \log_2 \frac{1}{64}$

$2^{x-4} = \frac{1}{64}$

$2^{x-4} = 2^{-6}$

$x - 4 = -6$

$x = -2$

8. $\log_b \sqrt[4]{\frac{8}{25}} = \frac{1}{4} \log_b \frac{8}{25}$

$= \frac{1}{4}[\log_b 8 - \log_b 25]$

$= \frac{1}{4}[\log_b 2^3 - \log_b 5^2]$

$= \frac{1}{4}[3 \log_b 2 - 2 \log_b 5]$

$= \frac{1}{4}[3(0.3562) - 2(0.8271)]$

$= -0.1464$

9. $5 \ln x - \frac{1}{2} \ln y + 6 \ln z = \ln x^5 - \ln \sqrt{y} + \ln z^6 = \ln \left(\frac{x^5 z^6}{\sqrt{y}} \right)$

10. $\log_9 28 = \dfrac{\log 28}{\log 9} \approx 1.5166$

11. $\log N = 0.6646$

$N = 10^{0.6646} \approx 4.62$

12.

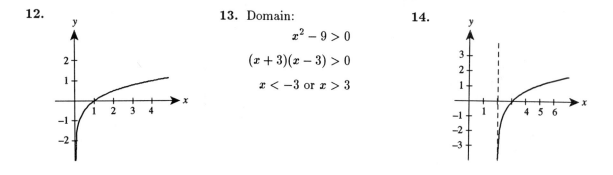

13. Domain:

$x^2 - 9 > 0$

$(x + 3)(x - 3) > 0$

$x < -3 \text{ or } x > 3$

14.

15. $\dfrac{\ln x}{\ln y} \neq \ln(x - y)$ since $\dfrac{\ln x}{\ln y} = \log_y x$

16. $5^x = 41$

$x = \log_5 41 = \dfrac{\ln 41}{\ln 5} \approx 2.3074$

17. $x - x^2 = \log_5 \frac{1}{25}$

$5^{x-x^2} = \frac{1}{25}$

$5^{x-x^2} = 5^{-2}$

$x - x^2 = -2$

$0 = x^2 - x - 2$

$0 = (x + 1)(x - 2)$

$x = -1 \text{ or } x = 2$

18. $\log_2 x + \log_2(x - 3) = 2$

$\log_2[x(x - 3)] = 2$

$x(x - 3) = 2^2$

$x^2 - 3x = 4$

$x^2 - 3x - 4 = 0$

$(x + 1)(x - 4) = 0$

$x = 4$

$x = -1$

(extraneous solution)

19.

$$\frac{e^x + e^{-x}}{3} = 4$$

$$e^x(e^x + e^{-x}) = 12e^x$$

$$e^{2x} + 1 = 12e^x$$

$$e^{2x} - 12e^x + 1 = 0$$

$$e^x = \frac{12 \pm \sqrt{144 - 4}}{2}$$

$e^x = 11.9161$ or $e^x = 0.0839$

$x = \ln 11.9161$ $x = \ln 0.0839$

$x \approx 2.4779$ $x \approx -2.4779$

20.

$$A = Pe^{rt}$$

$$12{,}000 = 6000e^{0.13t}$$

$$2 = e^{0.13t}$$

$$0.13t = \ln 2$$

$$t = \frac{\ln 2}{0.13}$$

$t \approx 5.3319$ years or

5 years 4 months

CHAPTER 7

Practice Test Solutions

1. $3x + 4y = 12 \Rightarrow y = -\dfrac{3}{4}x + 3 \Rightarrow m_1 = -\dfrac{3}{4}$

$4x - 3y = 12 \Rightarrow y = \dfrac{4}{3}x - 4 \Rightarrow m_2 = \dfrac{4}{3}$

$\tan\theta = \left| \dfrac{\frac{4}{3} - \left(-\frac{3}{4}\right)}{1 + \left(\frac{4}{3}\right)\left(-\frac{3}{4}\right)} \right| = \left| \dfrac{\frac{25}{12}}{0} \right|$

Since $\tan\theta$ is undefined, the lines are perpendicular (note that $m_2 = -1/m_1$) and $\theta = 90°$.

2. $x_1 = 5$, $x_2 = -9$, $A = 3$, $B = -7$, $C = -21$

$d = \dfrac{|3(5) + (-7)(-9) + (-21)|}{\sqrt{3^2 + (-7)^2}} = \dfrac{57}{\sqrt{58}} \approx 7.484$

3. $x^2 - 6x - 4y + 1 = 0$

$x^2 - 6x + 9 = 4y - 1 + 9$

$(x - 3)^2 = 4y + 8$

$(x - 3)^2 = 4(1)(y + 2) \Rightarrow p = 1$

Vertex: $(3, -2)$

Focus: $(3, -1)$

Directrix: $y = -3$

4. Vertex: $(2, -5)$

Focus: $(2, -6)$

Vertical axis;

opens downward with $p = -1$

$(x - h)^2 = 4p(y - k)$

$(x - 2)^2 = 4(-1)(y + 5)$

$x^2 - 4x + 4 = -4y - 20$

$x^2 - 4x + 4y + 24 = 0$

5. $x^2 + 4y^2 - 2x + 32y + 61 = 0$

$(x^2 - 2x + 1) + 4(y^2 + 8y + 16) = -61 + 1 + 64$

$(x - 1)^2 + 4(y + 4)^2 = 4$

$\dfrac{(x - 1)^2}{4} + \dfrac{(y + 4)^2}{1} = 1$

$a = 2$, $b = 1$, $c = \sqrt{3}$

Horizontal major axis

Center: $(1, -4)$

Foci: $(1 \pm \sqrt{3}, -4)$

Vertices: $(3, -4)$, $(-1, -4)$

Eccentricity: $e = \sqrt{3}/2$

6. Vertices: $(0, \pm 6)$

Eccentricity: $e = 1/2$

Center: $(0, 0)$

Vertical major axis

$a = 6$, $e = \dfrac{c}{a} = \dfrac{c}{6} = \dfrac{1}{2} \Rightarrow c = 3$

$b^2 = (6)^2 - (3)^2 = 27$

$\dfrac{x^2}{27} + \dfrac{y^2}{36} = 1$

7. $16y^2 - x^2 - 6x - 128y + 231 = 0$

$$16(y^2 - 8y + 16) - (x^2 + 6x + 9) = -231 + 256 - 9$$

$$16(y - 4)^2 - (x + 3)^2 = 16$$

$$\frac{(y-4)^2}{1} - \frac{(x+3)^2}{16} = 1$$

$a = 1,\ b = 4,\ c = \sqrt{17}$

Center: $(-3,\ 4)$

Vertical transverse axis

Vertices: $(-3,\ 5),\ (-3,\ 3)$

Foci: $(-3,\ 4 \pm \sqrt{17})$

Asymptotes: $y = 4 \pm \frac{1}{4}(x + 3)$

8. Vertices: $(\pm 3,\ 2)$

Foci: $(\pm 5,\ 2)$

Center: $(0,\ 2)$

Horizontal transverse axis

$a = 3,\ c = 5,\ b = 4$

$$\frac{(x-0)^2}{9} - \frac{(y-2)^2}{16} = 1$$

$$\frac{x^2}{9} - \frac{(y-2)^2}{16} = 1$$

9. $5x^2 + 2xy + 5y^2 - 10 = 0$

$A = 5,\ B = 2,\ C = 5$

$$\cot 2\theta = \frac{5 - 5}{2} = 0$$

$$2\theta = \frac{\pi}{2} \Rightarrow \theta = \frac{\pi}{4}$$

$$x = x' \cos \frac{\pi}{4} - y' \sin \frac{\pi}{4} \qquad y = x' \sin \frac{\pi}{4} + y' \cos \frac{\pi}{4}$$

$$= \frac{x' - y'}{\sqrt{2}} \qquad\qquad\qquad = \frac{x' + y'}{\sqrt{2}}$$

$$5\left(\frac{x' - y'}{\sqrt{2}}\right)^2 + 2\left(\frac{x' - y'}{\sqrt{2}}\right)\left(\frac{x' + y'}{\sqrt{2}}\right) + 5\left(\frac{x' + y'}{\sqrt{2}}\right)^2 - 10 = 0$$

$$\frac{5(x')^2}{2} - \frac{10x'y'}{2} + \frac{5(y')^2}{2} + (x')^2 - (y')^2 + \frac{5(x')^2}{2} + \frac{10x'y'}{2} + \frac{5(y')^2}{2} - 10 = 0$$

$$6(x')^2 + 4(y')^2 - 10 = 0$$

$$\frac{3(x')^2}{5} + \frac{2(y')^2}{5} = 1$$

$$\frac{(x')^2}{5/3} + \frac{(y')^2}{5/2} = 1$$

Ellipse centered at the origin

10. (a) $6x^2 - 2xy + y^2 = 0$
$A = 6, \ B = -2, \ C = 1$
$B^2 - 4AC = (-2)^2 - 4(6)(1) = -20 < 0$
Ellipse

(b) $x^2 + 4xy + 4y^2 - x - y + 17 = 0$
$A = 1, \ B = 4, \ C = 4$
$B^2 - 4AC = (4)^2 - 4(1)(4) = 0$
Parabola

11. Polar: $\left(\sqrt{2}, \ \dfrac{3\pi}{4} \right)$

$x = \sqrt{2} \cos \dfrac{3\pi}{4} = \sqrt{2} \left(-\dfrac{1}{\sqrt{2}} \right) = -1$

$y = \sqrt{2} \sin \dfrac{3\pi}{4} = \sqrt{2} \left(\dfrac{1}{\sqrt{2}} \right) = 1$

Rectangular: $(-1, \ 1)$

12. Rectangular: $(\sqrt{3}, \ -1)$

$r = \pm\sqrt{(\sqrt{3})^2 + (-1)^2} = \pm 2$

$\tan \theta = \dfrac{\sqrt{3}}{-1} = -\sqrt{3}$

$\theta = \dfrac{2\pi}{3} \quad \text{or} \quad \theta = \dfrac{5\pi}{3}$

Polar: $\left(-2, \ \dfrac{2\pi}{3} \right)$ or $\left(2, \ \dfrac{5\pi}{3} \right)$

13. Rectangular: $4x - 3y = 12$
Polar:
$$4r\cos\theta - 3r\sin\theta = 12$$
$$r(4\cos\theta - 3\sin\theta) = 12$$
$$r = \dfrac{12}{4\cos\theta - 3\sin\theta}$$

14. Polar: $\quad r = 5\cos\theta$
$$r^2 = 5r\cos\theta$$

Rectangular:
$$x^2 + y^2 = 5x$$
$$x^2 + y^2 - 5x = 0$$

15. $r = 1 - \cos\theta$
Cardioid
Symmetry: Polar axis
Maximum value of $|r|$:
$\quad r = 2$ when $\theta = \pi$
Zero of r : $r = 0$ when $\theta = 0$

θ	0	$\dfrac{\pi}{2}$	π	$\dfrac{3\pi}{2}$
r	0	1	2	1

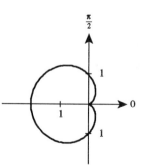

16. $r = 5 \sin 2\theta$

Rose curve with four petals

Symmetry: Polar axis, $\theta = \dfrac{\pi}{2}$, and pole

Maximum value of $|r|$: $|r| = 5$ when $\theta = \dfrac{\pi}{4}, \dfrac{3\pi}{4}, \dfrac{5\pi}{4}, \dfrac{7\pi}{4}$

Zeros of r: $r = 0$ when $\theta = 0, \dfrac{\pi}{2}, \pi, \dfrac{3\pi}{2}$

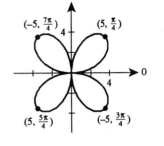

17. $r = \dfrac{3}{6 - \cos\theta}$

$r = \dfrac{\frac{1}{2}}{1 - \frac{1}{6}\cos\theta}$

$e = \frac{1}{6} < 1$, so the graph is an ellipse.

θ	0	$\dfrac{\pi}{2}$	π	$\dfrac{3\pi}{2}$
r	$\dfrac{3}{5}$	$\dfrac{1}{2}$	$\dfrac{3}{7}$	$\dfrac{1}{2}$

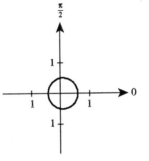

18. Parabola

Vertex: $\left(6, \dfrac{\pi}{2}\right)$

Focus: $(0, 0)$

$e = 1$

$r = \dfrac{ep}{1 + e\sin\theta}$

$r = \dfrac{p}{1 + \sin\theta}$

$6 = \dfrac{p}{1 + \sin(\pi/2)}$

$6 = \dfrac{p}{2}$

$12 = p$

$r = \dfrac{12}{1 + \sin\theta}$

19. $x = 3 - 2\sin\theta, \quad y = 1 + 5\cos\theta$

$\dfrac{x - 3}{-2} = \sin\theta, \quad \dfrac{y - 1}{5} = \cos\theta$

$\left(\dfrac{x - 3}{-2}\right)^2 + \left(\dfrac{y - 1}{5}\right)^2 = 1$

$\dfrac{(x - 3)^2}{4} + \dfrac{(y - 1)^2}{25} = 1$

20. $x = e^{2t}, \quad y = e^{4t}$

$x > 0, \quad y > 0$

$x = e^{2t} \Rightarrow \ln x = 2t \Rightarrow t = \frac{1}{2}\ln x$

$y = e^{4t} = e^{4(1/2\ln x)} = e^{2\ln x} = e^{\ln x^2} = x^2$

$y = x^2, \quad x > 0, \quad y > 0$

Alternate solution:

$y = e^{4t} = (e^{2t})^2 = x^2, \quad x > 0, \quad y > 0$